Advance Praise for *Unstoppable*

When we look at the most successful people, we usually look at their habits—their behaviors, their day-to-day rituals, their dedication. But what about the mind? Ben Angel hits this idea head-on in *Unstoppable*, tackling peak performance goals with biohacking strategies that will blow your mind.

—Dr. Ivan Misner, Founder of BNI and *New York Times* Bestselling Author

This is an essential read for not only entrepreneurs but anyone who is driven to achieve their goals and dream big. *Unstoppable* is a deep-dive into the human psyche that gives us the tools we need to crush negativity and manifest the best version of ourselves.

—Cynthia Henry Thurlow, Nurse Practitioner, Functional Nutritionist and Thought Leader

Take charge of your life and use this book as the catalyst to your success. Unafraid and unrelenting, *Unstoppable* is a guide to reaching your peak. With actionable steps, new-age techniques, and a real-world journey to follow, Ben Angel is about to open your eyes.

—Jeremy Bloom, 3x World Champion, 2x Olympic Skier, Former NFL Player, CEO of Integrate, and Author of *Fueled by Failure*

I have spent years trying to figure out why I often feel so disconnected. Thanks to the strategies in the book, I successfully overcame a 40-year-old phobia that had ruled my life in more ways than one. I will never be able to thank Ben enough! It's been life-changing.

—Trish Wumkes, Overcame 40-Year-Old Phobia

Ben Angel's thought-provoking journey into his own brain and psyche is a compelling read for anyone looking to achieve their goals and dream big. *Unstoppable* explores the complex interaction between mind and body and offers tools to support you in becoming the best version of yourself.

—Sam Marchetta, Australian Psychologist and ICF certified Coach

I highly recommend this book not as information on alternative treatments but as the basis of future discussions on the condition of your wellbeing with your healthcare provider, so you can look for the right assessments, treatment, and professionals that will help you become the productive and happy person you deserve to be.

—SIGLIA DINIZ, MD, MPH, HARVARD GRADUATE IN PUBLIC HEALTH, TRAINED PHYSICIAN, AND HIGH-PERFORMANCE COACH WORKING IN MEDICINE/PUBLIC HEALTH/ RESEARCH FOR MORE THAN 20 YEARS

Ben has beautifully shared his knowledge, encouragement, and heart in such an engaging, comprehensive, and practical way while providing an easy-to-follow plan anyone can apply. *Unstoppable* is an invaluable tool to help guide the integration of body, mind, and soul and goes where other books fail to go.

—TRISHA HOTHORN, CLINICAL SOCIAL WORKER

As a naturopath, I can't recommend this book highly enough, especially for people who have tried everything to get their lives back on track, but nothing has helped. I can't wait to give it to my clients!

—HETAL GOHIL, NATUROPATH, ADVANCED DIPLOMA OF NUTRITIONAL MEDICINE

If you are running on determination alone yet running in place or sliding backward, this book is your meaty, eye-opening, and well-researched guide to hacking your brain and your life to launch yourself forward. Ben shares his personal and dedicated journey, leading us to a detailed blueprint on how to hack our own brains to become *Unstoppable*.

—MARY-WEBB WALKER, FORMER ABC TELEVISION EXECUTIVE, COFOUNDER OF ACCENTHEALTH, ALZHEIMER'S ASSOCIATION LEGISLATIVE ADVOCATE, AND HEALTH COACH

Get ready to dive in and rethink everything you've ever heard about health and habits for success! This book will transform your life in a super short amount of time. It's an essential read for anyone wanting to excel in all areas of life.

—MAGGIE BERGHOFF, CELEBRITY HEALTH EXPERT AND FUNCTIONAL MEDICINE NURSE PRACTITIONER

Unstoppable is an excellent story about a man on a quest to heal himself. Ben Angel shares his personal story in order to help others who may be struggling with the same or similar issues. His story points out the importance of looking at your physical, emotional, and spiritual health and how to treat them holistically instead of just trying to find one solution. Ben not only tells his story, but he also creates a step-by-step guide on how you can heal yourself.

—MONICA BURTON, LICENSED MARRIAGE AND FAMILY THERAPIST
AND CLINICAL MEMBER OF THE AMERICAN ASSOCIATION
FOR MARRIAGE AND FAMILY THERAPY

Unstoppable is a must-read. This unique book dives into how fatigue and brain fog can halt your success, why the willpower argument provides endless guilt rather than results, how to tailor your body to target both well-being and wealth, and how to safely and naturally biohack your body and brain for a greater life. I've not read anything else that gets to the heart of what he shares (and my reading list is embarrassingly large). What I've found is that some books add to prior knowledge while others open new possibilities by clearly shining a light on previously unseen links. Ben Angel's *Unstoppable* is one of the few that fall into the latter.

—DR. REBECCA HARWIN

The ultimate body and mind hack. A groundbreaking, fresh perspective on an all-too-common problem many of us are ill-equipped to solve. Ben's inspiring experiences and unique journey will make you think twice about what's holding you back from becoming *Unstoppable*.

—CANDICE AVILES, CHANNEL 10 NEWS ANCHOR AND HOST OF *MEET THE CHEF*

Unstoppable is more than a self-help book—it's entertaining, enlightening, and empowering. Angel breaks down his advice for how to get the best out of yourself by looking after your inner health and focuses on the link between our bodies and our minds.

—KRISTY LIST, AWARD-WINNING BLUEGRASS SINGER

Get out of your vicious cycle of depression, fatigue, burnout—whatever is holding you back. *Unstoppable* is packed with inspiring storytelling, motivational boosts, and practical strategies to overcome your mental barriers and conquer more than you ever dreamed!

—Pete Williams, Author of *Cadence: A Tale of Fast Business Growth*

I find there is a large gap between reading information without application and retaining it for practical use. *Unstoppable* screams for you to make actionable change by giving you the tools to do so with full support along the way. I'm privileged to have read it and to pursue my 90 days of becoming unstoppable!

—Dean Haynes, Olympic Lifting and CrossFit Coach

Unstoppable is not only for the overwhelmed and overworked entrepreneur but for anyone struggling with bridging the gap between deep in your heart knowing exactly what you are capable of achieving and feeling let down by your body, mind, or out-of-date health "care." After reading *Unstoppable*, I have made considerable changes to my lifestyle, eating habits, stress management, and mindset—taking from Ben's journey what was applicable to me and working through my own challenges. As a result, I am my strongest, happiest, and more productive self. Once again, Ben Angel has nailed it.

—Sarah Louise Bidmead, Marketing Strategist and Owner of Bohemia Business Solutions

UNSTOPPABLE

A 90-DAY PLAN TO BIOHACK YOUR MIND AND BODY FOR SUCCESS

BEN ANGEL

Entrepreneur Press®

Entrepreneur Press, Publisher
Cover Design: Andrew Welyczko
Production and Composition: Eliot House Productions

This publication is designed to provide accurate and authoritative information
in regard to the subject matter covered. It is sold with the understanding that
the publisher is not engaged in rendering legal, accounting or other professional
services. If legal advice or other expert assistance is required, the services of a
competent professional person should be sought.

Entrepreneur Press® is a registered trademark of Entrepreneur Media, Inc.

Library of Congress Cataloging-in-Publication Data
    Names: Angel, Ben, author.
    Title: Unstoppable: a 90-day plan to biohack your mind and body for success /
        by Ben Angel.
    Description: Irvine, California: Entrepreneur Media, Inc., [2018]
    Identifiers: LCCN 2018022897| ISBN 978-1-59918-631-3 (alk. paper) | ISBN
        1-59918-631-4 (alk. paper)
    Subjects: LCSH: Success—Psychological aspects. | Self-actualization
        (Psychology)
    Classification: LCC BF637.S8 A527 2018 | DDC 158.1—dc23
    LC record available at https://lccn.loc.gov/2018022897

Printed in the United States of America

22 21 20   10 9 8 7 6 5 4

Contents

PART III

OBLITERATING FEAR AND FINDING YOUR PURPOSE

PART IV
YOUR PATH TO BECOMING UNSTOPPABLE

Introduction

Something was horribly wrong, but for the life of me, I couldn't put my finger on it. I was 34 years old and had just completed my last event on a national speaking tour throughout Australia. The second the audience left the room and the doors shut, I lay flat on the ground in utter exhaustion. I had been losing my train of thought all day, and at one point had even asked the audience what I was talking about in mid-sentence. This wasn't the first time it had happened, either.

After the successful release of my third book in 2014, *Flee 9 to 5: Get 6-7 Figures and Do What You Love*, I returned home from a solo trip to the U.S. and Canada and started experiencing severe depression, exhaustion, and anxiety. Depression, an old archnemesis of mine, used to be manageable. This time, however, it didn't matter how much personal development work, meditation, supplementation, exercise, or healthy eating I did or how much willpower I used. It clung to me like a bad smell. There was no amount of "positive thinking" that was going to get me out of this downward spiral. Everything had become overwhelming. Even music, which I used to love to listen to while working, became an irritant.

Suddenly, light, noise, and social interactions were too much for my brain to process. I couldn't manage social situations anymore and moved across Australia to cut off ties with friends. I barely had enough energy to stay awake, let alone hold a conversation or speak onstage. Reading and writing, my passions, became too exhausting for me to contemplate. My short-term and long-term memory were both failing, and my speech was slurred.

Everyone was beginning to notice, no matter how hard I tried to hide it. I became plagued with self-doubt and fear that made every waking moment painful. Worse yet, I began having suicidal thoughts.

I beat myself up because the soundtrack in my head was stuck on repeat. It kept saying, *I should know better! I should know how to fix this! Why can't I stay focused? Why can't I think my way out of this one? Why aren't I motivated and driven like I used to be? Where did my confidence and energy go? Why do I feel like I'm not good enough anymore?* And: *What the f—k is wrong with me? I know I'm capable of more!* I felt like I was falling out of an airplane without a parachute. I was just waiting to hit the ground, desperately hoping someone would catch me before I came crashing down.

Like many of you, I mistakenly thought I could self-medicate with self-help. For years, it had worked. This time, nothing worked, and I wanted to know why.

I shared my symptoms with doctors from Adelaide to Melbourne to Dubbo and was confronted with patronizing remarks like, "Most people never work out while they're fatigued," "You look fit and healthy; you should be fine," and, "Are you depressed?" I was but not for the reasons they believed. I walked out of the last office in tears, having been told I needed to accept these symptoms as my fate.

This was my first revelation that the medical field had been failing me for more than 20 years. Doctors are trained to diagnose the symptoms, not the underlying cause. I needed to seek out doctors who didn't follow this traditional approach and were willing to investigate deeper with the newest medical advances and scientific research. I needed to find visionary doctors who realized that the traditional model was doing more harm than good.

I wanted to dig out the underlying causes from the roots, not cover them up as the doctors would have me do. None of them had any answers. I felt more and more defeated daily, on the verge of a complete mental breakdown.

Have you ever had a goal you wanted to achieve, but it always slipped through your fingertips? Have you ever doubted yourself and your ability to the point where you gave up before you broke through? Have you ever given up on yourself, your dream, and your purpose because you felt you had nothing left to give? Have you known you were capable of more, but you didn't know how to unlock that capacity? Have you read countless personal development books, listened to podcasts, or participated in coaching or therapy just to end up right back where you started? No amount of willpower can unlock this dilemma for you.

Our "hustle until you die" culture that applauds those who work themselves into an early grave would peg you as weak-minded. They would say, "You're just making excuses! You're being lazy and failing because you're not working hard enough!" Worse yet, they would tell you, "It's all in your head; you just need to push through!"

But what if it wasn't just all in your head? What if your excuses were a symptom of a deeper problem, not a poor attitude? And what if there were countless scientific links between food, mood, nutritional deficiencies, gut health, inflammation, energy, medication, and psychology being ignored and leading to dangerous consequences?

What if the "hustle now" culture, personal development, and therapeutic and medical models were too simplistic in isolation? These models for success fail to take in the bigger picture of what influences human emotion, behavior, and performance. And, worst yet, what if people ended up believing they were worthless as a result of this culture?

Every time we log onto social media, we're overwhelmed with articles on the best time to wake up, blog posts on the productivity habits of the superwealthy, and images of people living their best lives (#Iwokeuplikethis), all designed to help us become smarter, faster, healthier, more productive, and more empowered. But what if we've had it backward all this time? What if there's more to success than simply hustling for our goals, waking up early, working late nights, and pushing ourselves beyond the breaking point?

Four years ago, I was at my peak physically, mentally, and in business. I was delivering online marketing courses to thousands of entrepreneurs internationally and speaking at business and personal development events in front of thousands of people across Australia. My audiences included local and state governments, universities, and companies like Toyota on the topics of business, marketing, sales, personal development, and personal branding. I was consulting with one-on-one business clients and helping them grow their businesses nationally. And I was traveling between New Zealand and Australia to work with high-profile clients. A regular in the Australian business media, I wrote articles and conducted interviews on a monthly basis, and I loved it! I was interviewed as one of Australia's leading personal branding and marketing experts for magazines including the Australian versions of *GQ* and *Marie Claire*, among countless others.

Every time I stepped onstage to present, I came alive. I used this energy to write my first three books, two of which became bestsellers and all three of which I wrote in 30 to 40 days each. My brain was firing on all cylinders, and I had focus like you wouldn't believe. Nothing was too hard, and no problem was too big to solve. I used this energy and focus to build an online education business that boasted more than $1 million in sales with two part-time team members and required only four to five hours of my time per day.

Then everything changed. I wanted to give it all up, and I couldn't work out why. I was trapped! I couldn't escape, and I certainly couldn't take on a full-time job as I was barely getting through the day. My resume would have read, "Proactive worker who naps a lot."

In 2017, I packed my bags and flew to America.

You see, I knew I had the capacity in me for more, but for some reason someone had changed the lock on the door, and I couldn't open it. My soul was willing, but my body was weak. Fearful of where my uncontrolled emotions would take me next, I drank several cups of green tea one hot summer's day and pushed myself to come up with a solution. I wasn't willing to give up on ten years of hard work. But I knew I wouldn't find the answers in a self-help book or at the doctor's office. I had tried and failed miserably. I wanted to know why!

In my exhausted state, I came across *New York Times* bestselling author Dave Asprey's audiobook *Head Strong: The Bulletproof Plan to Activate Untapped Brain Energy to Work Smarter and Think Faster—In Just Two Weeks*, in which he shares his journey of coming back from debilitating fatigue by biohacking his body and brain back to health. He gave me hope.

Biohacking is the practice of changing the environment inside and outside you so that you gain full control of your biology to enhance your body, mind, and life. It has grown in popularity in recent years as individuals are discovering the numerous benefits of taking control of their health and leaving nothing to chance.

So I did the most illogical thing of all—I pitched a book idea to *Entrepreneur* magazine in which I would go on a 90-day mission to biohack my mind and body and develop a plan anyone could use based on what I discovered from biohackers, neuroscientists, doctors, psychologists, and more. This didn't just mean getting better; it meant continuing to optimize and upgrade my performance. To do so, I had to ask the same questions we have asked repeatedly for years but look at them from completely different perspectives to come up with new answers we have never been able to arrive at before. I wanted complete and conclusive answers to questions for which I had received overly simplistic answers, questions such as:

▶ Why don't people really change?

▶ How can I improve my memory and my confidence?

▶ What really holds people back from becoming successful?

▶ What is the root cause of procrastination? Is it psychology, bio-chemistry, or a mix of both?

▶ Why do we get stressed, and what are the quickest ways to obliterate it?

▶ Why do we make excuses? Are we just lazy, or is there an underlying cause all the self-help gurus have overlooked?

▶ How can I upgrade my focus and increase my levels of motivation?

▶ How can I unleash my purpose and live a meaningful life?

▶ What is the best way to hack my own body for endless amounts of energy, clarity, and focus?

▶ How can I reboot my brain, reimagine my life, and reawaken my soul to become unstoppable, so that no goal or dream feels out of reach?

In hindsight, 90-day goal looks insane, especially considering I could barely string a sentence together at the time I pitched the book. All of a sudden, I was going to not only attempt to solve a problem even the doctors couldn't but also write a book on the new science of success using neuroscience, biohacking, technology, and psychology. But what did I have to lose?

I thought I was at the end of my writing career because my cognitive abilities and motivation were no longer accessible. Thankfully, the magazine and its publishing division jumped at the idea. To be honest, I didn't know how this journey was going to unfold. But because my options were fast becoming limited, I threw every last ounce of my willpower and energy, including traveling from Australia to Canada and the United States, into seeking answers.

If willpower is the fuel in your reserve tank, mine had one drop remaining. I was going to use it as wisely as possible to completely refuel and reboot my body, brain, and soul.

The only way I could achieve this mission would be to close my "identity gap." The identity gap is the distance between who you are and who you need to become to reach your goals. Our identity dictates our thoughts, behaviors, and actions and either sets us up for success or primes us for failure at both a conscious and subconscious level. It limits or expands our thinking and our ability to succeed, depending on which identity we hold at any given time. You can't be a good accountant if you're a painter at heart.

Our capacity for success is limited by who we believe ourselves to be, to the degree our biochemistry allows us to be it. We hold various identities throughout our lives: mother, father, brother, sister, entrepreneur, employee. But what about an identity that allows us to unlock our potential and live a life unleashed? We need to evolve into a person who can be more, do more—and have more, someone who can become a catalyst for change and never-ending improvement. This is the beautiful self-evolution of who you are becoming in the pursuit of your goals—an evolution that stretches us and encourages us to grow. When we fail, it is because we have failed to evolve into the person we need to be to solve the necessary problems to break through.

To find new answers, I traveled the world and met with the top biohackers, neuroscientists, doctors, and microbiome experts. I tried out the latest wearable technology designed to unlock human potential. Many of these devices, funded by the Pentagon and the Defense Advanced Research Projects Agency (DARPA), are being used by the military and Olympic athletes. I tested the latest smart drugs to boost my focus, mood, and cognition and met with the best of the best working in revolutionary medicine, who performed comprehensive lab tests to uncover any physiological problems affecting my mood and motivation.

You'll discover how my medications, nutritional deficiencies, and foods influenced my behavior; what changes I embraced to correct that behavior; and how these factors could be impacting your life. You'll also discover how using the latest neurotechnology devices trained my brain to focus, and how I tested my body with a four-week CrossFit challenge. You'll see the changes I went through when I experienced intermittent fasting, experimented with various dietary protocols, tracked my sleep, took countless supplements, and tested technology that reduced my stress in less than 30 seconds. I even walked across hot coals to find some answers—literally, not metaphorically! Although, that might not have been as nerve-wracking as the colonic irrigation I had.

What I found was truly jaw-dropping. By using the real science of success, I was able to bring myself back to full health and help others in the process. In the following pages, I dive into the real science of success, not just the simplistic version we have subscribed to that is far too limiting. Along this journey, you will also meet others who through persistence have overcome serious challenges to become unstoppable in their fields by biohacking their way to the top.

I welcome you now to join me on what ended up being an incredible journey. Buckle up; you're in for a ride like no other—one that will result in an incredible paradigm shift into the science of success you never saw coming.

—Ben Angel
The Accidental Biohacker,

PART I

DECIPHERING YOUR IDENTITY GAP

CHAPTER 1

A Paradigm Shift Decades in the Making

Closing Your Identity Gap

I was on the verge of a breakdown and beginning to have suicidal thoughts, and I didn't know where to turn. My life at this point was an absolute lie. I was touted as "The Agent of Influence" to hundreds of thousands of devoted entrepreneurs and companies, yet I couldn't even motivate myself to look at my next goal. And I was angry about it.

It was my dream to move to New York and continue my career as an author. I had visualized this goal countless times. I could see myself walking the busy city streets, going to cafes and restaurants, and, yes, even having my very own Carrie Bradshaw moment writing in the window of a classic New York City townhouse (don't judge me). However, for reasons that eluded me, I couldn't even bring myself to look at my to-do list; it was too overwhelming. I was fast becoming what my industry sees as a has-been. My dream was getting further and further out of reach, and it didn't matter how I tried to convince myself that I was OK. The truth was, I wasn't all right, and nobody had any answers as to why.

You may be able to relate. You know you're capable of more, but for some reason you can't unlock the capacity to thoroughly express it through your purpose, your vision, and your goals. Your dreams always feel just out of reach. And, no matter how hard you try to stretch yourself to grasp it, you always fall short. You try to convince yourself that you'll get up earlier, work harder, and do whatever it takes to achieve your goals, but time after time, you miss. Is it us? Do we just have a poor attitude? Do we just need to toughen up? What are the super-successful people doing that we're not? I followed their strategies, but I didn't get their outcomes. Why?

We are taught that if you're sad, you need to be more positive. If you're angry, you need to find peace. If you're procrastinating, you're lazy. If you're making excuses, you're weak. It's all in your head. Pick up a self-help book and get over it.

And yet if you go to a doctor complaining of these same symptoms, you'll get a medical diagnosis of depression and be put on antidepressants to fix a chemical imbalance in your brain. Even then, the doctor can't take the time to find out the cause of your decline, thanks to training, attitudes, and time constraints.

What's worse is that the self-help industry looks at these same symptoms and believes an injection of motivation and an inspirational story is the answer. It's not interested in finding out the underlying cause either.

This realization led me to ask: If these are my symptoms, what is the cause?

We all experience setbacks to varying degrees throughout our lifetimes, some more severe than others. In a 2018 online Facebook survey my team conducted of 2,000 entrepreneurs internationally, we discovered the following revelations:

- ▶ 75 percent experienced brain fog.
- ▶ 82 percent experienced procrastination.
- ▶ 82 percent were easily distracted.
- ▶ 65 percent were easily overwhelmed.
- ▶ 71 percent experienced high levels of stress.
- ▶ 58 percent did not wake up feeling refreshed.
- ▶ 47 percent experienced sadness.
- ▶ 62 percent had inconsistent energy throughout the day.
- ▶ 65 percent got caught in a negative mental feedback loop.

These numbers are astonishing in that they demonstrate a large percentage of people experiencing symptoms that could be related to depression. In this specific demographic, we have highly motivated people who are passionate about their goals and embedded in a workforce that is usually made up of the movers and shakers of the business world, yet an overwhelming number of them are not enjoying complete wellness when it comes to their mental health. How many of them will burn out before they can achieve their dreams due to biological factors?

By looking more carefully, we can see that there is an underlying cause triggering these symptoms. I firmly believe we can cure ourselves of this "disease" of elusive well-being. Especially in the United States, we are seeing an epidemic of prescription drugs as the answer to these symptoms, and the medical industry is not yet willing to trade in their prescription pads for questionnaires to discover the root causes of our decline.

Closing the Gap to Who You Are Supposed to Be

My story is not the exception to the rule; it is the rule. These are all symptoms of an underlying issue completely ignored by the personal development industry and the medical profession.

Like a frog, which will slowly die when put into tepid water that's then brought to a gradual boil, we, too, will adapt to our suffering without conscious awareness until severe symptoms appear and medical intervention is required. At that point, a scorched-earth approach is taken instead of a preventative one.

All these symptoms decrease our mental ability to process new information, with hazardous implications when it comes to closing the identity gap from our current self to who we need to become to reach our goals. In particular, it limits who we believe ourselves to be and our perceived ability to bring our visions to life. Even if mild, it snaps us back into who we are at our worst.

It wasn't until after visiting a doctor in the rural city of Dubbo in New South Wales, Australia, that I had my first major realization after what ended up being another patronizing interaction.

Looking at the Conundrum

I wasn't tired because I was depressed; I was depressed because I was tired. I want to know why I'm tired! Being depressed as a result of fatigue was the first of many discoveries that helped me uncover the solution, not just to my symptoms, but to reaching my goals and rewriting my model for success from the ground up. If I could discover why I was tired, making excuses, and procrastinating, everything else would fall into place. I would finally get my motivation and drive back, quit making excuses, and reignite my energy and passion for the projects I used to love.

Like millions of other people, I had started off with mild symptoms that I quickly dismissed as the result of overworking, a weak mental attitude, or late nights and tight deadlines. I had subscribed to the philosophy of "just do it" without being fully aware of the consequences.

When the soul is willing but the body is weak, the body can't fulfill the mission the soul is on. My soul was more than ready, willing, and able. Despite reading countless self-help books, attending seminars, and drowning myself in motivational strategies for 15 years, I realized that the information I had was sorely incomplete.

We've been taught that our psychology is the number-one key to success; our biochemistry doesn't get a mention unless you're an elite athlete or experiencing severe physical symptoms that are obvious to others. But even mild biochemical problems can prevent you from reaching your goals.

Strategic planning, mindset, and willpower are essential for one's ability to think and compete on the job and in life. These factors can make one a legitimate competitor. However, biochemistry, which fuels one's endurance and tenacity, provides the speed to succeed.

We tend to automatically assume that we're all biochemically on par with the likes of Tony Robbins, Richard Branson, the Dalai Lama, and other peak performers. But some of them actively work to hack their biochemistry. Others, through a combination of factors we'll be talking about in this book, got lucky; their biochemistry naturally makes them less susceptible to stress, brain fog, and sadness, helping clear the path for their success.

That's not to say they don't experience these ailments; they do but to manageable degrees. Nor is it to say they don't work hard; it just doesn't seem as hard because they are biochemically sound, establishing a firm foundation on which everything else can flourish.

We imitate their strategies. We want to know what time they get up, what they eat, how they think, what their core beliefs and reading habits are, but not for one second do we consider that each of us is biochemically unique. We each process our food, thoughts, and emotions very differently due to numerous factors—factors we ignore in the quest for personal success, unless one of our goals is to lose weight.

Anyone can apply the same psychological principles as the ultrasuccessful, but if you're severely depleted on things like vitamin D, omega-3s, vitamin C, vitamin B12, dopamine, serotonin, or even testosterone (both women and men), you could experience mild to severe brain fog, fatigue, lethargy, anxiety, stress, and depression, all of which will severely impede your ability to remain focused and reach your goals. It's like putting a plant in toxic soil and willing it to grow. It doesn't matter how much you tell it anything is possible, that f—ker is going to die!

Ignorance of biochemistry undermines the psychological principles we're taught to apply. It's the invisible factor that derails us—an unseen hand that holds you back from crossing the finish line. Without this information, any strategies for productivity and peak performance are incomplete and ineffective.

Instead of realizing our biochemistry is out of alignment, we attach a negative emotional mental state to our goals and decide the goal itself is too hard or too lofty. We end up with self-defeating thoughts, such as, "I'm too tired," "I haven't got time for this," "What's the point?", "I feel too overwhelmed," or "I'm so stressed." To avoid that scenario, perhaps we should ask ourselves a few questions:

- ▶ What if instead of just studying the habits of highly successful people, our best creative minds, and multimillionaire game changers we compiled a database of their medical data that examines their serotonin and dopamine levels and microbiome makeup and compares it to those who routinely quit, make excuses, or experience more intense negative emotions?
- ▶ Would poor biochemical results impact their ability to cross the finish line? Do these biochemical levels impact the abilities of the highly successful to overcome setbacks and cross the finish line? Would these biological processes provide a real and complete understanding as to why successful people behave a specific way, not based on their mental attitude and upbringing alone?
- ▶ If a person were able to deplete their dopamine and serotonin levels, how would their behavior change?
- ▶ Could a successful, confident person be incapacitated physically and mentally as a result of nutritional deficiencies?
- ▶ If we were to look at their biochemical levels when they encountered a major setback, what would we discover?
- ▶ Upon examining other aspects of a person's life during a major physical and emotional setback, what would we find? What were they eating at the time? How did their behavior change? What occurred in the body, not just in their attitude?

(We are of course setting aside the ethical dilemma of compiling such a database; these questions are purely hypothetical.) The only time we consider biochemistry is when we're in decline or attempting to lose weight, not when we're trying to become a better version of ourselves. When we fail to reach our goals, it's implied we have a weak mental attitude, not a biochemical weakness that can be rapidly rectified with the right help. True personal transformation requires both biochemistry and psychology for lasting change. Otherwise, we'll default back to what's easy.

When the brain is weak, the output will be meek. One finding in our survey of 2,000 entrepreneurs was unexpected, but is blindingly obvious in hindsight: 57 to 65 percent of those experiencing brain fog were easily distracted, often procrastinated, lost their train of thought, and felt overwhelmed and sad, and were *also* experiencing food cravings. This was a *major* contributing biochemical factor as to why their day was being derailed and why they tended to give up. This discovery further led me to believe that success isn't only in the mind or body; it's in both.

To be truly successful means not only hacking our minds, but hacking our chemistry as well. Looking at this conundrum from a new perspective challenged everything I believed about self-help. I, like others, had been led to believe that you can will your way out of your excuses, procrastination, brain fog, negative thoughts, and sadness, but if you're depressed, you need a drug.

But what if that's not true?

How much does psychology play a part in your success and how much does biochemistry play a part?

The reality is that you cannot use mental ability to compensate for inadequate biochemistry. It can help, but unless you address and understand the underlying issues, avoidance and procrastination will continue. Your personal development practices will only be effective when your biochemistry is working at peak efficiency and supporting your body to its fullest.

New Approach to Old Problems

What do you tackle first, your mindset or your biology? In the past, we'd pick up a self-help book or seek out a therapist, who might or might not address our nutritional deficiencies.

These approaches might have been fine a decade ago, before the major changes to our environment and food supply, light pollution, and the psychological impact of social media began affecting our daily behavior. However, our prehistoric brain hasn't caught up with today's technological advances; our biochemistry is stuck in our evolutionary past. As a result, we're glued to our computer, phone, and notebook screens 24/7, and this addiction to technology is having a profound impact on how we behave.

Studies show that social media and app companies are using their technology to create addictive platforms, for which we unknowingly pay the price.[1] They are using cute emojis and keeping track of how many times we use their app, thus creating an addictive social media habit. These habits become pleasing to the user, embedding the need to do it again for that brief hit of pleasure. Facebook has admittedly hijacked one of our neurotransmitters, dopamine, for financial gain. Dopamine, otherwise known as the "reward chemical" due to it being in charge of our brain's pleasure-reward system, can give us the drive and focus we need to be productive. Unfortunately, we aren't always aware that this is happening until we feel it impacting other areas of our life.

Dopamine is a key component in various brain functions involving sleep, learning, motor control, working memory, and our ability to focus and concentrate.[2] Parkinson's, attention deficit hyperactivity disorder (ADHD), and other conditions are at the extreme spectrum end of abnormally low dopamine levels. In other words, is social media addiction a result of lower dopamine levels due to stress and the modern world we now live in? Excuses, procrastination, and brain fog are possible symptoms of deficient levels of dopamine, not the causes.

That's when I was hit with a blinding flash of the obvious: My excuses, negative thought patterns, and lack of drive and motivation weren't simply the result of a weak mental attitude. The problem was a neurotransmitter deficiency combined with various other factors. No one is inherently unworthy, useless, or weak; we all fluctuate throughout our lifetimes. Life, as you'll find out through the course of this book, is not a controlled experiment.

Positive thinking isn't a substitute for a nutritional deficiency. Unfortunately, we don't associate vague symptoms such as low self-esteem, anger, carbohydrate cravings, digestive complaints, feeling overwhelmed, insomnia, joylessness, brain fog, and poor cognitive function with low serotonin levels. Instead, we beat ourselves up for not being as good as everyone else.[3]

> *You are not your excuses; your excuses are your biochemistry.*

With that in mind, could my internal chemistry be triggering my procrastination, fear, anxiety, and greater willingness to quit? I had only ever experienced these fleetingly in the past, and they always subsided. This time they had laid roots I had to dig up. The short answer is a resounding "YES!"

Diagnosing Failure

The greatest problem with our old approach to success is that it fails to bridge the gap between biochemistry and psychology. The two are so intertwined they cannot be separated, and yet our medical system, the personal development industry, psychologists, naturopaths, nutritionists, and therapists have drawn lines between their methodologies for decades that have led to emphasizing psychology over biochemistry, or vice versa—but not a combination of both.

The true evolution will occur when we have a convergence of all practices of medicine. This is beginning to occur in the field of functional medicine, and it will revolutionize health care and the way we think about ourselves and the science of success. But before we address success, let's talk about failure.

Why We Really Fail

Failure isn't just due to low dopamine levels. It's also a question of managing our "fight or flight" response. When we're stressed, the body's somatic nervous system triggers what is known as the fight or flight response. The body kicks into high gear and shifts its energy resources toward fighting off a threat or fleeing from an enemy.

The fight or flight response releases the hormones adrenaline and cortisol, which sets off a cascade of internal processes, including increased respiration, fast heartbeat, and blood vessel dilation in the arms and legs, which triggers our digestive system to increase our bloodstream glucose levels to deal with the emergency. Once the emergency is over, everything returns to normal.[4]

However, if it continues over an extended period, chronic stress can cause problems ranging from cognitive impairment and emotional instability to physical illness. Emotional symptoms include agitation, moodiness, feeling overwhelmed, an inability to relax, low self-esteem, worthlessness, depression, and isolation. Physical symptoms could include headaches, low energy, upset stomach, muscle tension, chest pain, insomnia, colds and infections, loss of desire, nervousness, shaking, or difficulty swallowing. Stress can also lead to cognitive symptoms: racing thoughts, forgetfulness, disorganization, inability to focus, brain fog, poor judgment, pessimism, and constant worrying.[5]

Stress, Food Cravings, and an Inability to Focus on What Matters

Stress also plays a role. A staggering 71 percent of our 2,000 respondents said "yes" to experiencing high levels of stress, and here's where it gets fascinating: Stress causes food cravings, specifically for sugar and highly processed food. The digestion of this food releases the neurotransmitter serotonin, which brings us waves of calm and relaxation, allowing us to regain our focus temporarily, until the serotonin levels taper off.

Between 57 and 65 percent of our respondents who reported being plagued with brain fog, feeling overwhelmed, worrying, and sadness also experienced food cravings.

Carbohydrate cravings can be spurred on by low serotonin levels as this "feel good" chemical is released during the consumption of food. This results in a negative feedback loop driving people to consume excessive amounts of carbs to alter how they feel for the better. These cravings are often seen in individuals who are exposed to high levels of stress.[6]

The connection to our inability to succeed lies in two factors that are at play on a day-to-day basis. When we experience food cravings or stress, our fight or flight response is triggered. This takes blood away from our prefrontal cortex, which controls a myriad of executive functions, including complex behaviors like coordination, impulse control, emotional reactions, personality, focusing, organizing, complex planning, and prioritizing simultaneous information.[7]

This sets up a nasty cycle: Our blood sugar drops, our cravings increase, and our cortisol spikes, limiting our ability to control our impulses, attention, and emotional reactions. We reach for sweet or highly refined carbohydrates and our blood sugar increases, followed later by a sudden drop, which results in brain fog, inability to focus, loss of motivation, and the inability to reach our goals.

We attempt to address this cycle in our children by limiting their sugar intake, and yet we dismiss it when it comes to our own psychological well-being. We've also been duped by companies that are putting a "healthy spin" on their products, even though many of them are high in sugars, sucralose, refined carbohydrates, caffeine, and preservatives, all of which impact our ability to think clearly.

When your blood sugar drops or you experience high levels of stress, your brain switches into survival mode, driving you to take more risks and putting your primal brain into high gear. This shift causes your personality, mood, and identity to fluctuate throughout the day. Your motivation may be high in the morning, but by the afternoon, you'd rather sit on the couch and watch TV because you've used up all your mental capacity for the day.

In this primal state, the brain's key purpose is to sustain life, not keep you focused on achieving your goals. That doesn't even get a rating on the scale of critical functions necessary for your life to continue. In this state, otherwise known as self-preservation mode, you default to maintaining the status quo and nothing more.

The problem is that most of us can't switch it off, or if we do, it quickly comes back on again later, creating a roller-coaster ride of emotions and an inability to complete projects on time. How easily it comes on is directly linked to how we've learned to process possible threats. This is based on numerous factors, including our upbringing, genetics, and hormone levels like serotonin and dopamine just to name a few. If your serotonin or dopamine levels are low, you're more susceptible to dealing with setbacks poorly and more likely to have a reactive instead of responsive internal environment.

Our current lifestyles bombard us with stress factors daily once the pebble starts rolling downhill from something that seems inconsequential at the time. Examples of these stress factors could be a reaction to unhealthy foods, allergies, bad news, insomnia, pollution, hostile co-workers, financial stress, too much caffeine, relationship conflicts, family issues, constant stress, or a dirty look from someone on the street. The stress begins to pick up pace, and other problems appear as a result. It happens so slowly that we don't notice it initially.

At that point, any attempt to get out in front of it becomes futile because our cognitive functions have been disabled; it's like searching for a key in a room with the lights off.

To find the switch, we have to change identities and fuel sources, even if just for a moment, to reboot our spirit, body, and mind in unison.

The Old Models of Treatment

While speaking with experts in the field of medicine, psychiatry, personal development, biohacking, neurofeedback, biofeedback, and neuroscience, I discovered something interesting. They each have their own unique formula for success, but they rarely merge them into one cohesive framework to create lasting change for those of us who are asking more from ourselves. Some of these frameworks include:

▶ *The Medical Model*: diagnoses and treats illness, often prescribing pills to manage symptoms without always uncovering and addressing the root cause, resulting in possible side effects. It views the body as a collection of independent organs that gets divided up by medical specialties.

▸ *The Self-Help Model*: drives awareness, uncovers self-sabotaging behavior, inspires through storytelling, and encourages clients to change their beliefs and model the ultrasuccessful with drops of psychology thrown in for good measure. Unfortunately, it fails to identify any nutritional deficiencies that could be contributing to these behaviors, potentially resulting in short-term success without lasting change. Clients receive an injection of willpower, but when that runs out, they default back to their old "preset mode."

▸ *The Therapeutic Models*: of which there are many, including cognitive, mindfulness, behavioral, and interpersonal therapies. Similar to the self-help model, these therapies may result in patients not making fundamental changes to their biochemistry, giving them only one piece of the puzzle as to why they may lack motivation, drive, focus, and calm.

The field of functional medicine is changing the way illness is treated. It seeks out and addresses the root causes of disease. Unlike traditional medicine, where the body is viewed as a collection of independent organs, functional medicine views the body as an integrated system. Its objective is to treat the whole body, not just the symptoms.

The insights I received from the experts I spoke to and the countless supplements, diets, mindfulness strategies, and wearable devices I trialed during this 90-day period resulted in me reworking the science of success from the bottom up. Learn as I take a complete functional medicine approach to peak performance to guide you from finding the gap in your identity to being at the top of your game and becoming unstoppable.

CHALLENGE ONE

Halo Sport: Technology built for athletic training and used by Special Operations (S.O.) forces.

Unwrapping my first wearable device excited me to no end. It was Halo Sport, a pair of black headphones used by elite athletes from the Olympics, Major League Baseball, NBA, and NFL to improve everything from endurance and power to muscle movement.

Halo Sport works by sending electrical stimulation across the motor cortex, the part of our brain that controls muscle contraction, during training to establish stronger and more optimized connections between your brain and muscles, putting you into a state of "hyperplasticity."

The research behind the device is extensive. In August 2016, a project was announced with the U.S. Department of Defense to help train their S.O. The partnership was the first commercial contract signed by the Pentagon's Defense Innovation Unit, which aims to use technology to improve military defense.[8]

I chose it over other similar devices due to the heavy-hitting research that had gone into it, which others had failed to provide.

During the first 30 days of the 90-day challenge, I tested it using a CrossFit workout I'd completed multiple times; I had documented every workout over the past four years, so I had extensive baseline stats to compare it to. Lo and behold, it was beyond anything I'd ever experienced before. Every single day, despite experiencing fatigue, brain fog, and lethargy, I was able to break personal bests.

Not just by a little bit, but by a lot!

CHAPTER 2

Unlocking the Keys to Your Kingdom
Your Bridge to Being Unstoppable

It took me four months to track down Dave Asprey and secure an interview with him on his farm in an undisclosed location in Canada. I was willing to do anything to find answers even if that involved international travel. I wanted to feel better, have more energy, and most importantly, have the mental clarity I needed to reach my goals. This was my last-ditch attempt to succeed where I had constantly failed before.

To get to him, my partner and I took two flights and a ferry in the height of winter at the end of 2017. The ferry ride across the inlet was picturesque yet freezing! The fresh Canadian air was a welcome relief from hot and humid Florida.

I stood shivering on the ferry as the questions I wanted to ask him rattled around in my head, such as *What do you know about unlocking our human potential that others don't?* And *What do I need to do to become an unstoppable version of myself?*

I knew Dave, one of the world's top biohackers, would have the answers. No one else had gone to such extreme lengths to optimize human performance through biohacking. Dave is also a *New York Times* bestselling author of *The Bulletproof Diet* and the creator of Bulletproof Coffee and a supplement range. He is followed by more than 1 million loyal fans globally and has even launched Bulletproof Labs, based in Santa Monica, California. While it looks like a gym, it isn't. They take a scientific approach to training your mind and body by using the most cutting-edge, science-backed technologies to achieve the highest state of physical and cognitive performance. I was heading to Dave's own personal lab to get an insider's look at how he thinks and operates.

I first heard of Dave when I was at my lowest point. Listening to his audiobook gave me a sense of relief that my fatigue and illness wasn't all in my head. I wasn't unwell because I was weak-minded. There was something biochemically wrong with me that was influencing my mindset and ability to succeed.

The problem was no matter how many doctors I went to, none of them saw things from the perspective of a biohacker. A biohacker seeks to understand illnesses at the source and create a plan of attack. The interactions left me unsatisfied.

I soon realized that if I was going to change my life, I had to seek out others who had taken unconventional approaches to solving their problems. Dave fit the bill. He'd spent more than $1 million hacking his own biology over the past two decades. His objective was to help people succeed at levels far beyond what they would typically expect.

The Snapback Effect and the Identity Gap

To do this required an identity shift, not just at the psychological level but at the biochemical one as well. I realized I would always default back to my original psychological settings if my biological settings weren't brought up to speed with the new requirements placed on them.

I call this default setting the snapback effect. You cannot outperform your current concept of "self" or your existing biochemistry. I will go into more detail about the snapback effect a bit later, but first, I want to explain to you why we have an identity gap between who we are and who we want to become. Then I will show you the steps to create a biohacking and psychological model for successful, long-lasting change.

Change can be phenomenally hard unless all the factors are taken into consideration, especially when we need to identify anything that is holding us back from success. The objective is to escape our self-imposed echo chamber: those negative thoughts that reinforce and echo back our beliefs, ideas, and values in a way that reinforces and amplifies them through repetition.

There are myriad ways our echo chamber sets us up to fail. For example, in order to keep you coming back, Facebook's algorithm is designed to show you what you want to see based on your online behavior and biases. This acts to reinforce all the existing beliefs you have about yourself and the world, as do your physical environment, relationships, and biochemistry.[1]

> *A change in attitude will only hold for as long as your biochemistry supports it.*

Your biochemistry, when in mild to severe disarray, can lead to negative thoughts that are difficult to suppress or eliminate.

Think of the last time you tried to reach one of your goals. Maybe it was one that had you really excited at first, but as time progressed, you fell back into your old routine until you forgot about it. This is what I call the snapback effect.

Anytime we try to evolve from who we are to who we want to become to reach our goals, we create tension between our old and new selves, both psychologically and biochemically. This is what I call the identity gap. Each "self" is fighting for residence within your mind. The one that wins is the one that avoids triggering your "fight or flight" response. Therefore, you are creating a "gap" between who you are and who you want to become.

The greater the distance between the biological resources you have available and the psychological needs required to reach your goal, the greater the likelihood is that you'll snap back, give up, and default to your old self.

Why?

The new psychological needs deplete your biochemical resources. When you cross the threshold, your brain switches modes and seeks to preserve the limited energy supply left for critical biological functions. This can manifest behaviorally via excuses, brain fog, lethargy, and avoidance. And you thought you were just lazy!

You Under the Microscope

Thinking of adding another goal to your already full task list is like a power station lighting a city at maximum capacity and then suddenly adding another city to the grid without additional capacity being added. The new city will max out the entire system and a safety switch will flip, defaulting back to its original settings to protect itself from damage, much like our brain.

Our primordial brain is that safety switch. When it comes on, it reduces our available output in areas we're not even aware of, thereby changing our behavior.

In this state, our brain seeks to preserve the status quo. To do otherwise would jeopardize our life. Our brain must guard its resources and defend against further attacks, such as attempting to leave our comfort zone and seeking a new identity.

The first signs of this snapback will be mild symptoms, such as brain fog, slight headaches, and sleeping more than usual. You might simply brush them off. As you adapt to them, the symptoms will eventually escalate and become more extreme, manifesting as anxiety, stress, and possibly depression. Your body and brain will not stop reacting to the stimuli to reject change until you do something about it.

Attempting to leave your comfort zone and evolve into your new identity is like putting a stake in the ground, throwing a rubber band around it, stepping into the open loop, and trying to sprint as far away from the stake as you can, without building up your muscles first.

But if you don't have enough energy to push against the tension (the change created based on these new needs), you'll snap back into your old self hard and fast. This old self is drenched in behaviors the primal brain considers safe, since it doesn't exert your energy levels further.

The shock from the snapback can dramatically impact the way we see the world and ourselves, making us cautious about future attempts at change. The key is to evolve into our new self without flipping the switch that makes us snap back and resume our former status quo.

Turn Off Decision Fatigue to Reach Your Goals Faster

No matter how stable and rational we are, we cannot make decision after decision or maintain high levels of focus and output without paying a biological price. This is one reason why ordinary, sensible people lash out, make irrational decisions, buy junk food, make excuses, and ultimately quit before they experience a breakthrough.

As the day goes on, your mental capacity gets used up and slows down to a crawl, and it becomes less likely that you'll be able to sustain that newfound positive attitude. The more decisions you make, the harder each consecutive decision becomes, resulting in the brain seeking one of two shortcuts. One shortcut is to act impulsively without taking time to assess the consequences. The second is to do nothing.

In a 2011 study by the National Academy of Sciences, scientists demonstrated the impact of decision fatigue. Researchers Jonathan Levav formerly of Columbia Business School and Shai Danziger formerly of Ben-Gurion University analyzed more than 1,100 decisions from a parole board in an Israeli prison over a ten-month period. They discovered that prisoners who appeared early in the morning or just after a food break received parole approximately 70 percent of the time. Those who appeared before the board at the end of the day or just before a break received parole less than 10 percent of the time.[2]

These researchers found that the judges' decisions exhibited no ill intent toward the prisoners. The likelihood of receiving parole was purely linked to the countless decisions they had to make. This research demonstrates that there is a finite amount of mental energy for applying self-control, and it wanes as more decisions are made. The mental state can become further compromised by stress, nutritional deficiencies, and other environmental factors. You thought it was something innate about you that was keeping you from achieving your dreams, that perhaps you were meant to fail. But now there is a glimmer of hope that there is truly a way out of this rabbit hole.

It raises the question: Are you working with or against the tide? When we're in the zone, everything flows, it's easy, we remember names, stay on task, and tune out distractions. When we're going against the tide, our attention is easily stolen, misused, and spent on activities that take you further out to sea.

Anytime you feel yourself overexerting, it is an indication that something in your physical, emotional, or biochemical makeup is out of alignment. This misalignment causes a change in attitude and a switch in identity from confident, self-assured, and focused to unfocused and lacking in confidence and clarity. Everything becomes more difficult. You start making excuses and sit there glued to your phone, desperate for a hit of dopamine.

> *You're fueling your goals with one energy source instead of two, and because it's depleting, your brain has switched on "self-preservation mode" to save you from yourself.*

Based on countless discussions with psychiatrists, doctors, neuroscientists, and biohackers and the numerous experiments I conducted during this 90-day period, my understanding of what fuels success reaches well beyond mere habits of peak performers. Habits are critical, but not as significant as the entire system working as one toward a goal that lights up your soul.

Wouldn't you love it if you could take the weight of the world from your shoulders and place it lightly on your fingertips? Now you can! This new model brought an awareness that I hadn't been able to glean from one single source. It came from an entwined understanding of many individual connections. It empowered me to continue improving and allowed me to relax and reboot when something was out of alignment with my awareness. Something *was* out of alignment and not just in my head.

The problem will always be when we switch into self-preservation mode. We go from conscious thought and deliberate creation to unconscious thought and unintentional creation with our impulse controls turned OFF.

Try solving a problem when you're not even aware you have a problem in the first place. That's 90 percent of the population at any given moment.

Your mission, if you choose to accept it, is to burn that light bulb bright. To do that and get on your way to being unstoppable, you first need to close your identity gap (see Figure 2.1).

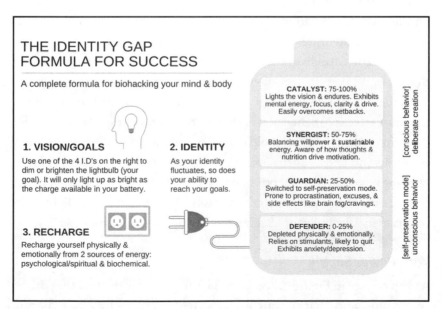

Figure 2.1 **The Identity Gap Formula for Success**

The Identity Gap Formula for Success

The first step in closing the identity gap is to choose your goal, defining who you are by the achievement of the goal. The light bulb represents your purpose, your goals (an expression of your purpose), and the person you wish to become.

Your mission is to light the bulb and keep it lit without flickering. Any flickering can result in a loss of momentum. If your battery runs flat, the light bulb will go out, any progress made will be halted, and even more effort will be required to relight it. The entire system may even need to be rebooted.

The second step is working with your identity, which is the battery that powers this light bulb. And, just like any battery, it can run flat at any point during the day, week, month, or lifetime. Also like any battery, it will begin to hold less charge over time.

This battery is broken into four levels, each representing a different identity. As we've seen, our identities fluctuate throughout the course of a day, not just a lifetime, and depend on our energy levels, mental clarity, biochemistry, and decision fatigue. When we're fully charged, we're unstoppable, but when we lack energy, we're as useless as a cell phone with a dead battery.

The four identities that make up your battery are the Catalyst, the Synergist, the Guardian, and the Defender. When an identity is running the show, it takes control of everything, consciously or unconsciously. Both the Catalyst and Synergist sit above the 50 percent line—these are the most effective mental states for you to reach your goals.

Fifty percent is the threshold mark that indicates the difference between conscious and effective behavior and unconscious and ineffective behavior. Dipping below 50 percent, our brain switches into self-preservation mode to save our energy for more critical tasks. At this point your light bulb begins to flicker, and your likelihood of giving up significantly increases.

Your Power Supply

As you can see in Figure 2.1 on page 23, the battery is the fuel that drives your vision and shapes your identity. It is recharged by two specific energy sources:

▶ *Psychological/Spiritual energy* incorporates your beliefs, values, outlook on life, willpower, focus, and attitude. This energy is nourished via ongoing education, spirituality (for some), and life experiences that lead to heightened levels of self-awareness and emotional IQ.

▶ *Biochemical energy* encompasses various factors, including nutrition, genetics, environment, allergies, overactive/underactive immune system, oxygen supply, neurofeedback, stress, movement, and electricity. All these factors must work in unison to be effective. When one factor is missing or inactive, it can cause disequilibrium to all the others, to the detriment/destabilization of your mental and physical well-being.

However, psychological and biochemical energy do not necessarily play equal roles in creating your identity. As it turns out, psychological energy is more reliant on biochemical energy.

In effect, your biochemistry, when lacking in energy, can become the thief of your psychological energy. It can steal your drive, willpower, motivation, clarity of thought, and focus. Your willpower can override it for only so long before your brain is forced into self-preservation mode and your battery drops below the 50-percent threshold. While positive thoughts and expectations can boost your serotonin levels, it may only do so temporarily, resulting in a short-term identity shift that fails to stick.

You can't simply will more vitamin D into existence. Consider your attempts at materializing a bag of money from thin air: How's that working out for you?

Stress, prescription pills, and poor nutrition can hijack our thoughts. If some prescription medications can trigger suicidal thoughts through altering our biochemistry, then could we also generate positive thoughts by hacking our own biology?

> *You can't outthink bad biochemistry by medicating it with self-help. You may get better, but will you get well?*

Closing this gap is one of the first and most crucial steps to setting yourself up for success.

Rethinking Your Body/Mind Connection

When we understand that our identity, mood, and behavior can fluctuate throughout the day, it highlights just how flawed traditional personality models are. This is why we experience a disconnect when we look at these models. When our body and mind are in alignment, we can demonstrate the personality traits assigned to us by such models (extrovert/introvert, sensitive/cautious, etc.). However, if things shift a few millimeters the other way, perhaps due to a change in their biochemistry, even a peak-performing extrovert can become an unproductive introvert. Personality is only as fixed as the biochemistry that supports it. An individual who is dedicated to their beliefs, behaviors, and patterns can suddenly throw caution to the wind and fail to assess the consequences of their actions if they are depleted of energy.

This also explains why personality test results can vary greatly depending on the time of day or the mood you are in when you take them. This demonstrates the need for a test that incorporates all elements that are key to your success, including the underlying factors that drive an individual to succeed.

Your Quest for Success

Trying to hold on to a specific identity 100 percent of the time is futile. No matter what you do, change is inevitable. We will forever encounter setbacks that will force us to embrace multiple identities at varying times of our lives. It's normal—and more important, it's life!

By breaking down the four identities I mentioned earlier, we kick off our quest to lift our awareness, achieve our goals, and let that light bulb shine. Once again, the identities are the Catalyst, the Synergist, the Guardian, and the Defender. In the sections below, I've broken each down into their vital functions and characteristics, including their strengths, emotional characteristics, cognitive functions, physiological characteristics, and energy sources. Once you read through all four, you'll understand which level you've been operating at and why. Soon you will discover why all your efforts to succeed have been trapped in a vicious cycle, like a psychological and biological tug of war. Let's dig into the specifics of each identity.

The Catalyst (75–100 percent)

The Catalyst feels they've bypassed the battery and plugged directly into the power grid, making them unstoppable.

This is your natural state. When it is eluding you, you feel a deep internal disconnect between who you are and who you know you can be. This leaves you feeling restless and anxious.

The Catalyst identity paves the way for your success and provides the fuel for the journey. Catalysts have an abundance of mental energy, focus, clarity, and drive. They are the key driver for change in society, both globally and locally. They endure even in the face of monumental setbacks. They light the way for others.

While their path may not always be easy, they are biochemically and psychologically wired to believe that it is. Catalysts are proactive and go with the tide, and when they feel themselves beginning to struggle, they take action to correct their course and continue. They are not afraid of seeking help; that's the reason they've made it where they are. (See Figure 2.2 on page 28.)

There's only one way to become a Catalyst, and that's by recovering from major setbacks that force them to be consciously aware of how they got there in the first place.

To do this, the biochemistry of a Catalyst must be healthy enough that they can still cognitively process this awareness and take corrective action. We can see this play out in rags-to-riches-to-rags stories. Many times, the person becomes hugely successful without fully understanding that it was a mix of psychology and biochemistry that helped them succeed. New success brings new challenges. For example, in celebrities, these often manifest as problems with alcohol and drug dependency.

If their psychology or biochemistry is compromised, their lack of awareness can turn them into a Defender, in which they become depleted of both types of energy. As a result, their body and brain enter self-preservation mode just to get through the day. Unless major intervention

Attributes of the Catalyst	
Strengths	Quick to adapt, problem solvers, undertake new challenges with positive expectations, deliberate creators, outgoing/reserved depending on what's required, not susceptible to criticism, not easily distracted, focus on long-term sustainable success, social media kept to bare minimum.
Emotional Characteristics	Inner strength, calmness, optimistic, even mood, friendly, high self-esteem, unstoppable, high drive to succeed, motivated, sense of satisfaction, love of learning.
Cognitive Functions	Fast thinking, conscious behavior, decisive decision making, high-functioning memory, organized, mental clarity, mental resources available to fully assess consequences of their actions, easily get into the "zone."
Physiology	Shoulders back, head up, posture in alignment top to toe, deep breathing, clear skin, confident stride, balanced digestion.
Weaknesses	Sometimes overly reliant on willpower to drive success during intense work periods. If they have become an "accidental catalyst," they will often perceive anyone less than them as weak-minded, albeit based on good intentions for others to succeed.
Energy Source	Their batteries are charged by two fuel sources: biochemical and psychological energy. Their fuel sources are clean, running on healthy fats/ketones, instead of sugar/refined carbohydrates that would cause them to crash midafternoon. While their energy levels still fluctuate throughout the day, it is not as extreme as others. They understand how to manage it with proper nutrition, rest, and recovery.

Figure 2.2 **Attributes of the Catalyst**

and help from others is available, they may remain stuck in this state. But when they recover, oh boy, do they make a comeback! Robert Downey Jr. is one of Hollywood's biggest career rebound stories. It wasn't that long ago that no one wanted to hire him, due to his drinking and the drug abuse that landed him in prison; now he's paid hundreds of millions to star in blockbuster films like *The Avengers* and *Iron Man*.

The Synergist (50–75 percent)

Synergists, although in a state of conscious awareness and deliberate creation, are still learning to balance willpower with sustainable energy that keeps them moving forward.

They're in the process of becoming more and more aware of how their psychology and biochemistry affect their motivation, their self-esteem, and their view of the world. They are future Catalysts who require some simple fine-tuning to make the next leap successfully and sustainably.

Synergists can benefit from ongoing education that teaches them how to coordinate and optimize their biochemical and psychological performance. They will have some off days, but they won't beat

Attributes of the Synergist	
Strengths	Medium to high adaptability, problem solvers, undertake new challenges with expectations of positive outcomes, deliberate creation, not easily distracted, focus on long-term sustainable success, waste energy on social media from time to time.
Emotional Characteristics	Inner strength, calmness, optimism, relatively even mood, friendly, medium to high self-esteem, drive to succeed, motivated, fluctuating sense of satisfaction, love of learning dependent on other demands for energy/attention.
Cognitive Functions	Moderate to fast thinking, conscious behavior with some aspects out of conscious awareness, do not always fully assess consequences of their actions, organized, solid memory.
Physiology	Shoulders back, head up, posture in alignment half the time, deep breathing, clear skin, confident stride.
Weaknesses	Because they are finding their balance, it makes them susceptible to biochemical and emotional setbacks, including criticism from others. Either one may deplete their battery. The consciousness of the need for change is there; they're just slightly slower to reach full-blown awareness, when action can be taken. This may cause their light bulb to dim now and then but not entirely go out.

Figure 2.3 Attributes of the Synergist

Attributes of the Synergist	
Energy Source	We've all been the Synergist at one point or other. However, an overreliance on one energy source throws us out of step (e.g., relying on sugar/refined carbohydrates in times of high stress). If left unchecked, this behavior can devolve a Synergist into a Guardian or Defender. Because they've previously experienced a level of self-awareness, it makes them less likely to remain there, however. A Synergist may also eat clean yet experience symptoms of a nutritional deficiency. As you'll discover, you can eat healthy but still have nutritional gaps that prevent you from being all you can be.

Figure 2.3 **Attributes of the Synergist,** continued

themselves up about it. They realize that rest and rejuvenation are required for long-term, sustainable success.

The Guardian (50 percent and below)

Guardians are protecting their current resources, but not defending themselves from an attack. The Guardian's body has switched to self-preservation mode, which triggers them to preserve their energy for critical functions. Keeping that light bulb lit isn't one of them. They can keep it going briefly through sheer force of willpower, but even that has its expiration date if it doesn't get biochemically replenished.

They still have their goals in sight, but for the life of them, they can't work out why they're unattainable. Self-doubt starts to creep in, and excuses amplify. They're not where they want to be, but they don't know why. They have a win from time to time, but they don't have the energy to sustain it.

Numerous factors got them here, including chronic stress and nutritional deficiencies. In this state, troubleshooting their way out requires external intervention or relying on willpower to research a solution. If they don't find one fast, their willpower will become so depleted that their body will defend the few resources they have left, turning them into the Defender.

Attributes of the Guardian	
Strengths	Their willpower is attempting to override self-preservation mode. They can endure for a period of time before the brain takes over and puts them into rest and recovery mode to heal.
Emotional Characteristics	Lowered self-esteem, mood fluctuations, friendly to abrasive, overwhelmed, poor memory recall, decreased satisfaction, agitated, anxious.
Cognitive Functions	Cognitive functions beginning to decline, harder to remember names or crucial information, impulse control beginning to turn off, limiting their ability to make educated decisions, decision fatigue beginning to kick in, easily distracted, brain fog, getting stuck in negative thought patterns.
Physiology	Slouching posture, drooping head, mild to severe digestive issues, posture out of alignment, shallow breathing, oily or dry skin, increase in food cravings, possible insomnia, mild anxiety, inflammation in the body.
Weaknesses	Susceptible to procrastination and criticism and sensitive to their surroundings, making them easily overwhelmed.
Energy Source	Rely on caffeine, sugar, and refined carbohydrates to motivate them and give them enough energy to get moving. While this may relight their light bulb, it quickly dims after they crash from the side effects of these dirty fuel sources.

Figure 2.4 Attributes of the Guardian

The Defender (25 percent and below)

Defenders are simply focused on guarding what's left over and defending themselves from further attacks.

Defender mode can be triggered by a number of changes, including a change in the stomach's microbiome, a course of antibiotics, chronic stress, a traumatic event, or a severe nutritional deficiency that crept up so slowly you weren't even aware of it until it trapped you in your own toxic echo chamber. Remember the poor boiling frog?

Any attempts to escape using only one fuel source, such as willpower or biochemistry, will only result in your battery becoming even more depleted. At this point, people may tell you that depression is a choice. But when your biochemistry is pointing you in an entirely different direction, you will continue to default to this mode until the

Attributes of the Defender	
Strengths	Finding a clear thought in this state is like searching for something in a dark room with a flashlight with a failing battery. You know the answer exists, but you don't have enough light to find it in time. There's a deep underlying desire to feel better; you just don't know where to start.
Emotional Characteristics	Lack of self-awareness, low self-esteem, abrasive to depressive behavior, extreme ups and downs, highly sensitive to other people's comments, criticism cuts like a knife, reactionary instead of responsive, sense of numbness, easily agitated, isolating self from others to preserve energy.
Cognitive Functions	Cognitive functions in serious decline, forgetting key dates/names/information, lack of self-control, inability to make decisions, brain fog, inability to focus on anything for an extended period.
Physiology	Slouching, digestive issues, drooping head, posture out of alignment, shallow/erratic breathing, oily or dry skin, intensified food cravings (especially toward sugar), joint pain, muscle atrophy, insomnia, mild anxiety, inflammation in the body.
Weaknesses	All systems have been depleted. External intervention by professionals is your best bet.
Energy Source	Caffeine, sugar, and refined carbohydrates are being relied upon for short bursts of energy. It never lasts. If you're like me, you'll be eating well, but you will be deficient in key vitamins and minerals. This has more to do with food supply. More on this paradox in Chapter 3.

Figure 2.5 Attributes of the Defender

underlying cause is addressed by the right professionals—specifically, experts in functional medicine.

In this state, you are fighting the current, fighting your thoughts, and fighting change. This takes even more energy, depleting you psychologically because you're unsure what is going on. This added stress can also trigger further physiological symptoms. Some may pinpoint these symptoms as the cause, but they most likely are not, as you'll discover later in this book.

Before you start freaking out because you recognize yourself as a Defender, this is precisely where my journey began. These are the symptoms I exhibited when I was at my worst. At best, I would only sit in "Defender Mode" for a few hours and then self-medicate with caffeine to turn myself into a Catalyst so I could get some work done. This never lasted, and I ended up bouncing between these two extremes.

The great news is that it's not all in your head: It's in your biochemistry, and once your biochemistry becomes balanced, your head will clear. At that point, you'll really get to ramp up and focus on what you want because you'll finally have the energy to do so.

It is crucial to remember that if you recognize yourself as a Defender (remember, we can fluctuate throughout the day, week, month, or year), it's because of a few simple issues you can begin to rectify, such as:

▸ You are nutritionally deficient in key areas.
▸ You have been relying on unstable fuel sources, such as sugar, refined carbohydrates, or fatty foods, resulting in the more extreme ups and downs.
▸ You have been relying too heavily on one of two fuel sources, i.e. biochemical or psychological, and they're burning smoke, making you choke on your own internal environment.
▸ You are experiencing inflammation in your body. (There'll be more on that in Chapter 3.)

If this is you, your internal environment has become toxic. Your body is doing everything it can to preserve your existence, which reduces your available energy, causing you to further isolate yourself. This isn't weak-mindedness; it's an inbuilt strategy designed to support us when our needs intensify. At this point, it's key to go easy on yourself. Don't beat yourself up because you're not driven or motivated. Instead, methodically work toward a solution, doing what you can when you can.

What's your identity gap? Visit www.areyouunstoppable.com to take the free online quiz now.

So why don't people change? Based on this new way of thinking about identity, it's clear why self-help intervention alone doesn't always result in people changing their behaviors—especially if they are already guarding their current resources from further depletion or fending off attacks such as inflammation or stress. There is no energy left to spark or maintain that change.

With this in mind, we can have greater empathy for ourselves or those people in our lives who are struggling. It's not that we're incapable; it's that we can't become who we want to become while we're applying the same old self-help, medical, and psychiatric models in isolation to our problems.

All is not lost. In fact, this new awareness may have just lit up your light bulb, if only momentarily, with the hope that there is a way forward.

It is from here that we revolutionize the game plan.

CHALLENGE TWO

Muse: the Brain Sensing Headband: The first tool in the world to provide accurate feedback on what happens in the brain during meditation.

Who was I kidding? I was still fluctuating between Defender and Guardian. Meditating in that state is about as useful as trying to vacuum your house with the power turned off. Nonetheless, I persisted.

The Muse looked promising. It promised to provide real-time tracking of what was going on in my brain while I meditated and audio feedback by

CHALLENGE TWO, continued

the sound of waves crashing when my thoughts became overactive or birds chirping when I entered a state of calm.

My goal was to use the device every night before I went to bed for a minimum of 30 days.

I put on the headset, connected it to the app, and began meditating, something I'd never really done before. I've always used visualization to imagine my day unfolding the way I wanted. I'd view this video in my mind's eye and rewind, fast-forward, and rewind it multiple times to trick my subconscious into thinking I'd already completed the tasks I needed to. Hence, there was no need to be anxious about a large workload. Having used this practice for more than ten years, sitting there just observing my thoughts was challenging.

The Muse app gave me a score at the end of each session. After my first session, I scored 48 percent calm. It took me more than two weeks to score higher than 70 percent. During this time, I made some interesting observations. I felt a lot calmer, although I was still exhausted, and I was having random flashes of beautiful memories I hadn't thought about in years.

As a result, my mood started to improve, and it was easier for me to relax. Little things that would have triggered my anger before no longer had the same sting to them. Instead, I would acknowledge them and then let them go. I even noticed that I would slip into a peak meditative state while working out at the gym during my CrossFit challenge. Combined with Halo Sport, my workouts became far more effective. It was still a struggle to meditate at times due to the meager power supply available to my brain, but I felt the meditative process was still beginning to rewire my brain for the changes yet to come.

PART II

TAKE CONTROL OF
YOUR DESTINY

CHAPTER 3

Under the Radar
How to Hack Your Emotions and Take Control of Your Energy and Your Life

> **WARNING:** *Please DO NOT STOP ANY MEDICATIONS without first consulting a physician since doing so could be hazardous to your health. You could suffer serious withdrawal symptoms.*

When I was ten years old, I woke up gasping for air. My parents ran into the room at lightning speed and rushed me to the nearest hospital, ten minutes away. They knew exactly what was wrong; it had happened before.

It wasn't from a bad dream but from a severe asthma attack. I don't know if you've ever experienced what it's like to have your air supply cut off without warning in the middle of the night. It feels like someone is choking you, but when you grab for their hands, there's nothing there. The thought of dying immediately pops into your head: *What if I don't make it this time?*

When I was growing up on a cattle and cropping farm in southern Australia, asthma was a daily part of my life. It is a respiratory condition that triggers spasms in the lungs and difficulty breathing. You can be on top of the world one moment, and the next, you're fighting for your life in full-blown Defender mode. Asthma short-circuits your entire system and can affect your learning, memory, processing speed, and attention.[1]

Worse yet, it's sneaky. The physical symptoms can trick you into thinking you're anxious when you're not. It triggers a psychological response to a physical reaction. It often leaves people asking, "Am I anxious because I have asthma, or do I have asthma because I'm anxious?" It can be both: Sometimes it's one and sometimes the other.

Why You Really Quit and What You Can Do About It

You're likely wondering what asthma has to do with becoming a peak performer and reaching your goals. It's simple: It's the perfect example of a symptom that has two possible underlying causes. Asthma can create a *psychological* response to an allergen, or a *biological* response to a thought. Either trigger may ignite a significant shift in mood, behavior, and, most important, identity.

As you have seen with the identity gap method, the key to success is to manage our energy, emotions, thoughts, and behavior as part of a complete system, as well as protect our power supply. What's the point of owning a Ferrari if there is no fuel in the tank?

This becomes extremely difficult when there are factors, like medication, food, and toxins, that deplete our battery and cut off this supply, resulting in an inability to think clearly, feel good, and provide enough fuel to light our vision.

Ingesting caffeine or sugar (say, by downing an energy drink) may give you a sudden burst of energy to power through a task and turn you into a Catalyst momentarily, but by no means is it a sustainable energy source. These are dirty fuel sources that can hijack our thoughts and mood, especially when we crash, or when we become reliant on these fuel sources to get going in the morning.

Our Thoughts Are Getting Hijacked

In March 2017, I had had enough of my asthma and went to the doctor in hopes of finding an answer. I was using Ventolin as a preventive medication multiple times a day, to no avail. Any suggestion of getting off the medication and finding a healthy alternative was quickly shot down as absurd. I felt like an idiot for asking. Instead, the doctor gave me a new preventive medication. That night, I woke at 2 A.M. on the verge of a full-blown anxiety attack. In the dim light, my eyes immediately went to the medication on the dresser. Could a side effect be causing this fearfulness and agitation?

I grabbed my laptop and spent the next two hours delving into the research and side effects of this commonly used medication. I became shocked when reading patient reviews for the Ventolin that had become so ingrained in my daily life. I didn't even think to question it. Reports on Ask a Patient (www.askapatient.com) cited patient reactions such as anxiety attacks, manic behavior, nervousness, hyperactivity, impatience, and instant severe depression. One individual wrote that they were planning their own suicide until, thankfully, they realized it was their medication causing this effect.[2]

This started me thinking:

▸ Are my behaviors truly my own and free from manipulation?
▸ Could medication cut off or limit access to my willpower?
▸ Could my depressive episodes throughout my life be attributed to an increase in using Ventolin due to seasonal allergies?
▸ Had medications been triggering my anxiety all this time and limiting my ability to succeed?

> ▶ Were side effects of the inhaler a contributing factor to brain fog and fatigue that almost cost me my career as a writer and professional speaker?
>
> ▶ Was I set up for failure as a result of my understanding of asthma and the medications I was being prescribed?

If these inhalers were hijacking my emotions, then I was going to reclaim my emotions and take control of my health! However, I wasn't going to stop there. I wanted to know what else I was missing, what was manipulating my behavior and potentially affecting the general population, limiting human potential.

It wasn't just the pharmaceutical medications that are marketed as safe while altering our moods, depleting our batteries, and turning capable individuals into empty shells. It went much further than that. I wanted to uncover the real underlying issues behind my escalating behavior changes and explain why millions of people worldwide struggle to reach their goals and question their self-worth.

We have countless interactions on a daily basis with medication, food, and toxins that can mimic psychological disorders. These interactions influence our thoughts, behavior, mood, energy, and identity, and are far too often overlooked or dismissed with a, "It's just in your head. Get over it!"

Foods, medications, and toxins can mimic psychological disorders, cloud our thinking, and create self-sabotaging behavior without us realizing it.

These interactions can either charge or deplete you. The problem is that when we become depleted and shift into Guardian or Defender mode, we're not aware it is an external cause that we can gain control over. Instead, we simply believe we aren't trying hard enough. In actuality, we're having a real psychological response to a biochemical reaction.

A sudden shift in diet or symptoms can become so severe that medical attention is sought. Then this cycle of blame, either by ourselves or the medical community, continues to repeat unless it naturally corrects itself.

After speaking with Dave Asprey of Bulletproof; Daniel Schmachtenberger from the nootropic company Neurohacker Collective; Julia Cheek of EverlyWell, which provides at-home health tests; and Richard Lin, the CEO and cofounder of Thryve, a company that provides microbiome tests and probiotics based on extensive research, I found they all had one thing in common. They were all failed by the primary medical professionals from whom they had initially sought help. The experience increased their determination to not only heal themselves, but to also set up companies that help others perform at their best.

> *If the symptoms are mild, you blame yourself. If the symptoms are severe and the doctor can't find a cause, they blame you and treat the symptom, not the cause.*

These previously peak performers had the willpower, but not the biochemistry, to keep working at the levels to which they were accustomed. They uncovered formulas that gave them enough biochemical energy to research a solution, even if it was just for a few hours of clarity per day before they found a more permanent solution.

All of them fluctuated between Defender, Guardian, Synergist, and Catalyst modes when they were at their worst. In their cases, as in mine, their problem couldn't simply be defined as a lack of willpower. Their physical system, which had previously fueled them to become peak performers, had become compromised. They were only running on one power source, creating an imbalance along with a myriad of symptoms.

My experience was no different. Not only did I have to assess my personal identity and question who I was, I also had to assess the doctors I was seeking help from and discover any biases they had that would prevent me being treated appropriately. The biases were many, and the arrogance was abundant. Instead of simply saying that they didn't know what was wrong with me, they ran the same blood tests they always did, regardless of who I saw, which always came back as "You're fine." I was far from fine. I wanted to feel great and become unstoppable.

In a Skype call with Richard Lin, he shared the story of one of his doctors telling him, "I'm not in the business of curing people!" Richard and I were not the only ones to have experienced this when seeking medical advice.

We each must become advocates for our health if we want to live a life free from the shackles that hold us back. We need to look for answers where we would least expect them and not stop until we find them.

Less Than 90 Days to Find a Solution

I needed answers, and I needed them quickly. I had less than 90 days to not only heal my debilitating fatigue, brain fog, and lack of mental clarity, but also become unstoppable and write this book. At that point, I could barely write a coherent email, and it took me more than an hour. I knew I was making mistakes, which meant I had to triple check everything.

In discussions with my neighbor and research writer, Debbie Holmén, in Saint Petersburg, Florida, I was introduced to Dr. Carlos M. Garcia of Utopia Wellness in Oldsmar, Florida. Debbie shared her recent experience of biohacking her health, starting with Dr. Garcia's wellness center.

After working in hospitals for years, Dr. Garcia realized, like many of us, that traditional medicine was being driven more by the profits of hospitals and pharmaceutical companies than by providing the best patient care. In 1996, he redirected his focus to natural alternatives, including holistic medicine, chelation therapy, IV vitamins, antioxidants, and integrative cancer treatment that has seen him featured in the controversial yet well-received documentary *Cancer Can Be Killed.*[3]

In the 30-minute Uber ride to his clinic, I became nervous, thinking this was just going to be a repeat of what I'd experienced over the past 26 years. I was wrong!

Before visiting Dr. Garcia, I completed an extensive questionnaire. In less than five minutes, he was able to diagnose my ailment and prescribe a treatment plan. I asked, "Why did the 20-plus doctors I had previously seen fail to identify the cause and gear each conversation toward antidepressants?" His reply, "They don't ask enough questions!"

What Do These Great Biohackers and Minds Have in Common?

All the people you meet in this book understand that communication within the body is bilateral. The brain and body communicate with each other. Either can drive the changes we want to see in ourselves (or prevent them). Our physiology and our reactions to food, toxins, medications, and allergens can influence our psychology just as much as, if not more than, our psychology can influence our physiology. It's a two-way street. Some days, there will be obstacles you need to swerve around, while other days you can put the pedal to the metal and hit all your targets. And on some days you will come to a complete standstill. The question is, why?

If one part of the system—in this case, biochemical energy—cannot meet your new goals' demands, or if it's simply overwhelmed with other bodily functions/toxins/medications/food sensitivities, the dominoes will begin to fall. This affects the entire system, including your ability to focus and ultimately succeed.

Think of the last time you attempted to make critical decisions when you were exhausted, your reaction time was impaired, and your resilience low. A physical symptom, labeled as harmless (if we're even aware it's occurring), can rapidly put us below the 50 percent threshold into a state of unconscious awareness and behavior, in which we can't see or dissect the problem. We no longer have access to our cognitive capacity to troubleshoot. We become about as effective as a dog turd.

Once we understand what depletes our battery and hijacks our thoughts, we can shore up both our psychological and biochemical energy resources so they start supporting and charging each other. This will enable your battery to recharge faster and redirect all your energy to achieving your outcomes instead of dealing with toxins or inflammation within the body. This also makes it easier to juggle distractions, focus for extended periods of time, push through when times get tough, and light that vision powered by an enhanced frame of mind.

Regardless of whether you're a Catalyst, Synergist, Guardian, or Defender, or if you suffer from asthma, low energy, lack of drive, or brain fog, all of us are susceptible to occasional lulls that take the life force out of us. At least this time, you'll have some commonly overlooked areas that you can focus on with the help of a great doctor in the functional or integrative medicine field.

The Seven Triggers Blunting Your Brain

First, we need to examine the possible sources that could be causing our adverse symptoms and holding us back.

Throughout my 90-day mission to become unstoppable, regardless of whether I spoke to psychologists, doctors, microbiome experts, lab testing companies, or biohackers, my attention was repeatedly drawn back to seven critical areas that depleted my battery and impacted my mood:

1. Medication
2. Food sensitivities
3. Nutritional deficiencies
4. Digestion
5. Hormones
6. Allergies
7. Toxins

All these triggers have one thing in common; They can cause inflammation within the body and the brain.

In his bestselling book *Head Strong: The Bulletproof Plan to Activate Untapped Brain Energy to Work Smarter and Think Faster—In Just Two Weeks*, Dave Asprey calls this "the muffin top in your brain." As he notes, the brain is the first part of the body to be affected, regardless of where the inflammation has occurred.

Inflammation releases chemicals called cytokines that can wreak havoc on cognitive processes and have been shown to alter behavior. Researchers have emphasized the role inflammation plays in a host of illnesses including depression and anxiety. This is not to say that inflammation is the sole cause of depression or anxiety.[4] To date, there is still no definitive cause for depression or anxiety, due to the many variables influencing those conditions. Hence pharmaceuticals alone aren't always effective, and a multipronged approach to treatment is often advised.

Short-lived inflammation is healthy and necessary to the healing process. The problem occurs when chronic inflammation takes over, and the immune system remains activated beyond the point of being helpful. Environmental factors, allergies, food sensitivities, diet, stress, and toxins may keep us in mild to severe states of inflammation on a daily basis, which may explain why some doctors find it hard to diagnose, due to there being more than one symptom and possible cause.

If an individual continues to interact with the trigger of the inflammation, causing it to become chronic, it can be serious, leading to the following side effects:

▸ Extreme fatigue
▸ Low mood
▸ Anxiety
▸ High fever
▸ Hot flashes
▸ Swelling/redness
▸ Nausea[5]

Data has shown that cytokines activate the protein kinase. This can have a significant impact on the metabolism of neurotransmitters like serotonin, dopamine, and glutamate. These neurotransmitters are key to ensuring you have the drive and motivation you need to succeed. Neurotransmitter imbalances can have mild to severe repercussions, including:

▸ Fatigue
▸ Brain fog
▸ Addictions
▸ ADD/ADHD
▸ Mood disorders
▸ Lack of attention and concentration

▶ Anxiety, panic attacks, PTSD

▶ Hormonal imbalances, low testosterone, hypothyroidism, estrogen dominance

▶ PMS[6]

The cytokines' effects can lead to changes in motor activity, motivation, arousal, and alarm.[7] At that point, your biochemistry is controlling your body's reactions. You can attempt to will your way out of these responses, but unless the neurotransmitters are brought back into balance and the inflammation is reduced, you'll continue to live in a state of fog and imbalance. This may also explain why some people benefit from therapy, while others return to their doctors year after year without improvement: The underlying physiological issues aren't being addressed.

The cycle can begin with some untoward interaction with a food, toxin, nutritional deficiency, or medication or a problem with digestion, allergies, or even prolonged stress. The reaction could be mild to severe and may impair an individual's ability to think clearly and stay focused on their goal. (See Figure 3.1 on page 49.)

If the symptoms are mild, typically the individual is criticized for being weak. If it's severe, medical help is sought, and medication may be offered to treat a symptom without a cause ever being found. This can lead to the prescribed medication having long-term detrimental side effects in other areas of their lives. Some medication, even once use has been discontinued, may leave patients with worse symptoms than the ones the medication was meant to treat.

If your body's resources are constantly fighting off inflammation, you will barely have enough energy to make it through the day, let alone progress toward your goals. Any energy you have left over is assigned to maintaining the status quo. Hence, many of us can occasionally get stuck, and wonder why our willpower isn't enough to push through the haze.

Learning to control inflammation is vital to enhancing our mood, memory, and day-to-day performance. To do so, let's delve further into the top seven triggers blunting our brains.

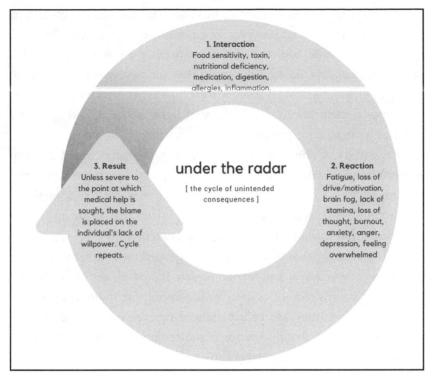

Figure 3.1 Cycle of Unintended Consequences

Medication

While you may not be one of the 25 million people in the U.S. who suffer from asthma,[8] you may be in the reported 70 percent of people who are taking a prescription medication of some kind.[9] Yes, 70 percent of the U.S. population are taking prescriptions!

The danger of that is that we don't all respond to medication the same way. People can experience a broad range of side effects, ranging from mild to severe. We might not even relate the symptoms to the medication we're taking, because our society believes that "doctor knows best." We fail to ask enough questions of our medical practitioners. We may even go back to the doctor and get another medication to treat our side effects—all without seeking to work out the underlying cause of our problems.

A close friend of mine confided to me that after his daughter had been in an accident and was prescribed opioids to deal with the pain, she became severely addicted. He was expecting a phone call any day saying she had overdosed. Obviously this isn't everyone's experience with painkillers, but it does demonstrate how seriously we need to treat prescription medications, particularly in light of the opioid epidemic America is currently experiencing.

Regardless of the medication, there are potential mood-altering side effects that aren't always clearly described by our doctors. Adverse reactions can be caused by allergies to the medication. Sometimes interactions can occur between two medications, creating severe symptoms that may be wrongly diagnosed as a new illness.

Below is a snapshot of some commonly used medications and their impact on our behavior and mental health. It is important to note that these medications can, of course, be life-saving for many people, and these side effects may not be experienced by everyone. However, they are serious enough to cause concern, particularly if they are only used to mask symptoms and not treat causes.

▶ *Ritalin.* Used to treat ADHD and narcolepsy. Side effects may include decreased appetite, nausea, anxiety, hallucinations, loss of contact with reality, suicidal thoughts.

▶ *Prozac.* Used to treat depression, OCD, bulimia nervosa, and panic disorders. Side effects may include nervousness, decreased sex drive, suicidal thoughts or actions, agitation, racing thoughts, reckless behavior, excessive happiness or irritability, or new or sudden changes in mood, behavior, actions, thoughts, or feelings.

▶ *Ambien.* Used to treat insomnia. Side effects may include memory loss, inability to concentrate, disorientation, emotional blunting, depression and/or suicidal thoughts, anxiety, insomnia, nightmares, confusion, sedation, or aggression. Withdrawal from Ambien can be life-threatening.

▶ *Lisinopril.* Used to treat high blood pressure. Side effects may include changes in mood, trouble sleeping, or general tiredness or weakness. Cases of suicidal thoughts have been reported online, although this isn't listed as a warning in the drug's pamphlet.

▸ *The Pill.* Used for birth control. Side effects may include depression, mood swings, anger.[10] A study published in the 2008 edition of the Proceedings of the Royal Society found women were attracted to more genetically dissimilar men before going on the pill. Afterward, they were more attracted to men genetically like themselves. This could result in no longer being attracted to one's partner once medication is discontinued.[11]

▸ *Requip.* Used to treat Parkinson's disease and restless legs syndrome. Side effects may include intense urges to gamble, increased sexual urges, intense urges to spend money, binge, or compulsive eating.[12]

New tests have been developed that analyze your DNA to gain a better understanding of what medication might work best for you based on your genetic makeup. One such test is the GeneSight® test (https://genesight.com/product/). This can help doctors personalize treatment plans, identify the right medication fast, and avoid medicines that may cause too many side effects. As with any health issue, a doctor must be willing to work with you to find the underlying cause.

Food Sensitivities

I took note of everything that had changed in my diet before my increase in fatigue, loss of drive and motivation, brain fog, and inability to think clearly. I'd just arrived back in Australia after three months of traveling around the U.S. and Canada, and I had done something out of the ordinary for me when I got back home. I started drinking one to two cups of coffee per day to deal with the jet lag. A couple of months later, I became suspicious it might be the cause of my fatigue and decided to remove it from my diet entirely for 30 days.

I made several key observations: My anxiety reduced, my energy improved, and I didn't feel as depressed as I had before. I was still extremely tired, but it wasn't as severe as it had been. It would later turn out that coffee wasn't the full story, but it was one crucial piece of the puzzle that could not be overlooked.

Further, diving into my research, I uncovered the harrowing story of Ruth Whalen. In her book, *Welcome to the Dance: Caffeine Allergy—A*

Masked Cerebral Allergy and Progressive Toxic Dementia, she recounts her physical and mental health deteriorating to the point that in 1999 she was diagnosed with both a personality disorder and bipolar disorder. Luckily for Ruth, a doctor finally realized it was extreme caffeine sensitivity triggering the episodes.[13]

Thankfully, stories like Ruth's aren't common, but in severe cases of food sensitivity, individuals can appear schizophrenic, experiencing paranoia, delusions, and hallucinations.

In my case, I had become extremely sensitive to caffeine, to the point that one cup would leave me feeling depressed for a week before the effects wore off. In later discussions with biohacker Dave Asprey, I would discover it might not be the caffeine or the coffee (the two are very different), but it could be a sensitivity to mold on the coffee beans triggering the reaction. We'll talk more about this in Chapter 6.

While these examples are extreme, they demonstrate that you might not always know what is holding you back from success. If you present with mild symptoms from the following list, a food sensitivity could be at fault:

▸ Fatigue
▸ Brain fog
▸ Respiratory issues (e.g., asthma, sinusitis, rhinitis)
▸ Headaches/migraines
▸ Eczema/acne/psoriasis
▸ Joint aches and pains
▸ Depression
▸ Anxiety
▸ Sadness

The challenge with a food sensitivity is that even if you remove one problem food from your diet, there may be another causing constant underlying inflammation, so your health may not improve. Antacids may help make your stomach feel better, but that just allows you to keep eating foods that you shouldn't be eating in the first place.

I knew I felt better when I didn't eat anything containing gluten, but I didn't know why. All the gluten sensitivity tests came back negative. I also suspected I had adrenal fatigue; I was constantly exhausted. But when I suggested this to my doctor, I was quickly dismissed. He said that was just a way for health practitioners to sell expensive supplements that we simply pee out in the toilet bowl. I decided I was going to find out for myself. During my 90-day mission, I came across a food sensitivity blood test by the company EverlyWell, which offers convenient at-home health testing kits. The tests are conducted by labs that have been around for decades, the same labs that doctors use in the U.S. to identify food sensitivities. EverlyWell is allowing individuals to run those same tests at a reasonable cost.

You may have seen them featured on ABC's *Shark Tank*. Julia Cheek, the founder and CEO, won one of the largest investments ever made on the show for a solo female entrepreneur. Shark Lori Greiner extended a $1 million line of credit in exchange for a 5-percent stake.

EverlyWell mails you a small, convenient testing kit. A little pinprick to the finger, a few tiny samples of blood, and you will have your results back within one to two weeks. I was blown away by mine. I was mildly sensitive to coconut, almonds, coffee, mushrooms, and sunflower.

Thinking I was supremely healthy, I had introduced coconut oil, almond butter, and milk to my diet around the time I became ill. I had never made the connection. Not for one second did I think these healthy recommendations were causing me a whole host of issues. I was also surprised to discover I had a mild sensitivity to baker's yeast, a common agent used in baking. Differing from gluten, which is a wheat protein, it is a strain of saccharomyces, a fungus. A positive result for baker's yeast could indicate a yeast imbalance in the gut.

Because baker's yeast is present in almost everything that contains gluten, I had immediately thought gluten was the problem. That's where food sensitivities get complicated unless you get a professional test done that checks a whole host of foods. Guessing which foods you are sensitive to could take years. A test shortcuts this process and can alleviate brain fog, fatigue, and insufficient mental clarity once these foods have been removed from the diet. This test checked my body's response to 96 foods.

These results drove me to reach out to Julia and EverlyWell's Executive Medical Director, Dr. Francis, via a Skype interview to find out more. Surprisingly, Julia's experience was very similar to mine. She started the company after suffering symptoms of chronic fatigue and unexplainable aches and pains.

"I had a lot of anxiety, and ultimately these were basic hormone imbalances and adrenal gland imbalances," Julia said. "But I spent this period—this odyssey—of six months going to tons of different doctors to try to get testing done and complete the issues. The doctors themselves were all excellent, but the problem was that they ordered a bunch of tests, and I was never given access to the results. I didn't even know what tests were run. I didn't have explanations.

"Then I started getting these bills coming in from requested lab work every few months, because I was on a high-deductible plan. I started figuring out that the high-deductible, noncoverage situation for Americans was just growing dramatically. The majority of Americans are having to pay so much more for these basic services, and the services actually don't always relate to them. So I really wanted to say, how can we use technology and digital health to disrupt the traditional experience for consumers and help them get access to this testing in an easier way? Access to tests consumers want, access to a more convenient process, or access to actually one price, a transparent price, is what was needed. You know exactly what you're gonna pay, and we won't charge you again. That message has resonated with thousands and thousands of people."

Julia's experience was shocking. I asked her how she felt being dismissed by doctors, specifically in relation to her adrenal fatigue. She said, "I was scheduled for a kidney stone removal that they stopped 12 hours before. The X-rays showed that I didn't have one. I had CAT scans, MRIs, and I was told I just had pulled a back muscle, and that I just needed to relax. I'm always about what are people's incentives and what are they trying to achieve, and so I wasn't mad at the doctors themselves. I was mad at the institutions. I was mad at the pressure put on doctors, and how they have to operate, and how they're incentivized. And they're often doing the best that they can, but that is with their own constructs. But that is, at the end of the day, not achieving the goal."

On her mission to biohack her way back to health, she took all her lab results to a functional medicine doctor and an acupuncturist. "They found all these areas, and it was certainly my cortisol that had completely gone just off-the-radar wacky," she said. "But my vitamin D was dangerously low, my magnesium, my vitamin B6, my vitamin B12, my iron. I was low on all of those, but nobody had put the picture together. I was not low enough, but it was this comprehensive set of things. I almost had very, very bad treatment as a result of not pinpointing the right issues. In looking back, it seems so ridiculous that I almost underwent a procedure when what I really needed to do was just make some lifestyle changes. I think that perfectly reflects this drastic gap in care, and what's really happening." Just like Julia, my doctors had failed to identify a severe vitamin D deficiency; they had also overlooked food sensitivities.

When I asked Dr. Francis how the reference ranges are set for vitamins, minerals, hormones etc., that doctors use to tell us if our results are normal or abnormal, she replied, "It's based on population studies. We have population studies for everything: for mineral levels, for vitamin levels, for what normal cholesterol should be. When you look at cholesterol, the population studies are based upon who developed heart disease vs. who didn't. So at what ranges is that considered normal vs. elevated risk for heart disease? These normal ranges are really set by society and set by population studies. Within the lab, the reference ranges, those are set based upon biological variability within your body. How much can that marker vary from day to day, from hour to hour within your body, and still be considered normal?

The standard guinea pig in medicine has always been the 70-kilogram [154-pound] man, which was originally set by the American College of Physicians (ACP) and the American Society for Clinical Pathology (ASCP) in the early 1900s. Now, obviously, we are trying to look at different populations because we don't all fit that mold. I will say that the U.S. Department of Health and Human Services (HHS) and the U.S. Department of Agriculture (USDA) has done a very good job at separating out pregnant and lactating women. Obviously, what their body needs and what is considered normal for them is vastly different than the standard 70-kilogram man. So we do have some population studies that have been separated out by gender, by race, and by pregnancy status.

When I asked Julia about their most popular test, she replied, "The food sensitivity test is not only one of the most popular, but we get more life-changing customer testimonials and physician testimonials around when they referred their customers to take the test. For women, hormone imbalances have actually improved, and they've continued their regular cycles again; even skin conditions have resolved. People with psoriatic arthritis that medication traditionally couldn't help found foods that were causing what they considered to be inflammatory flares, and their psoriatic arthritis was all but cured."

Dr. Francis added that other conditions cleared up as a result of the food sensitivity test are bloating, migraines, and sleep disturbances. They've even had people who lessened their anxiety and depression through dietary changes. She pointed out that she isn't saying that food sensitivity causes depression, but "when someone is being evaluated for symptoms of depression, we fail to look at their diet traditionally as a medical doctor. Which sort of confuses me, and it sounds silly, but we have that old saying: 'You are what you eat.' Why don't we look at diet as part of the puzzle when we're trying to figure out why someone has the symptoms that they do? I think it really does a disservice to our patients. Between all of the additives and chemicals in our food system right now, I think food is probably one of the biggest causes of people being unhealthy."

All I could think after doctors suggested antidepressants to me was: How many people are put on medication when the cause of their problem is really a food allergy? This research has yet to be done. EverlyWell will be undertaking an opt-in study of their customers that will be one of the biggest of its kind on food sensitivities.

This goes to show that sometimes it's the simplest things depleting our batteries and influencing our mood and behavior. Validation is crucial at every stage, but so is finding the right practitioner who can interpret the data. I discovered that I should avoid coconut at all costs. After I stopped eating it for a month, I ate a coconut Thai curry without thinking and had brain fog, fatigue, and general malaise for three days afterward. I only realized this link after I looked at my food diary and uncovered the slip-up. It's the small things that can make a big difference when you're upgrading yourself for success.

Nutritional Deficiencies

Ninety-two percent of the U.S. population has a vitamin deficiency; could you be one of them?[14] Why do deficiencies occur despite many of us eating healthy?

It comes down to farmland soil across the globe becoming deficient in micronutrients. In 2003, Canadian researchers compared the nutrient content of vegetables to data from 50 years ago. They discovered the mineral content of cabbage, lettuce, spinach, and tomatoes had depleted from 400 mg to less than 50 mg.[15] As soil quality continues to decline due to changes in farming practices and widespread use of pesticides, we can no longer rely on a balanced diet to get all the nutrients we need to feel alert and sharp.

To my surprise, when my test results came back from Dr. Garcia's office, they showed I was severely deficient in vitamin D. Vitamin D is crucial for more than just lung function and cardiovascular health. It supports the immune system, brain, and nervous system.[16] Vitamin D deficiency has also been linked to inflammation. Plus, having spent two months at the start of 2017 in the dead of winter in New York City fighting for sunlight didn't help.

To say vitamin D plays a vital role in mood, behavior, and cognition is an understatement. Despite its importance, vitamin D isn't always tested by doctors unless we ask for it. Here are some more interesting stats on vitamin D:

▶ One study found more than 40 percent of the U.S. population were vitamin D deficient. Some experts have referred to this as a pandemic.[17]

▶ Research has discovered that vitamin D may play an integral role in regulating mood and warding off depression. Another study found that individuals receiving vitamin D supplementation showed an improvement in depressive symptoms.[18]

▶ Cognitive impairment has also been seen in individuals with vitamin D deficiency. This can trigger forgetfulness, confusion, difficulty concentrating, and forgetfulness (see what I did there?).[19]

▶ Vitamin D deficiency is also related to low testosterone levels in men.[20] Testosterone is a powerful hormone that helps burn fat, increase sex drive, and make men happier.[21]

▶ Having a moderate vitamin D deficiency has been associated with a 53 percent increased risk of developing dementia and a 122 percent increased risk for those who are "severely deficient."[22]

It doesn't begin or end with vitamin D, of course. In Chapter 5, I will break down other key nutritional deficiencies that can trigger inflammation and harm your health and your most precious resource, your brain.

Digestion

Prolonged stress can cause inflammation and chemical changes within your digestive system. This can lead to nausea, diarrhea, irritable bowel syndrome, and behavioral symptoms, like procrastination, talking or brooding about stressful situations, difficulty completing assignments, and increased desire to either be with or withdraw from others.[23]

The brain has a direct effect on the stomach, as the stomach has a direct effect on the brain. This bilateral communication can leave you wondering what is causing your lack of focus, anxiety, and stress: a biological response to a food allergen, highly processed foods, lactose intolerance, or medication, or a biological response to a psychological experience.

Many people find their digestive issues resolve themselves after a stressful experience comes to an end (e.g., a divorce is completed, or they move locations). At that point, they are exposed to new microbiomes that positively affect their digestive processes.

As you'll discover in the next chapter, revolutionary research into the microbiome is showing it can have a positive effect on mental health, weight loss, tolerance for stress, inflammatory responses, the immune system, and more.[24]

It is estimated that 90 percent of our body's serotonin is made in the digestive tract. Microbes help produce serotonin in the gut. Serotonin is a brain neurotransmitter, and many antidepressants focus on increasing serotonin uptake, as low levels of serotonin are associated with depression and suicidal thoughts. Thus, optimal digestion is essential for a positive mood and outlook on life.

Hormones

Controlling everything from emotions, mood, hunger, reproduction, and critical bodily functions, hormones play a vital role in everyday well-being. A hormonal imbalance can cause chronic inflammation, a loss of sex drive, and behavioral changes. A hormone deficiency can wreak havoc in all aspects of your life. Our hormones fluctuate due to aging and dietary changes. Understanding the hormones estrogen, testosterone, and cortisol may give you insight into your personal experiences. Let's take a quick look at those:

▶ *Estrogen.* The main sex hormone for women, estrogen causes puberty, prepares the body for pregnancy, and regulates the menstrual cycle. Changes in estrogen levels can cause gastrointestinal discomfort, headaches, mood swings, and decreased sex drive. As reported by Medical News Today, hormone replacement therapy could be the answer to protecting cognitive function from declines related to aging.[25]

▶ *Cortisol.* Otherwise known as the "stress hormone," cortisol kicks in when we're at our worst and can cause mood swings, which can manifest as anxiety, depression, or irritability. If the cause of stress isn't eliminated, chronic stress may occur, leading to inflammation within the body and a lack of focus.

▶ *Testosterone.* The main sex hormone in men, testosterone causes puberty and increases bone density, facial hair growth, and muscle mass. Low testosterone can trigger excessive fatigue, loss of sex drive, anxiety, depression, and weight gain. Testosterone is known to protect against inflammation. Low testosterone has also been linked to asthma being more prevalent in boys than girls pre-puberty. Researchers believe that this may explain why women are more susceptible to asthma than men after puberty.[26]

According to Dr. Joseph Mercola, author of *Fat for Fuel: A Revolutionary Diet to Combat Cancer, Boost Brain Power, and Increase Your Energy,* to balance our hormones, we must start with our diet. That includes taking supplements such as magnesium to improve sex hormone levels and eating high-quality proteins, healthy fat, and fermented and cultured foods that promote healthy hormone levels.[27]

I have personally found that doctors in Australia are reluctant to check testosterone levels, potentially out of fear that it will lead to steroid abuse. However, research out of the New England Research Institute suggests one out of four men over 30 have low testosterone levels.[28] In March 2016, after almost blacking out from getting out of the car, I walked despondently into the nearest vitamin store and came across a naturopath named Hetal Gohil. Close to tears, I asked for her help. After an initial consultation that lasted one hour, she requested my GP check my testosterone levels. My GP refused.

Finally, in February 2018, I sent a blood sample to EverlyWell. My results came back within the lower range of normal. The problem is that I will never know if my testosterone levels were low when I first requested the test. As I was vitamin D deficient, which is frequently linked with low testosterone levels in men, and I had been supplementing with vitamin D for 60 days at this point, my testosterone levels may have increased due to the supplementation.

Allergies

If you suffer from hay fever, you know better than anyone it can knock you on your arse. The symptoms aren't just limited to congestion, runny nose, sneezing, and redness. It can also trigger fatigue and headaches. Current evidence indicates that individuals with allergies appear at higher risk (to what degree is unknown) for developing anxiety and mood disorders.[29]

The matter gets more complicated when specific medications are introduced to help mitigate symptoms. A 2016 study indicated that hay fever drug use could correlate to an increased risk of dementia and Alzheimer's as well as reduced brain size. Other common side effects could affect cognitive functions negatively, including use of short-term memory, problem solving, and verbal reasoning.[30] We may end short-term suffering, but the potential consequences in later years could be detrimental to the quality of our lives.

This only propels sufferers to seek out alternative treatments without the serious long-term consequences. Thankfully, with the introduction of air filters such as the Molekule and research into the microbiome and probiotics, there are ways to reduce symptoms without taking mind-altering medication that has the potential to affect your daily performance.

Toxins

According to the University of Southern California, aggressive behavior in teenagers could have something to do with an uptick in air pollution. This finding highlights the need for responsible public policy regarding the toxins we breathe, eat, or apply to our skin, which may be impacting the way we behave.[31]

Furthermore, neurotoxins like heavy metal toxins have been linked to elevated levels of violent crime as well as behavioral dysfunctions.[32]

While we can't always control our air quality, we can gain greater awareness of what we put in our bodies and on our skin. Below is a list of the top three toxins we most often overlook, which are linked to a variety of side effects and illnesses, such as headaches, anxiety, depression, brain fog, Alzheimer's, and hormonal changes. These substances numb our ability to become conscious creators.

1. *Aspartame*. Popular artificial sweetener, a.k.a. Equal® or NutraSweet®. Found in processed foods labeled "sugar-free," diet sodas, gum, yogurt, sugarless candy. Aspartame is harmful for your brain. Reported side effects include brain fog, migraines, dizziness, memory lapses, anxiety, depression, and amplified symptoms of ADHD.[33]

2. *Sucralose*. Another popular artificial sweetener. Sucralose, otherwise known as Splenda, is sugar bonded to chlorine, making it a toxic chlorocarbon. A surprising side effect of sucralose is that it prevents nutrient absorption and reduces good bacteria in your intestines by up to 50 percent.[34] And, as you'll find out in the next chapter, this could have a significant impact on your well-being. Stevia is a great replacement that won't impact your blood glucose or insulin.

3. *Phthalate*. Used in grooming products and plastics. Phthalates are in countless products, including deodorants, lotions, shampoos, conditioners, shaving creams, vinyl flooring, some cosmetics, organic spices, and more. Writing for *The Guardian* in 2015, Amy Westervelt reported that, "Researchers have linked phthalates to asthma, ADHD, breast cancer, obesity, type II diabetes, low IQ, neurodevelopmental issues, behavioral issues, autism spectrum disorders, altered reproductive development, and male fertility issues." They have also been shown to disrupt hormones.[35] It's hard to know which products have phthalates, but you can start by staying away from anything packaged in a plastic classified as "Recycle-Code 3." Instead, stick with containers made from glass or recycled products, and avoid products that list "fragrance" as an ingredient.

Before you decide to cut yourself off from society and hide out in the mountains, there is no reason to panic. Small doses of toxins may even be good for you, as mild stress makes your cells work more efficiently. Air pollution, plastic packaging, and pesticides are a daily part of life. You can reduce your risk by going organic, using an air filter, and detoxing. I'll step you through my top recommendations in the 13 Weeks to Unstoppable plan later in the book.

Collecting the Statistical Evidence to Back Up How I Felt

I hate guessing. I always have, which was why I didn't want to assume the cause of my low drive and motivation. I wanted statistical data I could interpret and apply to energize my battery and reignite my spark. After all, a 13-week period to not only heal myself but bring myself to optimal performance didn't allow much time for trial and error. The realizations had to come hard and fast, and they did.

The further I dove into the research, the more I started to uncover vital patterns that fly under the radar of the average Joe, especially if you're not a doctor, or work in that particular field of expertise. I found that doctors had multiple blind spots with countless biases, causing them to miss the connections. How could they know how best to treat you if they spend less than five minutes with you and, even if they are well-meaning, would rather give you a prescription than find a cause?

The problem I had to overcome was that each of the experts I spoke with had one piece of the puzzle, but not the entire picture. I was looking at a patchwork quilt, trying to work out what goes where: diet, nutrition, microbiome, psychology . . . What would have the biggest impact on my health and mind?

As I began to validate my findings, I began feeling vindicated. My symptoms weren't all in my head; the problem was with my entire system. Once I knew that, I could finally take action. But not before Dr. Garcia diagnosed me with something the experts claim is a silent epidemic most doctors ignore entirely, to the detriment of their patients.

CHALLENGE THREE

Health Tag and Spire Stone: A wearable device that tracks the rate of your breathing.

It started vibrating in my pants!

As I waited for the train home from the Tony Robbins "Unleash the Power Within" event in West Palm Beach, Florida, my fight or flight response hit maximum overload. A 7-foot man had just stormed into the train station yelling profanities at a much meeker man, accusing him of murdering his sister by giving her bad drugs. We watched in horror as he threw the smaller man like a rag doll at a vending machine in the corner. He quickly picked up the man again and slammed him into the concrete wall. In a deep, loud voice, the tall man demanded he get his luggage and get into the car.

The air was tense. I made eye contact with the other men present. There was no way any of us could have stopped this guy. Both exits were blocked by the altercation, and we were stuck until it was resolved one way or another.

I thought I was about to witness a murder. An elderly lady next to me echoed my thought. And then my Spire, a wearable device clipped to the inside of my jeans, started vibrating. It's designed to vibrate when it identifies tense breathing via rapid exhalation. This is an unregulated state associated with agitation, anxiety, and cognitive overload. This coincides with sympathetic activation, the "fight or flight" branch of the nervous system. While useful in times of real danger, repeated or frequent exposure is linked to adrenal fatigue, gastrointestinal disorders, a compromised immune system, and high cortisol levels.[36]

It made me painfully aware of my physical response to a psychological stressor. I had worn it for four weeks by that point, so I immediately sucked in a deep breath and started breathing normally again. I felt calm within 60 seconds. The Spire had stopped my fight or flight response in its tracks, no doubt reducing any potential trauma related to the experience by shortcutting the negative emotions.

CHALLENGE THREE, continued

After the police had arrived and taken the attacker away in handcuffs, I thought that the number-one reason we are not aware of our behavior is because we lack the tools to drive that awareness.

This was just one of many wearables I was using to provide real data and insight into the unconscious behaviors shaping my personality and my experience of the world. I couldn't just focus on mindset or biochemistry. I had to do both in tandem if I wanted to truly feel unstoppable.

CHAPTER 4

Fueling for Success
Upgrade Your Energy, Upgrade Your Life

"Have you done a finger prick before?" Geoffrey Woo, cofounder and CEO of HVMN®, asked me, as we sat in the company's headquarters in San Francisco.

HVMN (pronounced "human") believes the human body is a system that can be quantified, optimized, and upgraded. Their nootropic products are widely popular among Silicon Valley employees, whose aggressive "hustle culture" requires them to work harder, longer, and faster to appease investors and drive revenue. Nootropics are drugs, supplements, and other substances that enhance cognitive function, memory, creativity, energy, and motivation in healthy individuals. I wanted to learn more firsthand from a company whose investor list reads like the who's who of Silicon Valley, including Marissa Mayer (former CEO of Yahoo!), and Tony Hsieh (CEO of Zappos).

I had flown from Saint Petersburg, Florida, to San Francisco with one burning question: "How do we fuel ourselves for success by upgrading our energy to upgrade our life?" I needed more energy to help close the gap from who I was to who I needed to become to reach my goals.

Midway through the interview, Geoffrey stopped and asked if he could check my ketone levels via a blood test. He wanted my baseline before giving me a taste of HVMN's new product, Ketone, made from pure ketone ester. The ketone ester had originated from a program run by the Defense Advanced Research Projects Agency (DARPA). DARPA's interest in ketones was the result of an effort to enhance elite soldiers' performance during mentally and physically demanding missions.

After 15-plus years of research, $60 million in funding, and a collaborative effort between HVMN, Oxford, and NIH, they developed a drink that consisted of 98.24 percent ketones, with the remainder being water. The effects were astounding and kicked in within 30 minutes of drinking it.[1] Individuals on the currently popular ketogenic diet can take anywhere from two to seven days to get into a ketogenic state, depending on their carbohydrate levels. At this point, some may suffer flu-like symptoms as their brain switches from running on carbohydrates and sugars to healthy fats and proteins. This new optimal fuel is called ketones. The ketogenic diet has gained in popularity as more research has been conducted. Some scientists now believe ketones is a fourth fuel source for the body—one that has the ability to increase focus and energy and has countless health benefits.

The ketogenic diet was first used to treat epilepsy patients more than 100 years ago; it has been shown to effectively reduce seizures. Current studies into the treatment of Alzheimer's suggests that ketones might be useful for delaying cognitive decline in older individuals. Researchers now understand that in Alzheimer's disease, the brain loses its ability to use glucose to produce energy. Some believe ketones could help close this energy gap.[2]

"OK, nice. You bleed well," said Geoffrey.

My ketone levels measured at 0.3 mmol/L. Of course, I wasn't on the ketogenic diet. In fact, I was just coming off the candida diet (more on that later in this chapter). In a 2014 *Nourish Balance Thrive* podcast with Christopher Kelly, Dr. Dominic D'Agostino, a researcher at the University of South Florida, said he believed the optimal level of ketones, based on anecdotal data, is somewhere between 1.5 and 3 mmol/L.[3] I was nowhere near it.

I unscrewed the cap on the little clear bottle, leaned back, and drank it down in one hit. It was like having a shot of tequila at ten in the morning. I wasn't prepared! I tried hiding my reaction from Geoffrey but couldn't. I was tingling and twitching all over. This wasn't your typical sugary sweet sports drink—this was for the pros.

Geoffrey had told me they had been testing the ester on the NFL, the Grand Tour cycling series, and various military outfits. They were getting stellar results. If anything was going to give me energy, this drink was going to be it. The research that had gone into it was staggering.

We continued the interview, but 15 minutes later, I could see Geoffrey desperately wanting to ask how I felt. He patiently waited, then tested my blood again.

"OK. Let's see what happened here," he said. "Wow, your ketones are at 3.5. That's .5 above Dr. Dominic's optimal ketone level! To give you a magnitude of how interesting that is, that's equivalent to about five to six days of fasting." Fasting, whether it's intermittent or longer periods of clean fasting, can help reset your body's ability to optimize its fuel source. Fasting naturally creates a cleaner-burning fuel system for your brain and body; it takes about five days to create this pathway. That is intimidating for the novice faster. Going from a sugar-burning machine to using your own fat as fuel is the mechanism behind fasting to regain energy and vitality.

But after just one bottle of ester, I felt incredible. My brain was lit up like a Christmas tree. I hadn't had this much energy since I was ten years old.

As I sat back in the Uber after leaving the meeting, I felt like a little kid. I couldn't stop looking out the window. It was as if my brain had switched from viewing the world in 2D to 3D. The colors were crisp, and the energy felt clean and consistent. It wasn't like caffeine, which causes my heart to beat a million miles per hour; it felt natural.

I don't think Geoffrey knows how much that day meant to me. It helped me remember what it was like to feel great again. It reminded me of what was truly possible. It also reminded me of the survey we had done online, in which 75 percent of the people who responded admitted to suffering from brain fog. The unfortunate reality is that the general population doesn't feel great. We accept low energy as the new normal, but it doesn't have to be this way.

For the rest of the day, I was buzzing. Tasks I had been putting off since I had arrived in San Francisco were suddenly completed in a matter of minutes. The fear, procrastination, and general malaise I had been experiencing had disappeared. This continued into the next day. It was then that I realized something surprising: My need for willpower had completely vanished! I didn't need to convince myself to work.

When Your Energy Decreases, Your Need for Willpower Increases

This experience got me thinking. The ketone ester had turned me into a Catalyst for 48 hours. In this state, everything felt easy. I didn't have to fight through negative thoughts, fatigue, or brain fog. Trying to force myself to eat well, think positive, or stay focused simply wasn't required, because I had the energy available to effortlessly manage those activities outside of conscious awareness.

By definition, willpower means to exert control or restrain impulses. This had me wondering: If willpower is to exert control that implies something is out of control that requires management. The question is, what is out of control? If I could work that out, my life would become much easier. All my energetic resources could be aimed at achieving a greater level of success. Instead of managing energetic ups and downs that come with brain fog, slow response time, poor memory, mood swings, and cravings, I could achieve my goals.

What I found was that applying willpower results in more energy being expended, not just on the intended goal, but also on managing whatever is draining your battery behind the scenes. It's like the unnecessary "bloatware" of your cell phone, which drains the battery dry just when you need it the most. You must keep charging your phone throughout the day. The bloatware doesn't get blamed, because it's hidden from sight. Instead, your battery gets the blame for having insufficient power.

Simple activities that flow easily when you have energy (e.g., unloading the dishwasher, doing laundry, paying bills) suddenly become a battle of wills when energy is low. Think control vs. flow. When we master our energy, we master our state of flow. Everything comes together easily because there is no need to control our behavior. Low energy plays havoc on our body and mind.

In my case, my energy levels were impacting my drive and motivation much, much more than I had originally comprehended. I, like many people, had placed too much emphasis on the need for more willpower, not realizing that this way of thinking was throwing me into a greater state of disarray.

After this, I started observing my behavior and need for willpower on a daily basis during the final 60 days of my mission to become unstoppable.

As you can see in Figure 4.1 on page 72, as my energy went up, my need for willpower decreased. During the first 30 days, in which I was trialing Halo Sport and conducting the daily CrossFit workout challenge, my need for willpower was sky-high. At this point, I was still unwell. I was fighting food cravings, fatigue, brain fog, and an inability to focus, on top of trying to manage a highly demanding workout and research regimen for the book. I was also battling a barrage of negative thoughts, like *I don't know if I can finish this project!* I had less energy for decision making, and I hit my decision fatigue threshold earlier in the day, which limited my ability to get more done. This took energy away from the critical tasks I wanted to focus on.

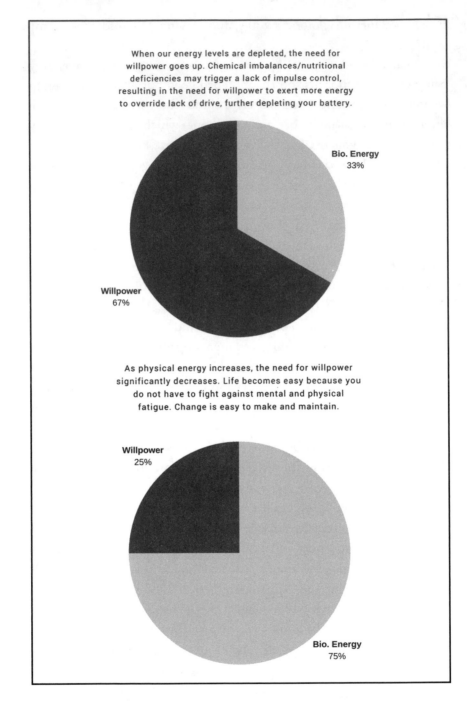

When our energy levels are depleted, the need for
willpower goes up. Chemical imbalances/nutritional
deficiencies may trigger a lack of impulse control,
resulting in the need for willpower to exert more energy
to override lack of drive, further depleting your battery.

Bio. Energy
33%

Willpower
67%

As physical energy increases, the need for willpower
significantly decreases. Life becomes easy because you
do not have to fight against mental and physical
fatigue. Change is easy to make and maintain.

Willpower
25%

Bio. Energy
75%

Figure 4.1 Is Willpower Really the Answer?

Procrastination and fear crept in because I had been unknowingly going into self-preservation mode due to inconsistent energy levels. My brain was trying to save what little energy it had for critical functions, and that didn't include working on my goals. The question is, which model are you working from, Model 1 or Model 2?

I started asking myself: Should an increase in willpower be the goal? The personal development industry rams it down our throats on a daily basis. They say that to be successful, you just need to follow these habits, but they don't ask why it's easier for highly successful people to follow these habits than it is for the rest of us. Yes, you need willpower to push through and complete certain tasks when your reputation or career is on the line, but you shouldn't apply it when there's an energy deficit. People recommend willpower like it's a pill, but they don't understand that low energy is influencing their behavior and mood. This simplistic way of thinking isn't just limiting—it's damaging. If we don't close the gap between our goal and the energy required to meet it, we're going to live in a constant state of struggling to gain control. Having an energy deficit means we will fall short of success—or, worse, we'll achieve it, but still be miserable because we don't have the energy to enjoy it.

Picture a racetrack. Everyone is stepping up for the 100-meter sprint, but with your low energy, you have to start 10 meters back from the starting line. The peak performers are starting 10 meters in front of the line. You have twice as much ground to cover as they do. You're not only going to have to exert greater willpower to make up for the disadvantage, which comes at a higher biological price, but you also must exert greater control of your thoughts, because your brain will be looking for every shortcut it can find due to insufficient energy available to power it. And, as we know from the decision fatigue study conducted by the National Academy of Sciences, this will result in choosing one of two options: 1) Making less effective decisions, or 2) Deciding to do nothing and sit out the race. In this state, Defender or Guardian mode, you are at a point of diminishing returns. No matter what you do, it's going to require twice as much effort as if you were in Catalyst or Synergist mode.

What Is Your Set Point for Success?

As you already know, you can't have a high level of psychological output without paying a biological price. You pay an even higher price when you have an energy deficit because you are trying to manage a body and brain in a state of exhaustion on top of the goals you have set for yourself. When we identify what our set point for success is, we gain instant awareness of what may have been holding us back.

> *Your set point for success is the point at which your energy supply becomes greater than what your goal requires.*

Having a surplus of energy available to not only maintain the status quo, but also to pursue your vision and manage any setbacks along the way, puts you ahead of the pack. This may also explain why so many of us default to our biochemistry when we're attempting to reach outside our comfort zone: Our brains have gone into self-preservation mode, and our energetic resources have been redirected.

To increase your energetic resources and become a Catalyst with an abundance of mental clarity and focus, you must turn your attention to three key factors: your mitochondria, gut microbiome, and fuel. Each of these factors will alleviate the need to exert willpower and increase your tolerance for internal and environmental stress that depletes your battery. Increasing your tolerance level for stress means you will bounce back from setbacks faster, regain your focus when it's been stolen from you, and methodically work through problems without getting overly emotional. And, in my case, eliminate my need for the asthma medication that I had inhaled daily since I was a teenager, a highly unexpected result of my mission to become unstoppable.

Marvelous Mitochondria: The Fuel Source for Life

A topic of intense fascination for Dave Asprey, and rightly so, is the mitochondria. These are the little cigar-shaped parts of our cells that create ATP, the energy our cells need to thrive. Mitochondria extract energy from what we eat and convert it into ATP. When your mitochondria are functioning at full capacity, you experience enhanced mental performance. ATP stores the energy you need to charge you both mentally and physically, the perfect balance required to keep you functioning as a Catalyst. This energy production, or the Krebs cycle, is one of the most important functions in your body. The brain uses its energy to think, remember things, learn, and make decisions. The cells in your brain are filled with mitochondria. They are the power supply fueling your entire system. When our neurons have lost energy, you can experience cognitive impairment, fatigue, and brain fog.

When the Krebs cycle converts sugars, proteins and fats into citric acid, it creates the raw materials for optimal energy. However, environmental toxins, as discussed in Chapter 3, impact our mitochondria. Our body's increased need to process a higher level of toxins in our food, medications, household products, and polluted air stresses our whole energy system. There are a number of important antioxidant enzymes found in the mitochondria; when not enough are available, we may suffer from oxidative stress. This is a sign of mitochondrial problems. Some scientists believe it may be linked to many diseases, including depression, chronic fatigue, Alzheimer's, autism, Parkinson's, and ADHD.

Dave said, "If you're suffering from a trauma, not a physical trauma but an emotional trauma, even then your mitochondria will sense that you're stressed, and because they think you're stressed they'll get you ready to run away from something scary, even if it's not present." He added, "When they do that, they stop turning on your rest, repair, and recover mechanisms. So no matter what, if you have any of these things going on, there's a likelihood that increasing your body's ability to make energy will reduce your stress and allow you to address depression, anxiety, and trauma."

Mitochondria are a critical fuel source required to keep you fully charged and alive. Without them, you would die. Taking simple, easy steps to optimize their function can have a significant impact on your overall well-being.

YOU AND YOUR MITOCHONDRIA: A TEN-STEP FUEL-YOURSELF-FOR-SUCCESS PLAN

To fuel yourself for success and enhance your focus, energy, and mental performance, there are ten easy yet critical steps you can take to boost your mitochondrial health, including:

1. Reducing toxins in your food and environment

2. Lowering your stress and cortisol levels

3. Oxygen therapy through effective exercise and circulation

4. Optimal hormone levels, including having a functional doctor check your thyroid level

5. Drinking filtered water

6. Testing for food sensitivities/food elimination diet

7. Ensuring your magnesium levels are optimal. Magnesium does important work in all kinds of processes that keep your body functioning normally from keeping blood sugar in check to making your muscles and nerves functioning properly. It also helps make ATP and improves mitochondrial function.[4]

8. Getting a good night's sleep (more on this in depth in Chapter 8)

9. HIIT (High Intensity Interval Training). One study reported that two weeks of HIIT significantly increased mitochondrial function in skeletal muscle.[5]

10. Rely on fat instead of sugar. Fatty acids are the best fuel for mitochondria and burn cleaner than carbohydrates. When they produce ATP via fats/ketones, fewer free radicals are created (and fewer need to be cleaned up).[6]

The second key factor we need to delve into is the microbiome. According to a 2016 article by Yann Saint-Georges-Chaumet, many studies report a link between the quality and diversity of microbiomes and mitochondrial function.[7]

Microbiome: The Key to Better Health, More Energy, and Better Mood

I constantly felt hung over, despite only drinking one to two glasses of wine per month. I'd never been much of a drinker; I knew it didn't agree with me, I just didn't know why. Sitting down in Dr. Garcia's office, bathed in fluorescent light, the pieces of the puzzle finally started coming together.

"What do I have?" I asked him.

"You have an overgrowth of candida albicans in your digestive tract," he replied.

Otherwise known as gut fermentation syndrome or a candida infection, this unusual digestive disorder can result in feeling intoxicated all the time. The symptoms include extreme difficulty concentrating on simple tasks, brain fog, chronic fatigue, depression, sinus infections, asthma, low mood, a weakened immune system, bloating, and constipation, to name a few. If the effects are severe and you drive, you can get a DUI. For example, CNN reported that in 2015, a woman's DUI was dismissed after she provided evidence that she had been suffering from similar effects, referred to as "auto-brewery syndrome."[8]

Candida albicans, often described as an opportunistic yeast, can be found in 80 percent of the human population. It normally lives in places like your mouth, skin, and digestive tract without any problem. But when the environment is right, it can quickly multiply and grow out of control. It's often thought of as a condition only experienced by people with suppressed immune systems, such as patients with AIDS or diabetes. But, surprisingly, astronauts whose immune systems have been compromised by space travel can also get it. According to Harvard Health Publishing, it can also cause symptoms in healthy people due to corticosteroid use (such as from asthma inhalers), malnutrition, and certain medications.[9]

This sentiment is echoed by the U.S. Department of Health and Human Services.[10] Research has shown an overgrowth of candida can occur after a course of antibiotics, from which our microbiome may not fully recover. Antibiotics take a scorched-earth approach, wiping out both good and bad strains of bacteria, which can spark the overgrowth.[11]

The Gut/Brain Connection

Our gut microbiome contains tens of trillions of microorganisms. It can weigh up to 4.4 pounds or 2 kilograms.[12] To put that in perspective, it weighs more than the average human brain, which comes in at 3 pounds or 1.36 kilograms.[13] Many scientists are now referring to it as our "second brain," as new research has discovered the communication between the gut and the brain is bilateral and has a significant impact on our mood and energy levels. I've come to think of it affectionately as an extra pilot helping to steer the ship.

There's been an explosion of research into our microbiome in recent years as scientists discover more and more vital information about it. There's even a field known as psychobiotics, the treatment of mental health issues by changing the gut microbiome through probiotics and prebiotics.[14] This gained further traction with the 2017 book *The Psychobiotic Revolution* by Scott C. Anderson. Once thought of as an out-of-the-box idea, a growing number of scientists have become interested in probiotics and prebiotics as possible treatments for depression, anxiety, and other mental health problems. A small study conducted at Leiden University in 2015, in which 40 subjects were given four weeks of probiotic treatment, showed a decrease in negative thoughts and feelings.[15]

This made me ask: Can we hack our own thoughts through our gut microbiome? It's not as crazy as it sounds.

Some experiments show that changes to diet can spark large, albeit temporary, shifts in a body's microbiome within 24 hours. This is key, as studies have suggested the intestinal microbiome plays an important role in modulating chronic diseases, including inflammatory bowel disease, obesity, type 2 diabetes, cardiovascular disease, and cancer.[16]

I sat down and thought about every significant event in my life in which I was at my worst and my best, and I noticed something interesting. My depression, fatigue, and inability to focus had flared up after each international trip or course of antibiotics. I wondered, was I just depressed because my holiday was over, or was I depressed because my gut had just been exposed to foreign microbes it didn't know how to deal with?

I reached out to Richard Lin, the CEO and cofounder of Thryve, for an answer. Thryve provides gut health tests and the world's first microbiome report. They have scientists from universities including MIT, Stanford, and UC Davis, as well as from the FDA, working on their team.

After submitting a sample, they begin by breaking down which bacteria are most active in your gut, and then create personalized probiotics that will be beneficial for your microbiome. They also recommend specific microbiome-boosting foods and where to source the ingredients with customized recipes.

About my travel theory, Richard said, "I don't think that's far off at all, actually. We've seen significant research because we have customers from around the world. Their microbiomes are completely different. That could be due to food and the environment. We've seen it with studies where when you actually travel across the world, due to your certain cycle changing, daylight savings and whatnot, the microbiome actually shifts pretty drastically. Sometimes it's not beneficial. You sometimes have microbes that cause inflammation. You have microbes that cause mood issues to be shifted to a larger population due to traveling. And then you're also exposed to microbes in that environment that you're not normally exposed to, so that's why people come back with traveler's diarrhea. It's not just you ate something bad, it's literally because the surrounding microbes are just completely foreign to your body and your body's trying to flush them out. They're not used to it."

Delving deeper into the research, I started asking myself, could a candida overgrowth be a silent epidemic many doctors have yet to recognize? I asked both Dave and Richard, and they both answered with a resounding yes. And that's when Richard blew me away with two incredible case studies that demonstrate just how much influence our gut microbiome has over our health.

He said, "We've seen, for instance, an example of a person balding due to an autoimmune disease, and who had *C. diff* [*clostridium difficile*, a serious bacterial infection], causing severe diarrhea. He got a fecal transplant. A fecal transplant is healthy stool from a person's gut, homogenized and turned into a slurry and transplanted into somebody who has a bad gut. So you're introducing good microbes back into a bad gut. The guy's hair actually started growing back."

Richard continued, "And we've seen results with Parkinson's. There's a doctor called Thomas Brodie from Australia. He's the one who led the fecal transplant and FMT movement here in the States. He had patients with Parkinson's that also had constipation symptoms, so he treated these patients with a triple antibiotic therapy. The three different types of antibiotic wipe out the microbes that cause constipation. Then he did a fecal transplant to reinoculate good bacteria. What he realized was not only did he remove the constipation symptoms, but he also reversed the Parkinson's symptoms."

Could Our Diet Kill Our Healthy Microbiome and Trigger Inflammation?

A 2018 study by the University of Bonn and published in the journal *Cell* likened a fast-food diet to a bacterial infection based on a similar acute inflammatory response in the body. In addition, the researchers found there can be long-term consequences for an "overly aggressive immune system." As such, we may be doing permanent damage to our bodies' immune systems by following a diet high in fat and sugar.[17] This, combined with the overuse of antibiotics and a diet laced in sugar, which the bad bacteria feed off, is a recipe for disaster, killing our energy and our drive to succeed.[18]

I wasn't just taken aback by Richard's answers, but by my original diagnosis. I hadn't known if I would ever get an answer or ever get better. One doctor had told me, "Most people with fatigue never work out what it is." My thought was, *Yeah, only because they have you as a doctor!*

Finally, I had an answer that explained the way I was feeling: the dizzy spells in the morning after breakfast, the general fatigue, the overwhelming anxiety, and the aggression. This was the underlying cause. Digging further into the research, I found I had unknowingly created a perfect storm for the overgrowth of this bad bacteria and for my asthma symptoms to become exacerbated. Here are the factors of my "perfect storm":

- ▸ Traveling throughout the U.S and Canada for three months exposed me to many unfamiliar gut bacteria.
- ▸ Corticosteroid overuse may have suppressed my immune system, making me susceptible to a yeast/candida overgrowth. I was getting sick constantly!
- ▸ A course of antibiotics I had taken to rid myself of a bad sinus infection had killed my healthy gut bacteria, allowing the candida overgrowth to take hold. My immune system was already depleted when I got ill. What happened next, an increase in my asthma symptoms, wasn't surprising since some studies suggest a correlation between taking antibiotics and later developing asthma and allergies.[19]
- ▸ My asthma symptoms heightened due to sensitivity to this bacteria, again, no surprise since asthma's connection to candida albicans is well-known.[20] Candida overgrowth can also prevent nutrient absorption, possibly resulting in my low vitamin D levels, further exacerbating my asthma and fatigue.[21]
- ▸ Vitamin D deficiency is prevalent in individuals with candida.[22] Sufficient levels of vitamin D reduce your risk of infectious disease by strengthening your immune system.[23]
- ▸ Food sensitivities may have contributed to the compounding problem.[24]

The candida overgrowth was confirmed when I took the EverlyWell food sensitivity test. It came back positive for being sensitive to baker's yeast and brewer's yeast—both indicators of a yeast overgrowth.

The surprising thing was that when I corrected my vitamin D levels, took a course of antifungals to rid myself of the candida, and eliminated foods I was sensitive to from my diet, my asthma disappeared. As I write this, it's been five months since I have taken any medication for asthma whatsoever. My personal experience doesn't constitute a cure for asthma; it may come back. But if it does, I know several steps I can take to deal with it.

What jumped out at me was how interlinked everything was, but my doctors had treated each symptom separately. Multiple vicious circles had come into play, resulting in my cognitive decline.

It all made sense. Dr. Garcia had asked if I had been treated with antibiotics as a child; the answer was yes. My symptoms had first flared up after the last course of antibiotics I had taken. Not only that, I was constantly sucking on asthma inhalers shown to spark candida overgrowth.

Taking Extreme Measures to Fix Myself

Per Dr. Garcia's advice, I tackled this challenge from multiple directions, including two vitamin IVs, a colonic irrigation, the candida diet (no or minimal carbohydrates and sugar) for four weeks, and a course of Diflucan, a commonly used antifungal medication. Interestingly, the colonic wasn't the most unpleasant thing I tried; it was the detoxing my body went through when the bacteria started dying off, which led to headaches, fatigue, and severe brain fog. My mood went up and down constantly. I either wanted to sleep or high-five someone in the face with a chair (demonstrating my anger/fatigue).

Then, finally, I started feeling better. My energy was beginning to return, and just in time, too. I had lined up interviews with experts in San Francisco and Canada. After I visited Dave Asprey in Victoria, Canada, I decided my partner and I would spend a few days in Vancouver. While there, to our surprise, we learned we didn't have all the required paperwork to reenter the U.S. It was going to take a full month to get what we needed! Needless to say, this put a crimp in my plans.

While I was involuntarily spending the month in Vancouver, I noticed something interesting. My digestion was working like clockwork. I had color in my face again, after looking like an even paler Anderson Cooper for four years. I was able to have sweets without putting on a pound of weight once I resumed my normal eating routine. My microbiome had balanced itself after the candida diet and the course of antifungals. But when we returned to St. Petersburg, my gut became completely imbalanced again, fatigue set in, and I felt like I was starting over from scratch.

However, this time I acted the second my digestive issues kicked in (bloating, diarrhea, and constipation). If I was to have the profound levels of energy I needed, I had to heal my gut. The shock of going from great to horrible had provided the wake-up call I needed.

Validating What Was Happening in My Stomach

For every part of this project, I wanted scientific evidence to back up what I was experiencing. My doctors had applied basic testing and guesswork, which is roughly as good as throwing darts at the board blindfolded. As I mentioned earlier in this chapter, I had discovered Richard Lin's company, Thryve, so upon returning from Canada, I decided to do their gut health test. They mailed me a testing kit, consisting of a specimen jar, a swab, and a prepaid box to send my sample in. I had been worried that I would have to somehow poo in a jar; thankfully, you only need to provide a rice-sized fecal sample. I received my results four weeks later, and they were unexpected.

Thryve gives you access to an online dashboard that explains in basic terms what your results mean, and tells you which foods you can eat to recalibrate your stomach and rebalance your microbiome. They also give you an overall gut bacteria wellness score. I scored 65 out of 100. (See Figure 4.2, on page 84.)

This score determines how well your body is functioning. The higher the score, the closer you are to achieving your health goals. Typically, Thryve notes, individuals in Western countries have a lower score. That's to be expected, considering the changes to our food supply and the prevalence of junk food. The usual score in Western countries is somewhere around 50 to 80 out of 100. I was smack in the middle of this range, but well below optimal. That's when I dove deeper into the data.

The graph (in Figure 4.2) pinpointed key issues that I would never have been able to learn about without taking the test. I was lacking specific types of good bacteria, which is what was causing my stomach upsets and digestive issues. One type flew off the screen at me: bacteroides. Bacteroides support gut integrity and provide immune support. I was well below the healthy average. The bacteria *alistipes*

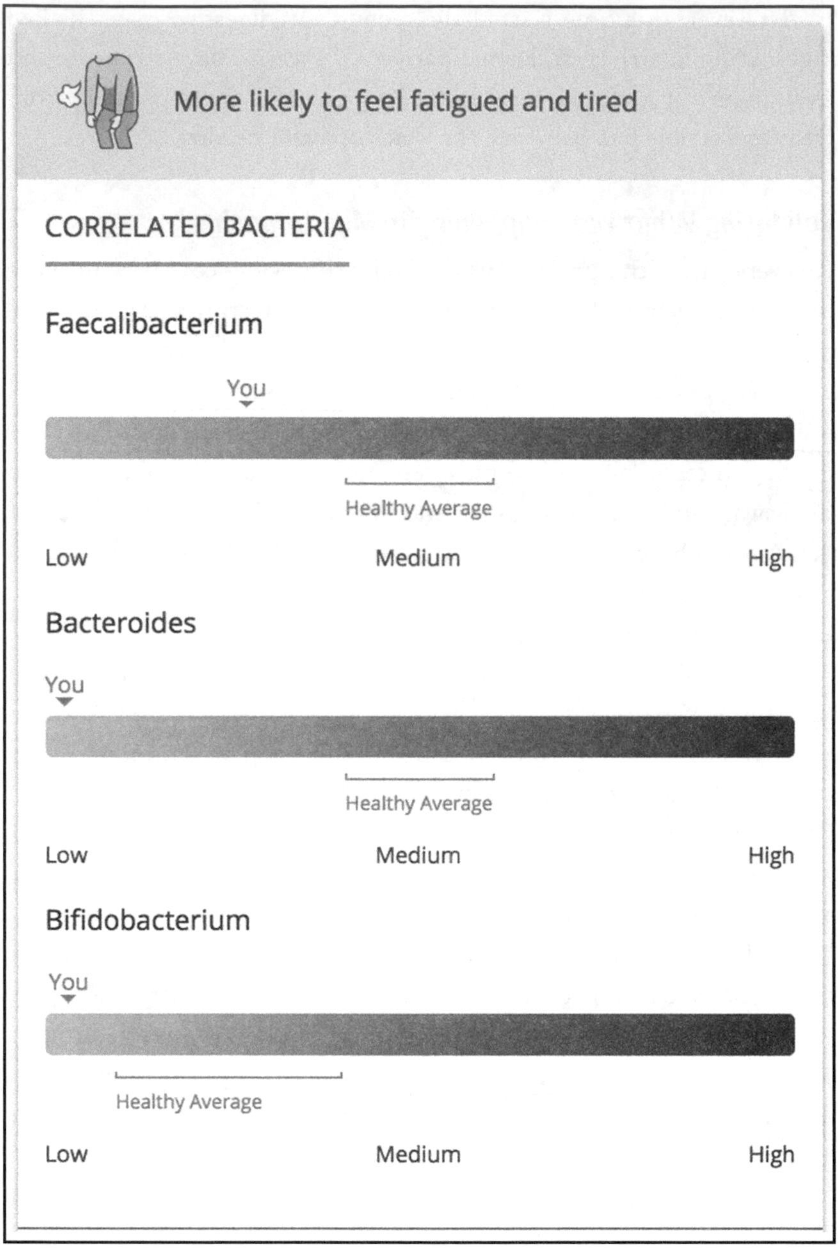

Figure 4.2 My Results from Thryve's Gut Microbiome Test

was also low. They aid in digesting fats, protect against pathogens, and assist in digesting whole grains, something I have had issues with for years. As a result, I have avoided grains, especially oats, altogether. *Lactobacillus* was another bacteria I was depleted in. Commonly found in probiotics supplements on shelves worldwide, its benefits are well-researched: It assists in breaking down food, absorbing nutrients, and fighting off unfriendly organisms; it has antifungal properties; and it is beneficial for those with Crohn's disease and IBS (irritable bowel syndrome).

Another bacteria I barely rated in was *bifidobacterium*, which aids in gastrointestinal and immune support and has anti-inflammatory properties. Other benefits include the inhibition of pathogens, which can include harmful bacteria, viruses, and other microorganisms that colonize and/or infect the gut mucosa.

If I could correct these imbalances, would my gut heal, brain fog lift, and energy increase again?

First, I started taking the personalized probiotic Thryve sent me based on my results. An off-the-shelf solution would have still left my gut imbalanced because they didn't have all the beneficial bacteria *my* body needed, or the diversity I required.

Second, I started eating foods that were known to have the bacteria I lacked, such as apricots, which contain bacteroides. I started noticing a difference within two weeks. My digestion improved, my brain fog began to clear, and my bloating dissipated.

I had thought I had tried everything to correct my gut imbalance, but nothing had worked. Now I finally knew why.

Our gut, just like our biochemistry, is like a fingerprint. The balance and makeup of our gut bacteria, good and bad, is unique. What is right for you may not be right for me, and vice versa. Once we recognize this, we can correct these imbalances based on data, not guesswork.

By focusing on increasing our gut bacteria diversity, we can influence a whole host of areas when it comes to our health, including weight, digestion, energy regulation, cognition, allergies, and our immune system. In fact, a staggering 80 percent of our immune system is in our microbiome. Thankfully, one easy way to tackle this is to learn the best foods to eat that can populate our gut with beneficial bacteria, which influence our mood as well as our digestion.

Fueling for Success: Why a One-Size-Fits-All Approach to Nutrition Does Not Work

The gut health test changed the way I looked at everything.

In Australia, I had been eating clean most of my adult life: avoiding refined sugars, carbs, and gluten as much as possible. I had adopted the popular dietary program Body for Life, created by Bill Phillips. This consisted of eating multiple times throughout the day and having one "fat day" per week. I could easily manage a healthy eating pattern the rest of the week. In no way did I feel restricted, experience food cravings, or suffer from brain fog or fatigue.

But now, I was eating the same way, but in a different country, and after a course of antibiotics, and I was gaining weight and body fat. Even after I cut calories, my body didn't respond. I could tell I was nutritionally deficient just by the way I felt, but I didn't know why: My diet, like always, consisted of a balance of healthy fruits, vegetables, and proteins.

New research has shown our gut bacteria don't just aid in digestion; they also play a crucial role in whether we lose or gain weight. According to a 2016 report in *Scientific American*, researchers conducting a study of twins who were both either lean or obese found big differences in the gut bacteria of the two groups. The guts in lean subjects were abundant in bacterial species, while those of obese subjects were less diverse. [25] I concluded most (not all) diet plans are questionable unless they factor in our microbiome health and how we each respond to food individually.

As a society, we have been quick to blame our genes for our weight gain. But we all have similar DNA. The real question is: Why do we each respond so differently to food? Why can some people eat carbs freely, and others gain ten pounds the second they glance at a slice of pizza? Why do some succeed on a ketogenic/paleo/Atkins diet, and others struggle with digestive symptoms due to severe detox? Why can some eat poorly, yet feel great?

While some companies are now claiming they can personalize meal plans based on our genes (backed by little research), one factor we fail to take into account is our gut microbiome genes, which outnumber the genes in our genome by about 100 to 1. The role they play in our relationship to food cannot be ignored.

Is it the diet or my microbiome that I should be focusing on to increase energy levels and focus?

I looked at countless dietary protocols, and for every positive effect, there was a reported negative one, or a case study showing an adverse response to the plan. Each had its benefits as well as setbacks, such as managing food cravings, or the side effects of going ketogenic in the first five to seven days, which are hard for some to endure. One minute, scientists say carbs are bad; the next they proclaim that carbs are good. The truth lies in the fingerprint of our microbiome. What's great for you may be detrimental to me.

With more than 100,000 papers published on nutrition in the peer-reviewed medical literature each year, it's hard to keep up. And all this research fails in one key area: It doesn't consider that everyone's microbiome is unique, which means our responses may vary greatly—especially from country to country, as I discovered from my conversation with Richard.

Any meal plan must be personalized to ensure we each have the energy we need to not just feel good but feel great, and have the energy to pursue our goals and navigate this minefield called life. This personalization will increase the likelihood of successfully following the plan and eating in a way that benefits us.

Regardless of the dietary protocol you choose, to improve mood, memory, and drive, the following are a few key factors that must be included and then tweaked to match your individual response to various foods:

▸ *Remove sugar and processed food from your diet.* This will rid the body and brain of toxins and inflammation. In a 2016 article in the *Canadian Journal of Diabetes*, Dr. Robert Lustig wrote we are inundating our bodies with so much sugar that they can no longer process it. It's a toxin our body must rid itself of, but it's losing the battle.[26]

▶ *Eat foods that increase your microbiome's diversity.* This includes fermented foods that populate your gut with healthy bacteria (e.g., pickles, kimchi, unprocessed yogurt, and kombucha). These foods are rich in prebiotics. Prebiotics feed probiotics and encourage the growth of healthy bacteria. Prebiotic fiber is a type of carbohydrate that we do not digest, but our gut bacteria thrive on. Since discovering my gut imbalance, I have been supplementing with a prebiotic fiber from Dr. David Perlmutter's doctor-formulated range. I add one tablespoon to a smoothie with a banana. This has been particularly useful in curbing my afternoon cravings when combined with a dash of medium-chain triglycerides, more commonly known as MCT oil. It helps prevent constipation, I no longer experience a midafternoon crash as a result, and it helps me maintain my weight by preventing me from snacking too much. According to research from the University of Calgary, prebiotics may even assist in the fight against childhood obesity by helping to "reduce body fat in children who are overweight or obese by altering their gut microbiota."[27]

▶ *Eliminate foods that cause you discomfort.* This includes any food you are sensitive to that causes constipation, diarrhea, sluggishness, brain fog, headaches, fatigue, or mood changes. For greater insight, have a food sensitivity test done. It would take years to methodically remove foods from your diet and work out which ones are the culprit. With the test, you can get your answers within two weeks.

▶ *Repopulate your gut with healthy bacteria.* I went to the extreme and did a probiotic enema every few days for one week to regain my gut health after returning home from Canada. This was based on Dr. Perlmutter's treatment approach. There will be more on this and the probiotic I recommend (and why) in the 90-day plan later in this book.[28]

▶ *Fuel up with fats.* I began supplementing with MCT oil, as well as upping my healthy fats from avocados and olive oil. More on this in Chapter 5. This helped curb my cravings and reduce the midafternoon energy slump and cravings.

▶ *Eat anti-inflammatory foods.* This includes green leafy vegetables, beets, blueberries, bok choy, broccoli, celery, chia seeds, coconut oil, flaxseed, ginger, pineapple, salmon, turmeric, and walnuts. Exclude any foods that cause you sensitivity.

▶ *Eat diverse organic fruits and vegetables.* This will increase microbiome diversity and promote overall gut health.

▶ *Drink filtered water.* Much is still unknown about the impact chemicals like chlorine can have on our delicate gut microbiome. Filtration is crucial regardless of which city or part of the world you live in to prevent unnecessary exposure to toxins from rusty pipes or compromised water supplies.

▶ *Switch trans fats and vegetable oils for olive, avocado, or grapeseed oil.* One study found the participants who took in the most trans fats increased their risk of depression by 48 percent. Those in the same study who consumed more than 20 grams of olive oil per day had a 30 percent lower risk of depression than those who consumed little olive oil or didn't consume it at all.[29] Trans fats are often hidden in highly processed foods at the supermarket and used to deep fry food at various fast-food chains. The Food and Drug Administration has required trans fats to be declared on the nutrition facts label since 2006 to help consumers understand their dietary intake.[30]

▶ *Consume more omega-3 and less omega-6.* Both are essential fatty acids important for good health, but we need them in the right balance to help protect our joints, pancreas, heart, skin, and mood stability. We consume way too much omega-6, commonly found in corn and vegetable oils. Too much can cause the body to retain water and raise blood pressure, which could lead to blood clots, thus raising the risk of heart attacks and strokes.[31]

▶ *Consume foods with antifungal properties.* This includes cayenne pepper, coconut oil, garlic, ginger, lemons, limes, olive oil, onions, pumpkin seeds, and rutabaga to help fight off bad gut bacteria. Do not consume any foods that you are sensitive or allergic to. Find substitutes that work for you.

▶ *Keep activated charcoal on hand.* Dave Asprey first introduced me to this when I mentioned I had been detoxing as a result of the candida diet. He mentioned that when detoxing, especially with such an intense dietary protocol, toxins can build up. The activated charcoal can assist by binding itself to these toxins, which are then excreted by the body. Activated charcoal has been used for years in emergency rooms for certain kinds of poisoning, including alcohol. It helps prevent the poison from being absorbed from the stomach into the body. I now use it intermittently, especially if I am feeling flat and have potentially consumed something that isn't agreeing with me. It can also assist with gas, bloating, and even lowering cholesterol.

▶ *Practice intermittent fasting (IF).* I grew up believing I would lose muscle mass if I didn't eat six small meals per day (a belief that has since been debunked). While this helped me maintain my energy levels throughout the day, it didn't help me maintain a lower body fat percentage. A month prior to beginning the 13-week challenge, I chose to do 30 days of intermittent fasting, and took a picture every day in the mirror to observe the changes and keep myself accountable. It is widely reported that IF is effective for weight loss, inflammation reduction, and boosting brain power by increasing ketones. IF was made popular by Hugh Jackman, who used it in preparation for his Wolverine movies. It is a pattern of eating, not a diet. It doesn't change what you eat so much as when you eat. Instead of consuming food all day long, you eat within a set window of time. The most popular protocol is to eat for eight hours per day and fast for 16. You can start by gradually closing your eating window until you hit the 8/16 goal, this being by far the easiest protocol to follow. I chose to eat between noon and 8 P.M. each day and allowed some flexibility on weekends. If I ate earlier, I would stop eating earlier. It was incredibly easy to maintain, and my gut benefited from taking a break from digesting food all the time. According to Mark Mattson, a professor of neurology at Johns Hopkins University, fasting has been shown to increase rates of neurogenesis (the growth and development of new brain cells and nerve tissues) in the brain.[32] Higher rates of neurogenesis are linked to increased brain performance, memory, mood, and focus. It has also been shown to boost production of BDNF (brain-derived neurotrophic factor). BDNF is considered "Miracle-Gro for your brain" and plays a role in neuroplasticity, which makes your brain more resilient to stress and adaptable to change. IF has been shown to boost BDNF by 50 to 400 percent.[33] It also has positive benefits for your mitochondrial biogenesis, the creation of new mitochondria. I didn't notice any physical changes in the first two weeks of IF. It wasn't until week four that I was pleasantly surprised when I compared my before and after photos. That stubborn back fat that I had never been able to get rid of, even when restricting calories, was gone. This protocol was far easier to follow than I expected, especially with the loss in body fat and boost in energy and mental clarity. I drank plenty of tea and sparkling water in the morning to keep myself satiated. It is an easy change to make, with numerous added benefits.

Find What Works for You

By following these easy-to-apply guidelines, you'll begin to notice a significant change in your energy levels, as well as your mental clarity. Don't allow yourself to be overwhelmed by all the different dietary protocols out there. Find one that works for you, but always stay focused on your microbiome health; this is the fundamental building block many fail to factor in. A dietary shift can help repopulate your healthy bacteria; however, if you do have a yeast overgrowth or an intestinal imbalance, you may need a course of antifungals to reset and reboot your digestive system. Talk to a functional doctor to learn more.

As we're learning, our willpower and our thoughts aren't just influenced by our upbringing. There are many factors that come into play when you're trying to become a peak performer and have energy to hit all your targets. Food and an increase in toxins may have added a barrier to your success you aren't aware of, because it happened so gradually. By removing these factors and fueling yourself with consistent, clean energy sources that keep you focused throughout the day, you can achieve a lot more in less time. Catalysts and Synergists rely on clean food sources; Guardians and Defenders rely on caffeine, refined sugars, and carbs to get them through the day. Which one are you? Once I corrected my gut imbalance, my cravings, brain fog, and fatigue vanished. I was eating a fraction of what I was previously and feeling better. I stopped counting calories and focused on how food made me feel. Instead of immediately blaming someone or something for my bad mood, I looked immediately to food. I hadn't felt this calm in more than ten years. The ketone ester drink I had tested provided the kick I needed to keep going. But before I could make the necessary dietary changes and turn them into habits that would reboot my entire body and brain, I needed a *MAJOR* kick-start!

I want you to stop right now and ask yourself if you feel great. I mean, *really* great. Or do you feel just OK? OK isn't OK. We want to feel amazing. But to get to that, we may have to give ourselves a major kick-start to increase our energy for long enough that we can make our new habits stick. To do that, we need to delve into the world of nootropics and supplementation.

CHALLENGE FOUR

More Fun with Colonic Irrigation: How I went from 16 percent to 13 percent body fat.

I jumped online and started seeking out research that backed the benefits of a colonic irrigation. Dr. Garcia had recommended it as a way to jump-start my treatment. I wasn't crazy about the idea, but I had committed myself to getting better. Colon cleansing has been around since ancient times. It was thought of as a procedure to help the body dispose of waste and toxins. It

CHALLENGE FOUR, continued

was then discredited by a number of professional societies, including the American Medical Association.

Coming up blank on well-researched benefits, I decided to go ahead with a skeptical attitude, after speaking with several friends who had done it on and off throughout the years and were willing to attest to its benefits.

The nurse made me feel welcome in the dimly lit room as she calmly explained the process and shared case studies of other clients, one of whom had not had a bowel movement for an entire month until his colonic! You can't tell me there isn't a benefit to be had there.

Here's the nonromantic version: I put on a gown, and she inserted a tube into my rectum. On the wall was a series of clear pipes that would show what came out. I swear she found a set of keys from ten years ago. I had felt relatively empty going into the procedure, but boy, oh boy, was I wrong.

My stomach felt queasy for the rest of the night, but when I woke in the morning, I felt incredible. Like a weight had not only been removed from my intestines, but from my head as well. Friends I told about the treatment dismissed it as water weight. The scales told a different story. I had lost 4.4 pounds, or 2 kilograms, and in the following weeks I continued to lose weight, as well as body fat. The colonic, in combination with the antifungals, had rebooted my digestion. I went from 16 percent body fat down to 13 percent. The last time I was at 13 percent, I had had to starve myself. This time, it felt natural and better, and my energy increased as a result.

CHAPTER 5

The Accidental Biohacker
Sharpening Your Mind with Nutritional Supplements

"What? We're stranded in Canada for over a month?" I angrily retorted to the immigration agent over the phone. What was meant to be a ten-day trip to the West Coast—Los Angeles to San Francisco and then back to Canada—was about to turn into a five-week unplanned stay. Everything had been mapped out months in advance for my experiments with nootropics, wearables, and supplements. Some interviews had taken several months to lock down; now, it was all about to be thrown into disarray. We had just learned that even though we had received the paperwork we needed to live and work in the U.S., we didn't have the required paperwork to reenter the country. With a backlog of meetings at the U.S. embassy in Vancouver, we had to wait one full month to secure an interview and then several more days to receive our passports. Due to the delay, I also had to make an expensive round-trip flight to Ottawa to update my Australian passport, in hopes that it would come in time for the immigration meeting in Vancouver. We suddenly had to be prepared for a white Christmas and New Year's in Canada. However, that wasn't my only concern.

One month before our trip, my partner and I had decided to foster Mitch, a beautiful little Yorkshire terrier in need of much love. He was the last of 40 neglected Yorkies rescued from a house in Florida. His shocking rescue story had been featured on the local news a month prior to us meeting him. He was the last one left in Pet Pal's Animal Shelter in Saint Petersburg, and he was petrified.

As soon as our plans were set for our trip, I asked our close friends Debbie and Rich to watch over little Mitch. Suddenly, a week later in Canada, I had to call to see if they were OK keeping him for another five weeks or so. Although I knew he was in amazing hands with our friends, my blood boiled as to how this was throwing a major curveball at us, financially and emotionally.

> If I had Botox, I would have cracked it because I was so ANGRY!

I spent the first week in Vancouver angry. I believed I had done everything required to ensure something like this wouldn't happen. It had already cost a fortune to book my itinerary, and now I was about to take another major financial hit for a five-week unplanned stay in Canada.

On top of this, my laptop went on the fritz. How was I going to write my book and finish all my research and experiments? The 90-day clock was ticking down, and I was reaching a critical level of stress!

As I sat in the airport watching people board the flight to Ottawa, I decided enough was enough. My 90-day mission to become unstoppable wasn't just about feeling great and closing my identity gap; it was about achieving a level of emotional control that would enable me to work through any challenge—including getting stranded overseas. My energy had improved greatly after the treatment of antifungals and dietary changes. Now it was time to upgrade my thinking, memory, focus, and motivation. This was an opportunity for me to test everything I had uncovered so far. Would it work? I decided to opt for a little extra help.

In the past, I had handled stressful life events through mental rehearsal and EFT, otherwise known as the Emotional Freedom Technique. This time, however, I was going to heighten my mental state prior to applying these two strategies and amplify their effects to make a lasting impact. I realized later that I had become the "Accidental Biohacker" out of necessity, to heal and rid myself of fatigue, depression, and memory loss once and for all.

The flight to Ottawa was the perfect time for my first experiment: the nootropics and nicotine Dave Asprey had introduced me to. My first taste of nicotine was in Dave's personal Bulletproof lab in the Canadian mountains, where he gave me my first taste of Bulletproof Coffee, a unique blend of grass-fed butter, MCT oil, and Dave's own coffee beans. In addition to this, he added a brand-new sweetener that he plans to bring to market. Dave told me he was going to light my brain on fire with a hit of nicotine and round it off with a nootropic chaser.

Within seconds of him spraying nicotine under my tongue, I got the hiccups. We both burst out laughing and had to pause the interview while I regained composure.

Are you crazy? I thought, as Dave explained that nicotine is a well-known, well-researched nootropic popular for its cognitive and performance-enhancing abilities. It tends to get a bad rap from its association with cigarettes. However, when nicotine is separated out from the 5,000-plus other chemicals in a cigarette, the research is surprisingly positive, as seen in the following results:

▶ It makes you more vigilant. For example, nicotine patches allow some people to focus longer on a mentally exhausting task.
▶ People who took nicotine had better memory recall of a list of words.

> ▶ Nicotine sharpens short-term memory.
> ▶ It heightens your ability to pay attention.
> ▶ It speeds up your reaction time.
> ▶ It suppresses appetite.[1]

Nicotine is currently being analyzed for possible therapeutic benefits for a host of issues ranging from Alzheimer's and Parkinson's to ADHD, schizophrenia, and obesity. In addition, it's an inexpensive and mostly safe option.[2]

Never having so much as held a cigarette, I was nervous at the effect it might have on me. After Dave sprayed the nicotine under my tongue and I drank the Bulletproof Coffee, within minutes I felt flushed, and then the coffee kicked in. I hadn't touched coffee for almost a year. Hello, world! What followed was a fast-paced and productive interview that ranged across all areas of biohacking strategies. I was getting a firsthand look at how this revolutionary neuroscience field was merging with hacking our own health.

A week later, just before boarding my flight to Ottawa, I sprayed the nicotine under my tongue. I wanted to observe the effects on my cognition in a controlled environment, free from distractions and interruptions. This time, my reaction was completely different. I became dizzy and came close to fainting. As I anxiously watched the other passengers board from the safety of the airport lounge, I began to wonder if I should get on the flight at all. I opted to board last and tried desperately to keep my shit together. Did I look like a paranoid drug addict? I felt like one. What had I done to myself before boarding a five-hour flight that still had to go through Toronto and then on to Ottawa?

I sheepishly boarded the plane, took my seat, and put on my headphones. Listening to a powerful mental rehearsal I had created for myself when I was in New York a year ago, I visualized how the rest of my stay in Canada would unravel and how great it would be to complete the project. After that, I continued my research for the book. Five hours later, I arrived in Toronto. I barely remember the flight.

Have you ever been so focused you lost an entire day immersed in your work? You look up and suddenly realize hours have flown by.

It had been years since I had experienced this level of focus. Not only did I read an entire book on gut microbiomes on the flight over, but I also wrote more than 3,000 words, which I subsequently lost due to an intermittent internet connection. However, that didn't bother me in the slightest, because I could easily remember what I had written.

My focus was dialed in, my alertness was at an all-time high, and I was experiencing a strong sense of calmness. My anger had dissipated after the mental rehearsal, and the nicotine had helped narrow my focus to what was in front of me. This cleared the path for me to enjoy not just this short trip, but also the rest of the stay in Vancouver. Later I would trial nicotine while meditating with the Muse headband and was floored by the results. I now had tangible evidence to quantify that the nicotine had enhanced my results.

Time to Bring My A-Game and Become "The Catalyst"

To become a Catalyst on my 13-week mission to becoming unstoppable, I had to drive a level of awareness that I had failed to achieve previously in my state of fatigue and exhaustion. This first required me to identify who I currently believed myself to be: Defender, Guardian, Synergist, or Catalyst. Then I had to incrementally remove foods and medications that had a negative impact on my emotions. After that, I had to position myself for success by switching fuel sources, eat anti-inflammatory foods, and focus on healthy fats to help recharge my brain after high levels of psychological output. Once the brain fog began to lift, I could focus on unleashing my full potential with nootropics and additional supplementation to light my vision of my true self.

When you're in Defender or Guardian mode, change is massively harder because you have further to travel. And, as we've learned, your cognitive abilities become the sacrificial lamb, limiting your ability to focus, make decisions, research a solid plan, take action, and sustain any type of change. We need to kick-start whatever can give us enough mental clarity and focus to effectively assess our options to make easy, incremental changes. I call this "progressive overload."

Progressive overload is when you start small yet make consistent changes on a daily basis until, 90 days later, you have evolved easily into the person you knew you could become. You'll get more on this later in my 90-day plan.

My objective at this point was clear. I needed to boost my energy and dial in my focus for change to occur. To do that, I needed to find supplements and nootropics that would help stack the deck in my favor long enough to gain some momentum.

> *Nutritional deficiencies will amplify your worst emotions and make you your own enemy.*

As we have seen, a healthy diet alone is no longer sufficient for all our nutritional needs, given the changes in modern agriculture. But it isn't just farming practices that are a problem. In a 2004 article by John Heritage, a then senior lecturer in microbiology at the University of Leeds, Heritage shared a study by Netherland et al. that shows "when humans digest genetically modified foods, the artificially created genes transfer into and alter the character of the beneficial bacteria in the intestine."[3] It's already an uphill battle trying to maintain a healthy gut microbiome within our body without having to worry about how the quality of our food is being genetically compromised. This study demonstrates the dire consequences that are occurring environmentally and nutritionally by genetic engineers accidentally altering organisms that affect the trans-kingdom genetic flow.[4]

We must understand that a diet that may have been more than adequate 50 years ago isn't today. Global populations are becoming nutrient deficient, which can lead to brain fog, obesity, fatigue, depression, anxiety, memory loss, weakness, brain function abnormalities, behavior changes, and more. It's the next unspoken global epidemic.

Eating a variety of healthy and organic foods is vital; however, it's no longer enough. We need to supplement our diets to ensure we close the nutrient gap and perform at maximum potential for more focus, energy, and drive. It's simply not possible to eat the amount of food now required to get the same nutritional value from it as a decade ago.

At a book signing at Tampa, Florida's, Oxford Exchange, Dr. Steven Masley, author of *The Better Brain Solution*, stated that up to 85 percent of the population is nutrient deficient. We just haven't realized it yet because many doctors are still peddling the belief that a healthy diet is enough. The science says otherwise. Tired, mineral-depleted soils grow mineral-depleted foods. It's up to individuals to educate themselves on the effects this has on our behavior and supplement accordingly.

Reboot Your Brain, Boost Your Energy, and Dial in Your Focus

Nutritional deficiencies slow our cognition and trigger an inability to make healthy decisions across all areas of our lives. To break this cycle, we must break down some of the most common vitamin and mineral deficiencies. Often, as you'll quickly discover with nootropics, you won't notice the full effects until you stop taking them.

Have you ever said, "I feel great! I don't need to take these vitamins anymore?" The reason you feel great is because you are taking them. A few weeks may pass, and you may not connect insufficient supplementation with your poor attitude and performance. Whenever you begin feeling down, this is your go-to list that will help you take immediate action to conduct a course correction.

I have purposefully left out dosage information. Why? This can change according to lifestyle factors, age, diet, and deficiency levels. Talk to your functional doctor or naturopath to advise you on what is right for you. Everyone is biochemically unique based on their microbiome, where they live, daily stressors, and foods they consume. What is right for me may not be ideal for you, and vice versa.

Deficiencies in any of the following areas may present symptoms that are indicative of other disorders or conditions. If you notice any of the symptoms related to the following supplement deficiencies, it's important to seek proper medical help straight away.

A study published in the *American Journal of Psychiatry* in 2005 indicates that children who previously were malnourished experience an increased rate of behavior-related disorders and behaviors as they age. Could this be one of the root causes of individuals giving up on their goals, their community, and themselves? Nutritional imbalances distort mental function, mood, and our response to stress.[5]

Top Six Supplements to Reboot Your Body and Brain

The following supplements are crucial for Defenders and Guardians, who are potentially nutritionally deficient and whose cognitive functions have been impacted. You will need to immediately address any nutritional deficiencies that are preventing you from becoming an unstoppable version of yourself. Your main objective is to rid yourself of any brain fog or fatigue you are currently experiencing.

If you're a Catalyst or Synergist, the following supplements may help you sharpen your mental sword even further and help increase your tolerance for physical and emotional stress during times of peak activity.

Vitamin D: Mood Regulation, Concentration, and Memory

As we discovered in Chapter 3, some experts have referred to vitamin D deficiency as a pandemic. As it plays an integral role in regulating mood, warding off depression, improving concentration, and memory, supplementation is vital. Sunlight alone isn't always enough. With the increasing amount of time spent indoors, supplementation, especially during winter months, can help prevent SAD (Seasonal Affective Disorder), a type of depression related to seasonal changes. However, for you to know how much vitamin D your body needs, have your doctor run a simple blood serum test for your levels. Then you'll have an idea of where to start. Your ability to absorb vitamin D, age, geographical region, and ethnicity all play a role with this vital vitamin. Don't guess on your dosage; get your data first.

Form: D3

Time taken: Morning

Recommended brand: Carlson Super Daily D3[6]

Magnesium: Mental Health and Sleep

Magnesium is crucial for the absorption of sodium, calcium, phosphorus, potassium, and vitamin D; vitamin D especially cannot be metabolized without it. A magnesium deficiency results in vitamin D being stored as inactive within the body for as many as 50 percent of Americans. Furthermore, one study suggests that up to 75 percent of people are not meeting their daily magnesium intake. Nutritional magnesium intake has decreased due to industrialized practices.[7]

A deficiency of this vital mineral has been connected to mental disorders, including apathy. Mental numbness or lack of emotion are notable characteristics of apathy.[8] Studies have shown that low magnesium may also increase an individual's risk of depression.[9] Furthermore, studies have speculated magnesium deficiency may promote anxiety; however, more research needs to be done. Another study found magnesium also reduces cortisol, the stress hormone, which can keep you up at night. [10]

> *Forms*: Magnesium malate for energy and muscle soreness, magnesium threonate for memory and brain function, and magnesium oxide for bowel regularity.
>
> *Time taken*: I recommend Colosan Capsules (of magnesium oxide), two daily in the morning, 30 minutes prior to eating to get things moving and to prevent toxins from building up in the body due to slow-moving digestion.
>
> *Recommended brand*: Speak with your functional doctor to find out which type of magnesium is best for you.

Iodine: Energy, Memory, and Brain Health

Your thyroid glands use the mineral iodine to create thyroid hormones, which assist your body with functions like repairing damaged cells, controlling growth, and regulating metabolism. Iodine deficiency is not uncommon—up to a third of the world's population is at risk for it.[11] Iodine enhances the immune function and helps prevent brain damage.

To my surprise, Dr. Garcia told me my iodine levels were at the low end of the normal range. He warned that if they dropped any lower, I could develop thyroid issues if I didn't supplement. This was another contributing factor to my fatigue, poor memory, and weakness. So although your test results may come back as normal, always ask the doctor a crucial follow-up question, "Is it at the high end or low end of the normal range?" If it's at the low end of normal, that clearly isn't optimal health or preventative medicine. Many of our lab values were created more than 30 years ago and based on a normal adult male, and they vary from lab to lab as well. You have to educate yourself on where you fall on this variant range. You may still be experiencing low-level symptoms of a deficiency that can quickly be corrected before it gets worse. Vague answers to test results do little to optimize our health. Remember, you're in control of your health. Speak up and ask questions and never be afraid to fire a doctor who is unable to provide you with the answers you need.

Physically active individuals are at a high risk of iodine deficiency because you lose it through sweat.[12] An abnormal thyroid can be problematic for the body in a variety of ways. For example, it can affect mood and has been linked to changes in both cognitive function and the course of some disorders, such as bipolar disorder.[13] Important note: If you have thyroid problems, speak to your functional doctor prior to supplementing with iodine.

Forms: Kelp powder, liquid or potassium iodide capsules

Time taken: Tablets taken once daily with food, or liquid placed in a small square patch on your lower abdomen.

Recommended brand: Bulletproof Iodine

Vitamin B12: Improve Mood, Regenerate Cells

Vitamin B12 deficiencies are related to a whole host of symptoms, including mood disorders, bipolar disorder, low energy/fatigue, sexual problems/infertility, depression, anxiety, irritability, memory loss, and even Alzheimer's, dementia, cancer, and learning disorders. This can be assessed via a simple blood test.[14] A vitamin B12 deficiency is present in 40 percent of adults in ages ranging from 26 to 83, with nine percent of them having a full deficiency and 16 percent with a "near deficiency," according to the Tufts University Framingham Offspring Study. Disturbingly, many in this group also presented neurological symptoms, including mood swings, sudden outbursts, decreased alertness, difficulty reading and writing, poor cognitive abilities, depression, and delusions.[15]

There are some connections between the presence of B vitamins and healthy brain chemistry and mood. One study discovered individuals with the highest B12 levels who were also in counseling also experienced the greatest success in managing symptoms of depression in conjunction with counseling.[16]

Forms: Capsule and/or lozenge

Time taken: Daily with food

Recommended brand: Bulletproof Methyl B12

Brain Octane Oil: Efficient High-Energy Fuel Source, Brain Boosting, and Crave Reducing

This energy-boosting fat can work wonders for your body and brain. brain octane oil contains MCT oil, otherwise known as medium-chain triglycerides. They are naturally occurring fats found in a small handful of foods. Unlike carbohydrates and sugars, which spike your blood sugar level, leading to a dramatic crash that can seriously influence your mood and behavior, MCT oil is rapidly absorbed by the body and converted into brain fuel, or fat-burning ketones. Ketones can't be stored as fat, so you get a quick boost of energy that lasts without adding extra weight. Dave Asprey claims that Brain Octane Oil converts into ketones more efficiently than coconut MCT oils that contain lauric acid, and he says it produces four times more ketones than coconut oil alone.

MCT oil is a clean and efficient energy fuel source that is extremely helpful when seeking to boost and keep your energy levels consistent throughout the day. When I added it to a midafternoon protein shake, my cravings for a snack vanished. My body fat percentage naturally dropped, and absolutely no willpower was required when it came to avoiding highly processed food. And, as we have seen, anything that switches our cravings on can render our impulse control meaningless, thereby impacting your ability to stay focused and driving our need for increased willpower.

You'll read Stephanie's story in Chapter 10, about her mission to rid herself of brain fog, depression, fatigue, and anxiety, but here's a quick preview: she lost 8 pounds, or 3.6 kilograms, in five days. The shift to high, healthy fats, including adding MCT oil to her daily routine, helped her manage her cravings without needing to exert willpower. She explained, "I didn't have to force myself to eat healthy, nor did I feel like I was missing out on anything. The only time I felt the lack was when I forgot to supplement efficiently. The MCT oil, prebiotics, and healthy fat completely curbed and controlled my cravings. It felt easy compared to all the other times I had attempted to get my health under control."

One study found that consuming 2.7 tablespoons of MCT oil improved cognitive function in people with mild cognitive impairment.[17] Bodybuilders and endurance athletes also use it to increase energy and decrease body fat while increasing lean muscle mass.[18, 19]

Form: Liquid. Start small with one teaspoon in tea/coffee/smoothie, then gradually build up to one tablespoon per day. Having too much too soon may result in an upset stomach. Slowly build up the dosage to identify what's right for you.

Time taken: I have one serving of MCT oil midmorning and another one midafternoon to curb my cravings and keep me energized.

Recommended brand: I recommend Bulletproof Brain Octane Oil from Dave Asprey. For those of us who are sensitive or allergic to coconut, you'll be relieved to hear it has been processed so that the coconut proteins are no longer present.

Zinc: Modulate the Brain and the Body's Response to Stress, Increase Immunity, Balance Hormones, and Aid in Nutrient Absorption

Zinc, a type of metal, is an essential trace element. Zinc is required in small amounts daily to help maintain health and perform other vital functions, including hormone production, growth and repair, improving immunity, and facilitating digestion. It also acts as an anti-inflammatory agent and helps modulate the brain and the body's response to stress. Zinc deficiency can result in symptoms of depression, difficulties with learning and memory, aggression, and yes, even violence.[20] Low zinc levels have been found in the serum of those suffering from depression. [21] The more depressed a person is, the lower their zinc level will be.[22]

Form: Capsule

Time taken: Separately from meals or supplements containing iron, calcium, and phytates, which can decrease absorption of zinc.

Recommended brand: Bulletproof Zinc with Copper formulation

Final Thoughts on Fuel

It's vital that you do not choose the cheapest supplements; some may be dangerous due to inadequate oversight. Many over-the-counter supplements are of inferior quality. Become informed and read reviews. You get what you pay for when it comes to supplements. While the cost of supplementation may raise your eyebrows, I have found that when I am able to perform at my best, my ability to increase my income grows exponentially. You make better decisions with greater clarity in fast succession, allowing you to achieve more in less time. If you are deficient in any of these areas, life becomes harder than it needs to be. Negative emotions are amplified, and the need for willpower to counteract this deficit will deplete your battery further and land you right back into Defender mode.

In our efforts to oversimplify the complicated problem of falling short of success and condense it to "It's all in your head, just get over it," we've become unable to treat the underlying causes. Yes, we can think ourselves out of some problems, as you'll discover in the upcoming chapters. But you cannot will yourself out of nutritional deficiencies and toxins, which present real physical symptoms that hinder creative thinking and effective problem solving. Uncovering the root cause means we end the tug of war between who we are and who we need to become. You suddenly stop having to force yourself to do something because you don't have the energy, and shift into your true state of being. That tug of war is not just our old identity holding us back from becoming our new, evolved selves; it's our old biochemistry keeping us trapped in the past because there isn't enough energy available to make the changes you need to enjoy a successful future. You can't outperform bad biochemistry for long. Eventually, it catches up with a vengeance. But when we switch fuel sources to clean, sustainable energy, we can meet the demands our grand visions and future selves place on us. And now we also have the option of various nootropics, which can help sharpen our mental state when those demands intensify. They could mean the difference between having enough fuel for the journey or falling just short of your goal.

CHAPTER 6

Enter the World of Nootropics
Improve Focus, Concentration, and Drive

Flash back to 2017, Dubbo, New South Wales, Australia. I had just come back from seeing my naturopath, Hetal, who holds an Advanced Diploma of Nutritional Medicine, among many other qualifications, but I needed more help. That day, I had already fallen asleep twice and was ready for nap number three. This was during the period when I was at my lowest point and on the verge of a total breakdown. I had yet to pinpoint all my nutritional deficiencies and needed help just to get through the day. I was desperate and willing to try anything.

Hetal sent me home with three supplements: L-Theanine, L-Tyrosine, and L-Carnitine. At the time, I had no idea they were considered nootropics. I just needed something that would boost me out of Defender mode and help me become a Catalyst, if only for a couple of hours a day, so I could keep running my business and my remote team. I had to film eight videos for Entrepreneur.com that week, and at that moment, I couldn't think of anything that sounded worse than stepping out in front of a camera with a smile on my face.

I didn't notice any changes the first few days I took the nootropics, but then suddenly I started feeling better. It wasn't a complete solution, but it definitely set me on the right path. I distinctly remember the fog beginning to clear and my overall attitude improving. It helped me get through shooting the videos and tackling my next challenge: relocating to the United States in a few weeks' time to reboot my life.

In our January 2018 survey of 999 entrepreneurs around the world, 90 percent of individuals who said they didn't have the stamina to achieve their goals were experiencing brain fog—36 percent higher than those who said they had the stamina to achieve their goals.

These same individuals were being blamed and blaming themselves for not having the wherewithal to push through and reach their goals. They felt worthless and lacked the confidence required to become successful. This was being compounded by the ever-growing chorus of self-help gurus shouting, "Just hustle!"

Nootropics: Feel More Alert, Concentrate with Ease, and Supercharge Your Energy

After countless interactions with doctors, I too was blaming myself for insufficient mental stamina, not realizing I was experiencing real, physical symptoms with causes that could easily be addressed with the right help.

After my introduction to nootropics, thanks to Hetal, I began experimenting further with various combinations of supplements. I didn't fully understand what I was doing. All I knew was that the supplements were helping. My memory was improving, I felt healthier, and I could concentrate better than before.

There are two distinct types of nootropics: pharmaceuticals, such as Modafinil, and nutritional substances derived from plants; both kinds are used to enhance cognitive function. I would have been skeptical had I not benefited from them in my exhausted state without fully understanding what they were designed to do. I chose to stick to nutritional nootropics, with one exception, nicotine (which you read about in the previous chapter). I wanted to avoid any unwanted side effects, such as feeling wired, unable to sleep, and anxious due to overstimulation.

Diving deeper into my research, I came across a guy by the name of Mansal Denton, founder of Nootropedia (www.nootropedia.com), a site dedicated to providing comprehensive information on countless nootropics. Mansal delved into the world of nootropics shortly after he ended up in a Texas state penitentiary for six months. Over an 18-month period, he stole thousands of dollars' worth of historical documents from a Holocaust museum and sold them to fund a trip abroad to see a woman he was in love with. The prison, filled with violent inmates covered in full-body tattoos, was foreign to him as a nerdy, upper-middle-class kid. His time there led him to reflect on his life and what it meant to become a successful entrepreneur. After being released from prison, he decided to do anything he could to become a better person, including diet, spiritual practices, and, of course, nootropics. I reached out to Mansal on my 13-week mission and asked, "What is the most profound lesson you've learned by testing various nootropics?"

He said, "The body always desires homeostatic equilibrium [balance], and if you take the same nootropics daily, your body will adapt, and you'll experience less of a benefit [in most cases]."

That was precisely what I had experienced. Three months after I started taking the L-Tyrosine and L-Carnitine, my fatigue began creeping back. My body had become used to them, and I was requiring a higher dose to feel better. That's when I realized that, unlike supplements that can be taken daily, nootropics must be cycled if you want to continue to benefit from them. Mansal continued, "Honestly, consider where else in your life you can make changes before jumping to pills and supplements. People need to have their foundations right, including a full night of sleep, healthy diet, and exercise, plus plenty of social interaction and relationships, before they jump in."

I had done it backward due to insufficient insight from medical professionals, who had failed to identify my nutritional deficiencies. I decided I would only continue my experiments with supplements once I had corrected my deficiencies. Once my energy began stabilizing, I set specific criteria for trialing them, including intended outcomes, like heightening focus, improving memory, gaining clarity, improving sleep, and enhancing mood. They also had to have zero to minimal side effects. This led me eventually to the following nootropics, which I currently cycle through on a weekly basis. They were incredibly useful in the process of getting this book written in a three-month window, which required an intense effort, given all the medical research I had to read and the countless interviews I conducted with doctors, biohackers, neuroscientists, and others.

Six Nootropics for Optimizing Your Mental Performance

To help make your life easier, I have not only tested the following nootropics firsthand, but I have also broken them down in an easy-to-understand way, without the hyperbole. As with everything when it comes to your health, speak to a health professional to determine what is right for you before beginning a new regimen.

Caffeine: High-Performance Brain Fuel

Caffeine is highly effective as a high-performance brain fuel that will almost immediately make you more alert. It is one of the world's most commonly used psychoactive drugs, affecting the central nervous system's control of things like brain function, mood, and behavior. Found in coffee and green, black, and white teas, just to name a few, caffeine's benefits have been long known. One exception is if you are sensitive to caffeine or coffee. Individuals can react differently to this powerful nootropic, and it's critical that you understand your personal tolerance level. That third or fourth cup of joe may be fine for one person, but for someone else, it could lead to caffeine-induced anxiety and inability to focus. Moderate caffeine intake is associated with a longer lifespan. It also works to increase serotonin, a key mood influencer, and it's powerful enough to measurably affect depression.[1]

Side effects: Depending on your tolerance, caffeine may cause insomnia, nervousness, restlessness, increased heart rate/ respiration, stomach irritation, or nausea.[2] And, like all nootropics, you can become desensitized to its benefits. Taking a break or reducing your intake can help reset your tolerance level.

Sources:

1. *Yerba Mate*: A favorite of famous biohacker Tim Ferriss, as discussed with Dave Asprey on episode 127 of his podcast *Bulletproof Radio*, Yerba Mate is a tea brewed from the leaves of the South American holly tree (*Ilex paraguariensis*). It is best to sip it throughout the day, as it contains less caffeine than coffee, but more than green tea. This is my go-to when writing for long periods of time. Taper off before 3 P.M. to ensure a restful night's sleep. WARNING: Do not consume while taking blood pressure medication. Yerba Mate also contains theobromine, an ingredient found in chocolate that contributes to feelings of euphoria.[3] Yerba mate is full of polyphenols and flavonoids, antioxidants that can strengthen our immune system, and has anti-inflammatory properties as well.[4]

2. *Black Tea*: Black tea is a powerful nootropic in its own right; not only does it contain caffeine, it also contains L-Theanine. Studies have shown that L-Theanine amplifies the positive effects of caffeine while mitigating the negative ones. We'll learn more about the properties of L-Theanine shortly.[5] It was previously believed that green tea had more L-Theanine than black tea. This has since been disproven.

3. *Coffee*: A favorite of billions worldwide, coffee has cognitive-enhancing abilities that can help dial in focus. Many people think of caffeine and coffee as the same thing; however, coffee can be stripped of its caffeine, and caffeine is present in many

other foods. In 2011, researchers reported coffee drinking is "associated with a lower risk of depression among women and a lower risk of lethal prostate cancer among men."[6] However, choose your coffee carefully. Dave Asprey argues that that some coffee may contain fungal toxins known as mycotoxins, which are documented to cause substantial suffering by disease and death in humans and animals.[7] In fact, a sensitivity to coffee (unless specifically tested) may actually be a sensitivity to mold, which may explain why some respond differently to it. One 1995 study published in *Food and Chemical Toxicology* found 52 percent of samples were contaminated with mycotoxins.[8] Check to see if there is any certification of cleanliness when you choose your beans.

Ketone Ester: A New Fuel Source for the Brain

As we have already seen, ketones are a powerful fuel source for the brain that can dramatically improve cognition and focus. As it stands, HVMN's Ketone is a superfuel that can be used to improve training, recovery, and performance. It doesn't come cheap, however. This is for when you need a serious edge, such as a competition, public speaking, or a tough deadline. For $99 (as of March 2018), you will get three pocket-sized bottles of HVMN Ketone, each containing a 25-gram serving. As Geoffrey explained, "We're working as hard as we can to get it down to a little more expensive than the cost of sugar. To give you context, it used to cost $25,000 a drink. Then, when it was being produced out of the Oxford chemistry basement, it was around $100 to $150 a drink. So getting down to $30 a drink is cool and exciting for us, and hopefully we'll get it down even cheaper and more quickly."

HVMN Ketone is classified as food by the FDA and holds GRAS status (generally recognized as safe). It has been validated through numerous safety and kinetic studies on both animal and human subjects.

Side effects: Gastrointestinal side effects have been reported as being very rare.[9]

Sources: A ketogenic state can only be entered into by consuming exogenous ketones, such as HVMN's, or following a ketogenic dietary protocol.

L-Tyrosine: Decreases Stress, Promotes Healthy Mood, Boosts Cognition

L-Tyrosine is a nonessential amino acid that is important for many cognitive functions. L-Tyrosine benefits are largely linked with preserving mental capacity while experiencing physical hardship. It's also known to increase dopamine, one of the key brain chemicals associated with happiness.

One study found that L-Tyrosine assisted memory in high stress environments. To find out how, researchers placed test subjects into cold settings and assessed their mental capabilities.[10]

It has also been shown to assist children with ADHD when paired with other nootropic compounds to help them maintain better attention.[11]

Side effects: Likely safe.[12]

Sources:

1. L-Tyrosine is found in chicken, turkey, fish, peanuts, almonds, avocados, bananas, milk, cheese, yogurt, cottage cheese, lima beans, pumpkin seeds, and sesame seeds.
2. It is also commonly found in various nootropic stacks, which we will explore shortly.
3. Can be purchased in tablet form from your local vitamin store.

L-Theanine: Reduces Anxiety, Promotes Relaxation Without Sedation, and Enhances Attention

This well-researched nootropic is unknowingly ingested by millions of people on a daily basis via black and green tea. As an amino acid, it has been used to improve brain health, anxiety, and attention for thousands of years. One of the top benefits, whether supplementing with tablets or consuming it via tea, is anxiety reduction. One study found L-Theanine can improve anxiety symptoms in schizophrenia patients.[13] Research has also discovered that while it is not as powerful as prescription drugs like Xanax, L-Theanine can promote relaxation and calmness under resting conditions.[14]

One study found L-Theanine improved relaxation via alpha brain waves within 30 minutes of consuming the supplement. Another study, this one on children with ADHD, showed sleep quality was far higher when taking this supplement.[15] L-Theanine makes its way into many nootropic stacks for day/night use because despite its relaxation-promoting properties, it also improves attention and focus without sedation. When combined with caffeine, it has been shown to improve performance on cognitively demanding tasks.[16] Many first-time users are disappointed when using this supplement because unlike other nootropics, it does not stimulate the nervous system, resulting in a quiet, calm focus. Often you don't notice the benefits until many hours later, as you realize precisely how focused you have been.

Side effects: Likely safe.[17]

Sources:

1. Consume it via black or green tea.
2. Supplement with tablets in combination with coffee or other sources of caffeine. Many find that when they use L-Theamine with coffee, the anxiety they might have felt previously disappears. This is one of the most profound naturally occurring nootropics we have access to.

L-Carnitine (ALCAR): Supports Mitochondrial Anti-Aging, Increases Focus and Attention, and Reduces Mental/Physical Fatigue

A supplement that comes highly recommended via my naturopath, Hetal, and one that I have used intermittently, is L-Carnitine, otherwise known as ALCAR. ALCAR is naturally produced in the body, but additional supplementation can help mitochondrial anti-aging as well as increase focus and attention while reducing mental and physical fatigue. In one 2004 study, 59 percent of patients with chronic fatigue syndrome who used ALCAR supplementation showed significant improvement in fatigue and concentration.[18] ALCAR is well-researched, well-tolerated, and a good option for nootropic newbies. And, just like combining coffee with L-Theanine, ALCAR combined with coffee has been shown to improve physical endurance better than either of the two alone.[19] ALCAR is a great addition to your nootropic regimen.

Side effects: Likely safe.[20]

Sources:
1. Accessible in tablet form.
2. Can be found in smaller doses in red meat, milk, pork, sea-food, and chicken, to name a few.

Nicotine: Create a Mental State of Flow and Creativity

The smart drug nicotine isn't without controversy. While nicotine is addictive, many scientists also question whether it can be safe in small, daily doses.[21] As we learned earlier, nicotine helps you pay attention to mentally tiring tasks longer, improves word recall, sharpens short-term memory, and heightens your ability to pay attention. However, the downsides must still be considered. One study showed nicotine by itself promotes cancer in rats and mice.[22] However, dosage must also be taken into consideration when looking at this research. The average cigarette has anywhere from 15 to 30 mg of nicotine in it; a nicotine spray that goes under the tongue contains only 1 mg. Reaching out to Dr. Jaya Vikraman in Melbourne, Australia, I told her I had been using 1 mg of nicotine three to five days per week to improve my cognition after four years of severe fatigue, exhaustion, and memory loss. I asked, "Does that sound weird?"

She replied, "Not at all. It works. It's been proven to improve concentration and memory. I used it for medical exams to help with focus and recall."

Side effects: As with the other nootropics, you may become desensitized to it after time and need more to experience the same effect, requiring a break from use. Hence, nicotine is only to be used now and then when you need your focus dialed in, e.g., presentations, exams, or study. Or, in my case, as a treatment plan to improve severe cognitive decline. Now I only use it prior to filming videos, memorizing scripts, presenting, or for lengthy periods of writing.

Sources: According to Dave Asprey, the best form is via the nicotine spray readily available at drugstores or online.

How to Get Into the "Zone" with Nootropic Stacks for Greater Mental Clarity, Focus, and Creativity

If you're averse to experimenting with various nootropics and would like to make your life easier, you may want to consider nootropic stacks. A stack refers to combining two or more supplements that can work together to positively affect concentration, learning, focus, and motivation. While you can create a stack yourself by experimenting with various supplements, there are many companies bringing out their own combinations.

This takes out the guesswork, trial, and error of personal experimentation. It is critical to determine which one is right for you. Often, the only way to figure this out is to try them out and then stop taking them, which allows you to assess their benefits and impact. And although these off-the-shelf combinations make it easy, you still need to experiment with the dosage to ensure you don't overstimulate yourself. Research the nootropics/vitamins in the stack you're unfamiliar with to see if there has been any negative news coverage highlighting gaps in the research.

For my 90-day mission, I spent countless hours researching various stacks and decided to hone my efforts to just a few, mostly ones not pharmaceutically derived, with the exception of combining nicotine with caffeine, as I talked about earlier.

They had to meet certain criteria. First and foremost, user feedback had to be positive; I wasn't going to try any supplements with negative reviews. Second, the ingredients had to be well-researched and widely known to have measurable benefits. And finally, they couldn't have any adverse side effects like negatively disrupting sleep or triggering anxiety due to overstimulation. I avoided supplements that had an overly generous dose of caffeine, unless they combined L-Theanine to negate those effects. Furthermore, I had to notice a quantifiable difference, either via an enhanced ability to focus for lengthy periods of time or by an alertness and an ability to easily enter "the zone." Being in the zone is one of the most effective states you can be in; unfortunately, it's often elusive due to social media addiction and distractions from co-workers or family members. When you enter the zone you not only achieve Catalyst status, but you also lose all sense of time and become completely immersed in your work, ignoring any distractions around you. Procrastination disappears and creativity kicks in. This mental state is highly valuable: It leads to enhanced productivity and a narrowing of focus to just the task at hand, which can help you achieve more in less time. I wanted to use the stacks to direct my focus and reduce the risk of using my limited mental resources on unfruitful tasks, like scrolling through social media. I decided to put them to the biggest test of all: completing an 80,000-word draft of this book, a task

IMPORTANT NOTICE ON NOOTROPICS AND MEDICATION

As with antidepressants, which may make people feel great for a while but fail to address possible underlying causes (e.g., nutritional deficiency, inflammation, toxicity, overgrowth of bad gut bacteria, hormones, or food sensitivities, to name just a few), nootropics can also mask symptoms. This does not, however, mean the underlying causes of whatever ails you have been addressed. The day I drank the ketone ester, I felt incredible. I wasn't physically or mentally showing any signs of vitamin D deficiency, and yet I was still severely depleted.

Nootropics and medication can make you feel great for a while, but your symptoms may later emerge in a different manner. If you're experiencing any symptoms, it's vital that you seek assistance from a functional doctor to find out the underlying cause. And, as in my case, it may be more than one factor that needs to be addressed before you can become unstoppable—and an upgraded individual who can reach your goals.

that included speaking to countless experts, reading dozens of books, looking over hundreds of research papers, and traveling between Saint Petersburg, Los Angeles, San Francisco, Victoria, and Vancouver. You know—only a small challenge!

Are nootropics the only way to get into the zone? Not at all! But in addition to helping me get there, many are packed with other beneficial vitamins and minerals that help with well-being and cognition.

Nootropic Stacks for Easy Consumption and Additional Firepower and Focus

This list, as with the vitamin and nootropic supplements earlier in the chapter, is by no means exhaustive. These are the stacks that I experienced measurable benefits from and continue to use to this day. There were other supplements I tested that had little impact. I have omitted them because my personal experience may not be reflective of the response you may experience when using them. Just as in personalizing your diet to improve your energy, increase your brain function, and power your battery, you must also determine the nootropics and nootropic stacks that work best for you.

Now let's dive into the world of nootropic stacks.

Qualia by Neurohacker Collective: Enhance Focus, Energy, Mood, and Creativity

I was skeptical about taking Qualia because, at first glance, it was as if they had thrown everything in there but the kitchen sink. It contains 40 nutrients, all aimed at enhancing focus, energy, mood, and creativity. But looking over its countless reviews, I could see it had developed a cult-like following of fans espousing its greatness.

I reached out to Neurohacker and secured an interview with Daniel Schmachtenberger, a senior member of the Qualia team, evolutionary philosopher, systems designer, and strategist. Daniel, a scruffy-looking fellow with untamed dark hair, graying beard, and intellect that could match those of the world's top scientists, dove into the philosophy behind the product. I'm glad I had taken Qualia before the interview, so I could keep up with him. Daniel expressed concern at reductionist approaches to nootropics. He explained there are too many findings and mechanisms, but no meta-analysis of the complex interactions that make up the whole. Meta-analysis is a statistical analysis that combines the results of multiple scientific studies. Neurohacker Collective had to bring together all the scientific research in their approach to developing Qualia to prevent any serious side effects, due to the impact each of the 40 ingredients has on one another. The ingredients had to work synergistically together to achieve the intended outcome. When I asked Daniel how to assist someone who was struggling to find the cognition and motivation to solve issues that were impacting their mental performance, he said:

> One of the reasons that we got into the field of nootropics was when people were working on complex illnesses, there's [so much they have to do], but even having the motivation and cognitive clarity to do [it], it's actually harder because they have this negative feedback loop. If they can enhance their capacity to perform, then they can actually do the things necessary for deeper underlying well-being. That's on the negative side. On the positive side are people who are already doing everything they need to for their well-being, so we can enhance what the top of their baseline could be.

I loved his blunt way of interacting, which was refreshing in a field of companies desperately trying to please the media. The first day Qualia arrived, I took the recommended dose, and I was pleasantly surprised. They say it can take five days before you see the full results, but I noticed it kicking in within a couple of hours. In fact, I wrote the first two chapters of the book while using it. One benefit, although I can't prove it, was being able to recall thoughts and words more quickly, which is especially useful when writing, as well as an intense focus that kept me dialed into one task at a time. I have experienced issues with word recall for the past four years, which was the main reason I gave up my speaking career.

You take Qualia in two daily doses. Step one is taken first thing in the morning, 30 minutes before eating. Step two is taken with breakfast or lunch. I found I had calmer energy if I only took step two. Step one has as much caffeine in it as one cup of coffee. While step one also contained L-Theanine, I found it still overstimulated me, especially since I had removed most caffeine from my diet some time ago. Others may not notice it at all. Step two, however, I used daily, Monday through Friday, for several weeks to great effect. However, we all respond to nootropics and supplements differently. Reducing the dosage if necessary will help you find your sweet spot.

The ingredients read like a health food store shopping list: vitamins B5, B6, B12, D3, C, zinc, magnesium, and ginkgo biloba (increases concentration, helps fight anxiety and depression, eases symptoms of PMS)[23] are a few of the more recognizable ones. You'll also find Acetyl L-Carnitine, L-Tyrosine, L-Theanine, green tea leaf extract, quercetin (reduces inflammation, fights allergies, supports heart health, protects skin), and many more.[24] Two ingredients that jump out are Cognizin® citicoline and lion's mane. Citicoline is a naturally occurring brain chemical used to treat Alzheimer's disease, dementia, head trauma, memory loss, Parkinson's disease, ADHD, and problems related to circulation in the brain.[25] And lion's mane is an edible mushroom widely used in Chinese medicine; it is gaining popularity in the United States thanks to companies such as Four Sigmatic. They supply more than 65 countries and 1 million consumers with functional mushrooms that can be consumed via lattes, coffees, and teas. Lion's mane's benefits include anti-diabetic, anti-fatigue, anti-hypertensive, and anti-aging properties; it's neuroprotective and improves anxiety, cognitive function, and depression.[26]

Before you decide to try Qualia, I recommend checking out all the information on its website (www.neurohacker.com).

Qualia Mind by Neurohacker

In our interview, Daniel from Neurohacker Collective mentioned their new nootropic stack that, at the time of this writing, had yet to be released. They sent me an unlabeled bottle with handwritten instructions. Unlike their original Qualia stack, with its two steps, which some may find complicated to take, Qualia Mind was much simpler, with just one step. They even trimmed the number of ingredients down from 42 to

28, bringing down the cost. This blend of 28 compounds includes neuro-vitamins, antioxidants, amino acids, and adaptogen extracts that help to increase focus, boost energy, and decrease procrastination. The first few days of taking it, I didn't notice a change. It wasn't until the end of the week when I went over my progress report on the book that I realized I had broken a record for how much writing and research I had completed. I preferred Qualia Mind to the original Qualia because it didn't give me a stimulated feeling; I just naturally felt sharper without realizing it. As I was in the midst of doing intense research and reading over countless research papers that week, I have no doubt it assisted me in deciphering information and determining what was relevant. I also found it was easier on my stomach. I had observed that Qualia initially caused mild stomach upset, which I didn't experience with Qualia Mind at all.

Rise by HVMN

After I drank the ketone ester with Geoffrey Woo at HVMN's headquarters in San Francisco, he laid out the rest of their nootropic range on the table for me to try, including Kado-3, Rise, and Sprint. I experienced noticeable benefits from Rise in particular. Sprint I only use occasionally when I need an extra kick. Unlike Qualia, Rise has only three ingredients, and the benefits come from long-term use, according to its website (https://hvmn.com/rise). It includes:

1. *Bacopa Monnieri*: Used for thousands of years in Indian herbal medicine, Bacopa has demonstrated that consistent long-term use can enhance memory,[27] as well as decrease anxiety.[28]

2. *Alpha-GPC*: Essential for learning and memory, alpha-GPC is a precursor to the neurotransmitter acetylcholine. It has been shown to improve cognitive decline in individuals suffering from neurodegenerative disease[29] and is capable of improving cognition in healthy subjects.[30]

3. *Rhodiola Rosea*: Rhodiola, a popular supplement among the bio-hacking community for its nootropic qualities has been shown to reduce severity of cognitive decline brought about by fatigue and stress,[31] as well as provide relief from anxiety.[32]

As you will have noticed by now, nearly all the ingredients in these nootropics and nootropic stacks focus on cognitive performance. Some effects can be felt immediately; however, don't dismiss the ones that take a while to build up in the system for long-term support. For this reason, Rise has made it into my daily routine.

Keto//OS® MAX by Prüvit™

I came upon Prüvit unexpectedly. Contemporary Australian illusionist and winner of five "Magician of the Year" awards Sam Powers, who has performed in 19 countries across the globe, reached out to me after learning of the experiments I was conducting. Sam, who has even been praised by Spice Girls superstar Geri Halliwell when performing on Australia's Got Talent, is a fan of not only the ketogenic diet but also Prüvit supplements, which aim to increase ketones. Performing 400 physically and mentally demanding shows per year that are both physically and mentally demanding, Sam requires additional help where he can get it. He came across ketones and ketosis when he only had two months to prepare for one of the world's deadliest escape stunts. At the time, he was 33 pounds (15 kilograms) overweight, depressed, and taking solace in alcohol. Sam said, "Every bit of research I did to transform myself into a superhuman performance machine pointed straight to ketones and ketosis."

I asked Sam if he followed a strict keto diet or if he supplements with Prüvit or a mix of both. He said, "I initially tried; however, it was extremely difficult to cut out sugar and carbs. That's when I discovered pure exogenous ketones that instantly elevated my ketone levels and transition into ketosis without the strict dietary regime. Now I use exogenous ketones daily to balance everything out."

I asked what the most dangerous stunt he has ever done was, and was he in ketosis while doing it? He replied, "The Jaws of Death is undoubtedly the most dangerous stunt I've ever attempted, where I'm suspended 150 feet in the air in a straitjacket under a flaming set of steel jaws, ready to be devoured once a thin rope burns through and the jaws come crashing shut. The most difficult aspect is the mental game, because there's no safety net or crash mattress. Being at a physical peak was important; however, having heightened mental alertness was critical, which meant being in a ketogenic state. Everything goes into 'high def' within 30 minutes of drinking ketones; it was easy to identify that superhuman state of perfect mental clarity." Sam automatically knew how much his physical energy impacted his cognition and alertness. But how did Sam prepare mentally for this dangerous stunt? You'll find that out in Chapter 8.

Sam continued, "Ketones put me in control of food instead of food controlling me. I no longer needed to find solace with alcohol, and the radical improvement in my physical condition was motivating and confidence building." As we have learned, when we control our cravings, we regain our self-control function in our brain that can impact everything we do in our daily life, especially when it's switched off due to cravings.

Sam arranged for me to sit down with Joe Rogister, an advocate of Prüvit from Australia. Joe had traveled to Prüvit's annual conference in Florida and gave me a few samples of Keto//OS MAX to try. Two of the key ingredients that stood out to me were beta-hydroxybutyrate (BHB) and L-Taurine:

1. *Beta-Hydroxybutyrate*: BHB is an exogenous ketone found in various supplements targeted at individuals who are on the ketogenic diet or want to get into ketosis, like Sam, without always having to follow the strict dietary regimen. Recognized as safe by the FDA, BHB is a metabolite produced during metabolism and fat digestion. BHB, a ketone body, is derived from fat while the energy from glucose is derived from sugars and carbohydrates.

   This is where fat stores are broken down into energy and the body/brain begins burning that instead of the energy from sugars/carbohydrates. Exogenous ketones can be taken even if you aren't following a strict keto diet; however, if you are consuming sugars/carbs on top of exogenous ketones, the body may begin to store the sugars/carbs as fat, as they are not being burned. A ketogenic or low-carb diet is preferred, especially if your objective is weight loss. If it isn't, you will get the mental alertness regardless.

So, what is the difference between taking MCT oil/Brain Octane Oil, as we discussed earlier in the chapter, and exogenous ketones? When you take exogenous ketones like BHB as a salt or a ketone ester, the body can use them for energy right away. MCT oil/Brain Octane Oil must be broken down before it can be used for energy. It also doesn't spike the ketone levels as high as BHB. MCT oil bypasses fat metabolism and goes straight to your liver, where it is converted to BHB. There are benefits to both, especially since MCT oil comes with other elements that can help with overall health, as previously discussed. Studies have shown MCT oils can offer neuroprotective benefits for a variety of neurological diseases, including dementia, Parkinson's, stroke, and traumatic brain injury.[33]

2. L-Taurine: L-Taurine is a sulfur-containing amino acid with an endless list of reported benefits, including anti-inflammatory, antimicrobial, and cardiovascular. It also has anti-anxiety properties and has been suggested for the clinical treatment of anxiety as well as assisting with alcohol withdrawal.[34]

As I wasn't in a state of ketosis when I started testing Keto//OS MAX, although I was on the low-carb diet I typically follow, it took three days before I felt the full effects. Come Saturday morning (the fact that I can remember what day I noticed the difference is telling), I felt completely alert and ready to run a mile. My mental and physical energy had increased significantly.

Honorable Mentions

These are the top four stacks that have made it into my regular routine, although I do still cycle them in and out. There are two more supplements worthy of honorable mention that I use routinely to this day:

▶ *Bulletproof KetoPrime*: designed to power the cells in your brain and body for maximum performance. It contains vitamins C, B12, and oxaloacetate. That last can help remove glutamate excess, which can cause brain fog and an inability to focus.[35] I use this when extra energy is required.

▶ *HVMN's Kado-3*: Kado's ingredients include vitamins D3, K1, K3, and omega-3. It also contains astaxanthin oil (known for its antioxidant properties). These ingredients are known to help in stress reduction and improve mood.[36] This one can be used daily.

Nootropics have become a daily part of my life to ensure I am on point when I need to be. Addressing nutritional deficiencies and normalizing my health was the first crucial step; upgrading my mind was the second.

My Experience

After four years of memory loss and inability to focus due to constant fatigue, I had to jump-start my brain. In trialing the various nootropics, I was able to increase my energy further, reignite my cognitive function, feel calmer, sleep better, reduce stress, and finally feel like myself again after years of feeling worthless.

My behavior in social situations also changed. I felt more confident because I could find words and recall stories that added to the interaction, instead of withdrawing because I didn't have the mental energy available to socialize. I was also able to start meditating again. I had been too fatigued to even consider it.

Filling gaps in my nutrition recharged my battery; adding nootropics to the mix turned me into a Catalyst. I was able to make creative links that I had been unable to connect for many years, boosting my creativity and helping me solve problems faster. I don't say this lightly: I credit nootropics as a major factor in not only writing this book but also reclaiming my mind. The difference I have experienced is life-changing.

To prevent myself from the placebo effect, as much as one possibly can when self-experimenting, I emotionally detached myself from any expected outcome. I simply observed my experience as if I was watching someone else. Some nootropics simply had no effect on me, even though other individuals rated them highly. With others, I didn't notice the difference until a few days in. In fact, I thought many of them had failed initially and was ready to consider them a waste of money.

But I chose to continue the tests for the recommended duration and document the results. Sometimes I was pleasantly surprised when the effects kicked in several days down the road.

When upgrading our minds to improve focus, increase drive, reduce procrastination, boost memory, and yes, even boost confidence, we can unlock our potential in ways that may have been shut off from us for quite some time. For some, it's a reboot; for others, it's a process of continual improvement to ignite new connections that help solve real world problems. Fueling yourself for success is the basis of closing your identity gap and any gaps between the energy you have and the energy you need to reach your goals.

Now it's time to turn from biochemical energy to psychological energy, by training our brains with the latest in wearable devices designed to reduce stress, increase focus, improve physical performance, and obliterate fears and phobias, so you can become unstoppable.

Let's dive in . . .

PART III

OBLITERATING FEAR AND FINDING YOUR PURPOSE

CHAPTER 7

The Switch

Obliterate Fear and Overcome Failure by Leveraging the Latest Wearable Technology

"Hurricane Irma is heading straight for us!" I stood in shock as I watched the latest news report come in, advising that Tampa and St. Petersburg were now in the direct path of one of the most powerful Atlantic hurricanes in history. We had been living in suspense for a week as we watched the supermarket shelves empty of water and the state of Florida go into a panic. More than 6 million Floridians had been ordered to evacuate, including low-level areas a walking distance from where we lived.[1] It was as if everyone in the bottom half of the state had evacuated to the top half, thinking they'd be safe, only to find out they were now in the line of fire with the rest of us, and emergency supplies were growing scarce.

Having experienced Hurricane Sandy firsthand in New York in October 2012, I wasn't taking any chances. I was having flashbacks to the flooded New York City subway, cabs precariously dropping off passengers in the days that followed, as half of Manhattan sat in darkness from power outages. These thoughts only added to my ever-increasing anxiety. Sandy moved in swiftly and caused devastating damage New York is still recovering from.

Irma, however, took its time. We bounced back and forth between "We're going to be fine" to "Oh, shit! We should leave NOW!" The slow buildup was emotionally draining.

Going through two hurricanes was such a bizarre experience for an Australian, who never grew up knowing this type of threat. I used to believe Americans overreact to everything. Not this time! Now I understood.

We watched for an agonizing week as Irma grew into a powerful and deadly Category 5 hurricane and inflicted damage across the Caribbean. Some of our neighbors evacuated, despite our living in a safe zone and (supposedly) in a hurricane-proof building.

Despite all our precautions, I was struggling to remain calm. I paced around my kitchen as I looked at the map showing Irma was going to plow straight through our town. *We need to leave*, I thought, but it was too late. I quickly called some friends back home in Australia to break the cycle of repetitive thoughts running through my head.

On September 11, Irma shifted course. It was still unknown how bad it was going to be, but the new update showed that we were back on the "safe" side of the hurricane, if there is such a thing! It was still going to carve a path not far from us, and we'd still be in the eye of the storm, if the weather report held true. But no matter the outcome of the storm, fear was the result inside my body.

Real Danger vs. Perceived Fear: What's Ruling Your Life?

There is a genuine difference between perceived fear and real danger. Unfortunately, our behavior is shaped by perceived fear more than we care to admit or realize. Real danger rarely occurs, and yet perceived threats can flip a switch and turn on the fight or flight part of your brain. This is otherwise known as the sympathetic nervous system taking over from the logical and rational part of your mind, the parasympathetic nervous system. The logical/rational mind slows our heart rate and lowers our blood pressure after our fight or flight response has been engaged. This system is the best state of mind to be in when working on your goals. Here, you can make rational decisions and assess future consequences in a state of calm, rather than a state of fear that may cause you to make rash decisions you later regret. The more time we spend in this state, the easier life becomes, the faster we find focus, and the less we procrastinate. We can talk through problems without getting overly emotional about them.

Stress caused by perceived threats can take us from being a Catalyst or Synergist (logical/rational mind) into a Guardian or Defender (fight/flight/survival mode) within seconds, regardless of how well-fueled your body and brain are. Anxiety and stress can override even the healthiest individual's psychology and send them into a state of panic. When this occurs, we go from conscious creation to unconscious behavior within seconds that can either save our life or sabotage our success. If the threat is merely perceived and repeatedly triggered by a particular stimulus (financial, work, relationship, business pressures, or exercise), it can eventually play havoc on your emotional state and your adrenal glands. Each time fight/flight is engaged, we receive a rush of adrenaline that can make us sick, our digestion shuts down, and our focus narrows to the threat at hand. If it gets stuck in this "on" position, it can result in chronic stress, severe exhaustion, and even adrenal fatigue.

Today, we're under constant stress, and our sympathetic nervous system is stuck in on more than it should be. It is unnecessarily firing off multiple times per day, giving our bodies little downtime to recover from the physiological and psychological effects.

The annual stress survey commissioned by the American Psychological Association found that 77 percent of Americans routinely experience physical symptoms triggered by stress, while 48 percent said it had a negative impact on their professional and personal lives.[2] If we allow certain stimuli to trigger our fight/flight and stress response repeatedly, we end up forming strong neurological pathways to that response. This creates a negative feedback loop that becomes harder to break because it becomes habitual over time, even if the stimulus is removed in some cases.

Imagine driving a different way to work. You take a road you have never been down before and need a GPS to navigate. Due to the unknown factors, you need more mental resources to find your way. Hence, more often than not, you default to the tried and true route because it requires less mental processing and energy. The old route, built through the fight/flight response, even though it is detrimental to our success, is the easier option for our brain, especially when resources are low and decision fatigue has kicked in. It's the pizza for dinner when you can't figure out what to eat. You know it's bad for you, but damn, it's easy and tastes so good. The only problem is you often regret it later.

Some people, even after years of therapy, understand their fears aren't real, but still react negatively. Their old neurological pathways haven't developed a new response system. Some therapy may even further solidify the fear response they're desperately trying to avoid. The act of simply discussing it can trigger the fight/flight response. The therapist MUST break these neurological pathways and form new beneficial ones. This can be achieved via neuro-linguistic programming (NLP) or a combination of strategies that we will uncover in the coming pages.

Habits and Highways: How We Form New Behaviors and Break Old Patterns (The Real Secret to Your Success)

To form new habits, we must lay the foundation for new neurological highways to be built, ensuring they are well-established and well-maintained. These new highways help you close the gap from who you are to who you need to become to reach your goals. The more you frequent these new paths, the easier they are to travel, until they unconsciously lead you to success. Once they are embedded in your memory and experiences, your need for willpower to force change diminishes. Change becomes easy. Attempting to use willpower to force yourself to change can result in negative neural pathways being built, to the point your brain views your goals as a threat because it requires too much energy to process the unknown factors surrounding it. This could trigger your fight/flight response because the goal is located outside your comfort zone, and you end up "snapping back" into your old self.

Our conscious mind rationalizes the difficulty and frames the goal as "too hard," while your subconscious mind is screaming, "It's going to kill you! Danger, danger, Will Robinson!" Hence, we come up with an excuse that has nothing to do with the real underlying cause.

As you can see in Figure 7.1, the response "most traveled" will eventually become the default response, regardless of whether it

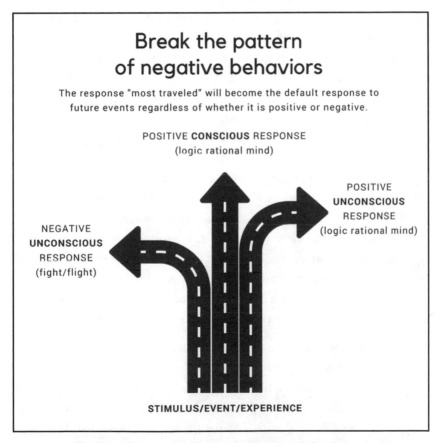

Break the pattern of negative behaviors

The response "most traveled" will become the default response to future events regardless of whether it is positive or negative.

POSITIVE **CONSCIOUS** RESPONSE
(logic rational mind)

POSITIVE **UNCONSCIOUS** RESPONSE
(logic rational mind)

NEGATIVE **UNCONSCIOUS** RESPONSE
(fight/flight)

STIMULUS/EVENT/EXPERIENCE

Figure 7.1 Road Map to Break the Pattern of Negative Behaviors

positively or negatively impacts your real-world outcomes. Because it's triggered while the mind is in fight/flight mode, this behavior becomes unconscious and can sabotage your success beneath the surface.

To change our behavior and ensure we reach our goals, we must make a conscious choice. This choice should occur while we are in the logical/rational mindset. After we have traversed this road repeatedly, it then becomes a "positive unconscious behavior" that naturally leads to success.

When we first attempt to travel down a new highway, it can feel incredibly uncomfortable. The unknown requires copious amounts of mental energy to process. Although going back to the old pattern could negatively impact your ability to reach your goal, it's still easier for your brain than learning something new. Furthermore, our tendency to repeat negative behaviors amplifies when we hit decision fatigue and our brain puts us into self-preservation mode.

Our objective is to demolish these old highways and build new ones using a strategic and long-lasting approach that works without turning on fight/flight. In my 90-day mission to become unstoppable, I used the latest wearable technology to reprogram my mind for success. Years of exhaustion, depression, and anxiety had me living in self-preservation mode. It took real effort to turn it off, and even then, it would only switch off for a short time before coming back on again. My identity devolved into a person who didn't believe I could reach my goals. I made decisions out of fear that painfully delayed my progress by years.

So let's look at how traumatic life experiences can shape our behavior decades after the events have been forgotten. While these events may not seem traumatic to others, perception is personal, and your response to a situation deserves respect. Fear isn't always rational—unless you're staring down the face of a Category 5 hurricane.

1. When you experience a traumatic event, your fight/flight response is triggered. This creates new neurological pathways that apply meaning to this event: fear, sadness, anxiety, grief, or anger. Your emotions are amplified in this primal state as your system is flooded with adrenaline and cortisol, increasing the likelihood of it being committed to your long-term memory,

both consciously and subconsciously. This reaction is meant to keep you safe and on high alert to future life/death situations despite the real/perceived danger having passed.

2. If similar events occur in the future that remind you of this experience (through sight, sound, smell, taste, or touch), your brain defaults to those old neurological pathways and responds based on your previous experiences. The past event is its reference point for future ones. Because this highway has been traveled repeatedly before, it's easy for your brain to default to it. In essence, you may be reacting to the old event out of habit, not the current one out of fear.

This physiological programming shapes the way we behave in every aspect of our lives, even if we attempt to convince ourselves it doesn't. It's like playing the same old album on repeat. It becomes comfortable. It reinforces who we believe ourselves to be, despite being in conflict with who we need to become to reach our goals. Hence, an internal battle for one's self continues until we select a new soundtrack for our life. When we short-circuit these neurological pathways and form new ones, we can quickly dismantle our fears and phobias. Change becomes easy, freeing us from our self-imposed limitations and allowing us to transform into the person we know we can become.

It is often only in hindsight that we are aware of how our behavior has been impacted by this change. When you're in a mental state of fight/flight, you see everything through an emotional, fear-filled lens. Your emotions become amplified, and sometimes uncontrollable. In this state, others may tell you to "calm down and breathe deeply." This can be completely ineffectual because your logical mind is not in control. You may sometimes be able to talk yourself out of it, or a pleasant distraction may interrupt the pattern.

But other times, your pattern may need to run until the adrenaline is released. The more often we allow stress to activate our fight/flight response, the harder it can be to rationalize fears we may have about stepping out of our comfort zones. If your goal engages your fight/flight response because it makes you feel too uncomfortable, your brain may come to view it as a real life-or-death situation. If this happens, you will forever be caught in a tug of war between who you are and who you want to become. Your identity gap will be harder to close, and you will feel out of alignment.

There's a constant battle between your primal brain's need to keep you safe and your spiritual side's need for you to shine. I haven't met anyone who hasn't faced this struggle at some point in their lives. There's no more painful way to live than fighting against your own primal instincts. And, as we've discovered, nutritional deficiencies, inflammation, medications, and more can amplify and even trigger your fight/flight response. When you address these problems first, managing the psychological side becomes much easier because you spend less time in fight/flight mode. Repeatedly experiencing fight/flight can manifest all types of unusual behavior that can sabotage your success, including:

- ▶ *Avoidance behavior*: Putting off what you need to get done, including overworking, so you don't have to deal with a particular situation. Spending countless hours scrolling through social media or watching TV.
- ▶ *Changes in mood*: Becoming angry or moody without realizing why and lashing out at others in an uncharacteristic way.
- ▶ *Increased anxiety*: This includes everything from racing heartbeat, fidgeting, and pacing to withdrawing from others and an inability to focus, all to keep yourself distracted from what's truly at play.
- ▶ *Identity shift*: You switch into Guardian and Defender mode and can begin to think you're the kind of person who just doesn't reach their goals or ever get what they want. This is the most detrimental one of all, but thankfully, through nutrition and brain training, there is a way forward.

Hurricane Irma posed a very real threat at the time, although it ultimately missed our area, and still impacted us psychologically in the weeks afterward because adrenaline had flooded our systems for an extended period before the storm. Daily stressors work similarly, although the threats are typically perceived rather than real; they can be everything from fear of failure, success, criticism, and feeling overwhelmed. And, like nutritional deficiencies, they also result in real physiological responses, including:

▶ Increased heart rate
▶ High blood pressure
▶ Adrenaline release
▶ Scattered thinking
▶ Chronic stress
▶ Depression
▶ Anxiety
▶ Fatigue

Reprogram Your Mind and Take Back Your Life

At the beginning of my 90-day mission, I felt like I was starting from scratch. Any semblance of my old driven self had disappeared. I had to remind myself who I used to be and what I was capable of, and imagine who I could become. Like everybody else, I tackled the problem backward by focusing on psychology first and nutrition second. But it was only after my nutritional deficiencies began to normalize that I could stay in my logical/rational mind most of the time. From there, I could begin to work on my psychology because my cognitive functions were slowly returning, and I could finally think problems through.

Now, though, I was going to step up my game. I was going to try out the latest in neuroscience and wearable technology being used by the Pentagon, Olympic gold medalists, PTSD sufferers, and peak performers. The wearable technology had to meet specific criteria, including being affordable to the wider population, practical, and cost less than the latest smartphone.

Not only did I want it to resolve any fears of failure or success that had plagued me, but I also needed it to do the following:

▶ Provide a drug-free solution
▶ Create new neural highways
▶ Reduce stress within minutes
▶ Tame my fight/flight response

▶ Break through physical limitations

▶ Speed up change and make it stick

▶ Provide a mental and emotional recharge

▶ Improve my duration and ability to focus

▶ Create spontaneous, positive behavior change

▶ Provide data that would give me insight into my mind/body

▶ Reduce my need to apply willpower when implementing change

▶ Create physiological change that would influence my emotional state

▶ Reprogram negative patterns I had failed to reprogram previously

And, most importantly, it would need to help me train my brain to switch tasks more efficiently and help me get into the elusive "zone" faster, so I could achieve more in less time and recover from disruptions swiftly. One study by the University of California, Irvine, revealed that distractions severely threaten your work output, disrupt your mental flow, increase stress and frustration, add time pressure, and compound the effort required to complete the task at hand. We all knew this already, but did you know it takes an average of 23 minutes and 15 seconds to refocus on a task after you have been interrupted?[3] Their results also showed interruptions lead people to change not only work rhythms but also mental states. This further drains your mental resources.

Wearables to Upgrade Your Body, Mind, and Soul

I spent several months before my 90-day mission began examining these objectives to determine which wearables lived up to their claims and which ones did nothing. What I found was fascinating. All the following devices work to calm the fight/flight response by building new neural pathways to the preferred behavior. Some devices also provide another benefit: They instigate what is known as a pattern interrupt. Derived from neuro-linguistic programming, a pattern interrupt disrupts a certain behavior from continuing while that pattern is being played out in real time. This is by far one of the most effective ways to short-circuit a negative behavioral response because the brain isn't expecting it to happen. The pattern interrupt has the ability to switch you back into your logical/rational mind instantly and drive awareness that can only occur in this part of the brain. It becomes even more effective when this pattern interrupt occurs without the brain expecting it. With this in mind, let's look at the four wearables I experimented with:

1. TouchPoints™
2. Muse™
3. Spire Stone
4. Halo Sport

TouchPoints: Used in the Treatment of ADHD, PTSD, Autism, Anxiety, and Phobias—The Ultimate Pattern Interrupt

He had blood streaming down his face! Rick, our close friend on his way back home from visiting his wife at work on St. Patrick's Day in St. Petersburg, came across an argument between a man and his girlfriend. He heard screaming and yelling from across the street and saw the man attempting to drag his much smaller girlfriend away by her jacket. Not one to walk past someone in distress, Rick grabbed the man's wrist and got between them in an attempt to calm the guy, who was absurdly drunk. Rick, a six-foot gentle giant with a bodybuilder physique, had previously worked in security. He said, "Listen, you need to calm down, the police are coming. You're way too drunk."

But while Rick was talking to him, two other men tried to attack the guy. In the scuffle, they all fell back, and Rick hit his head on a metal pipe. The paramedics sent him home to get cleaned up.

When I saw Rick, I winced as I looked at the cuts and the blood running from his hairline. He was pacing and appeared highly agitated as he described what had happened. His adrenaline was still high. Within minutes, our friend Ashley, a nurse, advised us he needed to go to the emergency room. The right side of his face had started swelling. His next-door neighbor went to get her car and told us to meet her downstairs. As we were waiting, I put my TouchPoints on Rick.

TouchPoints are two watch-type wearable devices that you wear on each wrist. They use what is called "bilateral alternating stimulation tactile" (BLAST) technology, which provides gentle haptic microvibrations that interfere with your body's stress response. Invented by neuropsychologist Dr. Amy Serin and brought to market by CEO and cofounder Vicki Mayo, the process can be explained in three steps:

1. An event or thought triggers our stress and fight/flight response. We experience sensations in our body—racing heartbeat, tightness in the chest, tension in our neck, and butterflies in our stomach.

2. When turned on, the alternating stimulation from the TouchPoints shifts you back into the logical, rational part of your brain. It feels like the gentle vibration from your phone shifting between your wrists.

3. If we think of something stressful without experiencing the physical sensations and while in the rational part of our brains, we create new neural pathways that neutralize the negative response. A stressful event or thought can become completely neutralized or even positive because you're seeing it through the lens of your rational mind, not the primal mind revving you up to fight or flee.

This has a lasting effect in your brain, reducing stress over time, and is why TouchPoints were derived from one of the few successful treatments for PTSD. User data confirms TouchPoints reduce stress by 74 percent in 30 seconds.[4]

I reached out to Vicki and asked her how she had come up with the idea.

She said, "About three years ago my daughter, who was four at the time, was having terrible night terrors. I happened to tell one of my wonderful friends, who is a mom, but also a neuropsychologist, Dr. Amy Serin. I put what would later become TouchPoints in my daughter's hands in the middle of a heinous night terror. She went straight to sleep and woke up happy the next day. I said, this is incredible. How can we bring this to the market and make this technology accessible to everyone?" Vicki's story had inspired me to put them on Rick.

By the time we got Rick to the emergency room, only a couple of minutes away, his persona had completely changed. He was relaxed and jovial as he checked in to get treated. He stopped biting the inside of his cheek and bouncing his legs up and down from agitation. His focus, scattered a few minutes earlier, softened, and he relaxed to the point he was joking around with others in the waiting room. Anyone who has ever been in a fight can attest to just how long it takes to calm down afterward. It can take many hours. Instead, this happened within minutes. This wasn't even the most surprising result I saw while I experimented with these wearables.

A 40-Year Phobia Gone in Less Than 40 Minutes

A week prior, I had sat down with Rick and Trish, his wife. Trish has thalassophobia, a fear of being in or near large bodies of water. When she was 16, Trish fell off a yacht off the coast of Florida. Her phobia was so severe that she couldn't even look at pictures of scuba divers or walk near the ocean unless Rick was holding her hand. It had affected her life for more than 40 years.

I sat her down and explained how TouchPoints work. For the next 40 minutes, I showed her deep-water pictures and had her rate her fear from a scale of 0 to 10 while they vibrated on her wrists.

The first few images were the toughest. She was visibly getting upset and had to turn away repeatedly. But within a couple of minutes, her level of fear dropped from 10 to 7. Then it went back up to 10, only to drop to 5. It continued to fluctuate as we exposed her to various images. Then she saw one of the images that used to send her into a panic: the *Jaws* movie poster. She picked up the computer, looked at it closely, and pointed out details of the girl's swimsuit. She was touching the screen and laughing in amazement.

Later that night, I received a message from Trish. She had sent me deep water ocean pictures with the message, "Look what I can do!"

"I Want to Go to the Docks! I'm Ready to Be Done with this Fear Once and for All!"

Trish was ready to confront her fear head on and visit the shipping docks in Tampa Bay, so we drove there one sunny Sunday morning. Being overly cautious, I had her put on the TouchPoints, despite her wanting to do it without them. As we walked to the docks, she began to get nervous as she saw the ships in the distance. I turned the TouchPoints on to calm her down before we went any further. As we were trying to work out how to get a closer look and get around all the security fencing, she walked straight up to a security guard and asked if we could get a closer look at the ship. He advised us to go to the terminal just meters away and head up the stairs. From there, she could get a great view of the ships.

At the top of the platform, Trish began to get nervous as the stern of the ship came into view. She took a few steps back and her knees went weak, unsure if she could go through with it. I asked her to recall the funniest thing Rick had ever done, but she couldn't—she was far too deep in survival mode. I had her turn and face the other direction and close her eyes. She laughed and started humming a song Rick would sing to make her laugh. (We wanted to interrupt her pattern in multiple ways, not just with the TouchPoints.) She calmed down and took a few more steps. We repeated this at least four more times before she got to the edge of the platform and peered over.

She couldn't believe she was face to face with a gigantic luxury cruise ship. We stood there for several minutes before she turned to the ship in front of it. She could see its massive propeller jutting out of the water, something that would typically send her into a panic, and wanted to get close to it. We took the steps down and began walking toward it cautiously. Having realized her phobia was irrational, with confidence and only slight hesitation, she walked up to the hull of the ship, leaned over, and touched it!

She jumped up with excited disbelief. This was the same shipping port she had previously refused to work at, something that had cost her income.

Trish messaged me a day later: "By the way, I watched a documentary on shark attacks. First few minutes was the habitual reaction, but then that passed quickly. Rick and I were totally shocked."

This is just one example of how fear can rule our lives. Trish could have gone to therapy for years to attempt to desensitize herself from the ocean. This may have resulted in her being able to rationalize the fear, but not being able to rid herself of it. Fear isn't a rational response. The TouchPoints had short-circuited the neural pathway that led to her reaction and completely neutralized it. In my 15 years of working in the personal development field, I can say with complete confidence that I have never, ever seen behavior change happen more quickly.

Side Effects and Results

Many of us try for years to overcome a fear of criticism, success, failure, or financial worries, to no avail. We know they aren't rational fears, and yet they can drown out any positive thoughts and lead us to behave in ways that are counter to our desired outcomes.

I asked Vicki if there were any side effects. "There is one significant side effect," she said. "Over time, you'll be calmer. We are creating new neural pathways in your brain, which over time you're learning not to handle situations in the same way. There's a certain spontaneous behavior change that just comes from using TouchPoints."

From my own experiences using the TouchPoints on a daily basis, I observed I could sit still for longer periods of time without becoming agitated. This was particularly useful when I was writing. Whenever I would get agitated because I wasn't getting enough done or got stuck, I would turn them on. This rewired the way I perceived the task in front of me, significantly reducing my stress levels and allowing me to regain my focus. This pattern interrupt was more effective than I had expected. What's more, I had noted spontaneous behavior changes before I talked to Vicki. I found myself speaking up and dealing with certain situations more calmly than before. This was particularly handy when searching for a new apartment in New York City without a credit history in the U.S.

I also used them in conjunction with a daily mental rehearsal to prepare myself for the day ahead. Tracking the results with the Muse meditation device, which records brain-wave activity in real time, I could see I was calmer by up to 20 percent in some instances. I've used them to reprogram stress around finances, topics of conversation that would normally get heated between my partner and me, and other activities that would typically stress me out.

One particular spontaneous behavior change I experienced was profound: I felt more confident when interacting with others. Any fears of what others thought of me suddenly diminished, and I was free to be myself. This was something I hadn't felt for years, nor did I consciously work on it while using the device.

While TouchPoints have been used to help ADHD, autism, Parkinson's, Tourette syndrome, and PTSD, Vicki makes no claims that they treat any of these conditions. She clarified, "What we do know . . . if you think about your body and all these, the verticals, ADHD, autism, Parkinson's, is that they're all conditions. Overarching above it all is this condition of stress. We know that stress exacerbates all of them, whether it's PTSD, fear of heights, anything that we experience in our daily life. Stress makes it worse. The way that your stress response works is it is initiated by your fight or flight. When you turn your fight or flight mechanism off, you automatically get this huge release."

This device can be used to reprogram anything, particularly when it comes to stepping out of our comfort zone, that may engage your fight/flight and lead you to give up on your dreams. It also has one other major benefit: You can turn it on in seconds. You don't have to wait to see a therapist, which comes too late, after the stimulus has passed. When we can short-circuit stress at the moment we sense it coming on, we can stop it from taking hold. Future versions of this device will have sensors that automatically turn them on without user intervention. This will make them even more effective than they already are at disrupting negative patterns from occurring in the moment.

Meditate with Muse: Reduce Stress, Improve Mood, and Relax

We've all heard of the countless benefits meditation can bring us. The problem for many of us, when it comes to sitting down and calming our mind, is that we can't tell whether we're doing it right. Thankfully this can be quickly overcome. First we must understand how deep the benefits of meditation run, and how much impact they can have on our ability to succeed in life and shape our identity. The benefits of meditation include:

- Increased immune health[5]
- Decreased inflammation at the cellular level[6]
- Increased positive emotions[7]
- Decreased depression[8]
- Decreased anxiety[9]
- Decreased stress[10]
- Improved ability to regulate your emotions[11]

All these benefits can help shape the way we perceive and respond to the world, how we present ourselves, and how we feel about ourselves. Most important, meditation has been shown to produce the opposite reaction of what occurs during the fight/flight response.

In a study published in the open-access journal *PLOS One*, researchers at the Beth Israel Deaconess Medical Center and the Benson-Henry Institute for Mind Body Medicine at Massachusetts General Hospital found that practicing a relaxation response a couple of times a day for 10 to 20 minutes improved its efficacy.[12]

Muse takes the guesswork out of meditation. Muse is a brain-sensing headband that walks you through a guided meditation and provides audio feedback in real time on how you're doing. A soundscape of your choice, like the ocean or rainforest, plays in the background. The seven sensors in the headband, which fits around the back of your ears and across the middle of your forehead, detect your brain activity. When you reach a deep sense of calm, birds start chirping. When your mind becomes overactive, the birds stop, and the soundscape becomes loud and chaotic, your cue to calm your mind. Through the "gamification" of the app, you receive calm points and awards. You also receive a percentage-based score of how calm you are, from 0 to 100 percent, so you can attempt to do better each time.

I found this style of meditation easy. The gamification supplied a real sense of purpose, and because it was guided, it was idiot proof. It provided a structure that many of us lack when we try to meditate on our own. My initial "calm scores" came in at under 50 percent. It wasn't until a couple of weeks into my daily practice with the device that I began to make significant improvements and score around 90 percent. My results also indicated my meditation practice was far more effective in the morning than nighttime, even though I needed it at night to wind down after a busy day.

I was able to achieve higher results after having 1 milligram of nicotine and wearing the TouchPoints in conjunction with the Muse. This was a huge step toward becoming the person I was meant to be and reaching my hefty goals.

Typically, it's suggested that when you meditate, you allow your thoughts to flow to whatever thought pops into your mind, which I did at first. However, after a while, I chose to recall a stunning beach on Koh Phi Phi Don, an island in Thailand where I took a holiday years ago.

Koh Phi Phi Don sits opposite Koh Phi Phi Leh, the beautiful island where they filmed the movie *The Beach* with Leonardo DiCaprio. I would visualize sitting in the sand, looking out over the crystal-clear turquoise ocean and listening to the waves hit the shoreline. After several days, I started developing the urge to meditate more. It felt like a holiday because I had hit a high level of calm during these meditations. Whenever I needed a quick recharge, I would slip on the Muse and be transported back to the island and the sense of calm I felt when I visited there more than ten years ago.

An unexpected outcome from using the Muse was that during the day I would have flashbacks to pleasant memories, many of which made me smile. I took this as my brain reprogramming itself with more positive neural pathways. I found this device useful for training my brain to focus on one task at a time, instead of flipping between internet browsers or social media sites.

After 30 days, I experienced a sense of calm I hadn't felt in years. It was as if I could finally breathe again. It is important to recognize if you have nutritional deficiencies, inflammation, or medications that are causing depression and anxiety, the Muse will be less effective in an environment with deficits. The real results didn't appear until I had corrected these problems.

Spire Stone: Interrupt the Stress Response Through Breathing

That day at the train station when my fight/flight response fired up tenfold, when the man came bursting in accusing the smaller guy of murdering his sister, was a wake-up call. Within minutes of observing what I believed was soon to be a murder, my Spire Stone, a wearable device hooked to the belt of my pants, vibrated and snapped me back into my logical/rational mind.

The Spire Stone tracks everything from steps, respiration, and sleep to how tense you are based on your breathing patterns. It measures these through the expansion and contraction of your torso. When it vibrates, it's providing a cue to take a deep breath. We often forget just how much our rate of breathing is affected by stress. When we become stressed, our breathing becomes shallow and tense. When we disrupt this pattern, we can bring ourselves back into our logical/rational mind and calm down.

The Spire Stone proved to be an effective pattern interrupt. It would occasionally vibrate when I was having a disagreement with my partner, at which point we would crack up laughing. The only problem I had with the device was that it wouldn't always connect or record the data. It is supposed to track how many minutes you are calm, focused, tense, active, and sedentary throughout the day and while you're asleep. Like the Muse, it has a real gamification element to it that kept me engaged. Since I tried out the Spire Stone, they have released a new device called the Spire Health Tag. This device is attached to your clothes and is even machine washable, making it even more user-friendly. Even though the data on the Spire Stone isn't hugely accurate, I would still recommend it as an entry-level wearable that can provide real pattern interrupts to beneficially influence behavior, turn off the fight/flight response, and reduce stress.

Halo Sport: Obliterate Limitations in the Gym Through Electrical Stimulation to Your Motor Cortex

I felt a strong tingling sensation across the top of my head. I had just put on Halo Sport: an expensive-looking pair of headphones with softly pointed foam pads under the top band that touch your head above the part of your brain called the motor cortex. Based on 15 years of scientific research, Halo Sport provides electrical stimulation during movement-based training, helping build stronger, more optimized connections between your brain and muscles. The function of Halo Sport is to place the brain in a state of hyperplasticity that refines the brain's ability to adapt to training. I had reached out to the company and secured a four-week trial of the device, during which I would undertake an intense CrossFit workout designed by a friend of mine, Dean Haynes, a CrossFitter from Adelaide, Australia. I had completed the four-week program multiple times over the past four years and had recorded all my statistics into an Excel spreadsheet. I knew what my average numbers were, and I wanted to improve them, as well as increase the intensity of my sessions and shorten their duration. I would compare what I used to lift with what I could lift with Halo Sport. This experiment had two core objectives: increase my workout intensity and break old neural pathways and my belief that I could only lift a certain amount without getting injured. This was a fight/flight response that had held me back from great performance in the gym. To feel unstoppable, I had to challenge my body and brain in a myriad of ways.

Different physical exercises can bring specific mental gains: dealing with cravings, reducing stress, improving memory—everything required to close our identity gap. An article included in *The Scientific Guide to an Even Better You* published these findings:

> *Lifting weights*: Assists the prefrontal cortex of the brain, complex thinking, reasoning, multitasking, problem solving

> *Yoga*: Helps the frontal lobe and helps integrate thoughts and emotions

> *High intensity interval training*: Focuses on the hypothalamus and appetite regulation, cravings, and addiction

Everyone from Olympic medalists to MLB, the NBA, the NFL, CrossFitters, and endurance athletes have praised Halo Sport. It's even been used to train special ops forces in the U.S.

During my first workout, something surprising happened. On my first exercise, a squat clean, a relatively complex movement that uses multiple muscles and requires perfect form to prevent injury, I lifted 936 pounds (424 kilograms), heavier across the set than when I had lifted previously. This is a movement I had not done in more than three months, as I rotate my programs regularly. I noticed something else interesting as well: I was sweating profusely. My personal trainers have always pushed me harder because I just don't sweat much. I thought this might be the placebo effect in full swing. But this type of gain continued daily for the entire four weeks I worked out with Halo Sport.

Remember Rick, the former bodybuilder and full-blown skeptic? I had him try the device while doing triceps presses. Rick had never been able to press the entire weight stack until the day he put this on his head. To say he was surprised was an understatement. He also noticed he sweated more than usual.

To find out more, I hopped on a plane to San Francisco and sat down with Brett Wingeier, the CTO and cofounder of Halo Neuroscience. He shared with me how they had worked with a comprehensive team of doctors, neuroscientists, athletes, designers, and engineers to develop Halo Sport. Before creating Halo Sport, the founding team had spent more than a decade developing the world's first closed-loop neurostimulation device for epilepsy patients. It received unanimous FDA approval after changing the lives of thousands of epilepsy patients. Here's what Brett said when I asked him more about it:

> *The roots of the company started when my cofounder and I spent most of our career in implantable medical devices. And we met at a company called NeuroPace, where we made an implantable responsive simulator for epilepsy. And what that means is it's an implant that sits in your head, lives there for the rest of your life, watches for seizures about to start, and then stimulates to stop them before they start.*

Unsure of how much he could tell me about their work with the military, he did say, "One of our first contracts was with the Defense Innovation Unit Experimental (DIUx), and they brought Halo Sports to numerous installations—special ops and other installations—and they've been getting great results with it. The basic science, also sometimes working with laboratory units, sometimes working with products like Halo, they've found results like this visualance where transcranial stimulation can accelerate sniper training. It can accelerate vigilance."

The military has also conducted placebo sham controlled randomized double-blinded clinical trials. "We've duplicated some of those studies," Brett said. "We've got our own data, and then the next step is we've gone out to athletes, and we've done randomized double-blind sham-controlled studies with the U.S. national ski team." They even have a stroke study going on at the Medical University of South Carolina with Halo Sport.

Each day I used Halo Sport, I made notes of my experience. Here's what I observed:

- The complex movements in my program became easier.
- After I lifted the first weight, without thinking, I added more weights to the bar. I just felt I could lift heavier weights natural-ly. Any fear that I couldn't had disappeared without consciously having to work through it.
- The extreme sweating only occurred the first two times I used the device.

The biggest change of all was that I didn't have the same level of muscle soreness. Typically, when doing this program, I ended up having issues with my right shoulder due to tight chest muscles; this time I didn't.

So where does Halo Sport fit in with obliterating fear and overcoming failure? It's simple. It showed my brain what my body was capable of. It broke the old neural connections that said, "I can't lift heavier or train harder than this!" And it rewired neural pathways that helped me lift heavier in the gym even after I had stopped using the device. Admittedly, my workouts did feel harder without it in the following weeks, but my brain knew I was capable of more. I could push through the discomfort. Sometimes we need a little extra help to reprogram our minds and open the door to greater success, in the gym and in life.

To track my progress, I not only recorded the weight I was lifting each day, I took a photo of myself in the mirror daily for the duration of the experiment. I will show them to you in Chapter 10. I was still nutritionally deficient in the first photo, as I had only just discovered what I needed to correct. Despite this, I lifted heavier than I ever have before.

This was one of the toughest experiments I conducted on my mission to becoming unstoppable. As it was one of my earliest experiments, I needed to use extreme levels of willpower to overcome nutritional deficiencies. While the workouts were easy and fun, they still put incredible amounts of stress on my body. The physical changes that occurred despite this, I believe, are a testament to what the body is truly capable of when we use devices that help us unlock our capacity. I look forward to conducting this experiment again now that my body has found a state of nutritional equilibrium. And, most critically, this transformation provided me with a real identity. As the shape of my body changed, so did my confidence in myself—not just in how I felt about the way I looked, but how I felt about myself. I had broken personal bests each day for an entire month. That has had a lasting impact on my psychology even to this day.

Applying the Latest Wearable Technology to Short-Circuit Behaviors That Stop You From Becoming Unstoppable

With today's technological advances, we possess tools that can unlock our capacity for great and lasting change. And as we've discovered, when our fight/flight response is frequently turned on, we become exhausted and overwhelmed and can convince ourselves we're not capable of reaching our goals. By leveraging the latest wearable devices, we can find new ways to transform ourselves into a Catalyst by interrupting the patterns that have held us back for years. They drive awareness in a way we can't when we're in self-preservation mode. By using these devices in real life-threatening situations as well as situations where the threat is only perceived, I've developed an ability to bounce back from setbacks within minutes, instead of hours, days, or even months. And now that we know how to short-circuit these disruptive, life-draining patterns, it's time to prime your brain for success and delve into one more life-changing wearable that tracks a key component to becoming a Catalyst, as well as a powerful technique for priming your brain for success.

CHAPTER 8

The Cusp of Brilliance
Advanced Strategies for Priming Your Brain for Success

"I don't think I can do this!" I said to Jonathan, who was sitting next to me. I was taking off my big, heavy Timberland shoes in preparation for the Tony Robbins fire walk experience. Tony had just completed a session of neuro-linguistic programming to prepare us to walk over smoldering hot coals behind the Palm Beach County Convention Center. During the visualization exercise, I felt unstoppable. But as soon as the lights came on to signal us to exit the building, my adrenaline kicked in and my thoughts became scattered.

I desperately tried to calm my nerves by reminding myself of the thousands of people who had done this before me. Logically I knew it was possible, but my primal brain thought it was crazy! My heart was racing, and my instincts were telling me to hightail it out of there. Despite this, I wanted to prove to myself that I could break through negative patterns that previously would have made me turn and run. It was time to let my subconscious mind know that I was writing the script.

As we began our journey into the pitch-black parking lot on a balmy Florida night, everybody began chanting, "Cool moss, cool moss, cool moss!" This was the anchor we were to repeat when walking across the coals to help us remain focused. We were to picture walking across cool moss instead of hot coals. As we came through the doors, my eyes had to adjust not only to the change in light, but to the chaos as well. We were among 5,000 others in the darkness. We couldn't see where the strips of hot coals began and the people ended. We just kept blindly following the people in front of us. Many of them were nervously joking: "BBQ feet for dinner anyone!?" I didn't know how close we were to the coals; all I knew was that my heart was about to jump out of my chest. Out of fear, I went back to chanting in my head, "Cool moss, cool moss, cool moss." I needed maximum willpower, if only for a moment.

Then, unexpectedly, I was standing right at the front of the line! *I'm not ready!* I thought. The woman in front of me charged through the coals, and I was next. I walked up to the front and felt the heat of the coals on my face. Was I ready to take the next step?

How to Align Your Biochemistry with Your Soul's Purpose

So far we have examined how to close your energy gap in a myriad of ways, as well as how to short-circuit your brain's fight/flight response that is holding you back from doing what you love.

Now it's time to dive even deeper, to bring your body and mind into alignment with that unstoppable version of yourself. Being out of alignment is like coming to a T-junction in the road: Your soul wants to go right, while your psychology or biochemistry wants to turn left.

This can feel excruciating, almost as if you are two people who can't agree on where to go next. When all three elements align (biochemistry, psychology, and your soul's purpose), your identity becomes strong and your resolve unstoppable. Suddenly your life makes sense; the many aspects of your body, health, and spirituality are aligned. A sense of relief washes over you as the fight between what your soul wants and whether your primal brain will let you have it ends. You transform into a Catalyst—an Oprah Winfrey, Richard Branson, or Tony Robbins—in which every part of you, your body, brain, and soul, is heading in the same direction, and when it isn't, you know precisely what to do to rectify the situation. This doesn't mean you won't ever experience self-doubt or fear. It simply means you'll know how to not let it cloud the road ahead of you. (See Figure 8.1.)

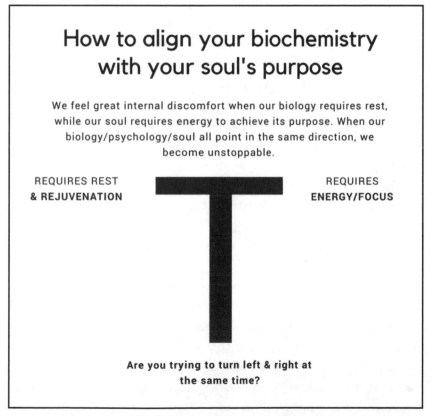

Figure 8.1 Aligning Your Biochemistry with Your Soul's Purpose

To achieve this blissful alignment, this step requires priming the brain for success and getting ready to take the required actions to fulfill your goals, without resorting to self-preservation mode, which will have you retreating back into Defender and Guardian mode. Doing this requires two crucial steps:

1. Optimizing sleep/rejuvenation
2. Visualizing/mental rehearsal

Many of us are on the cusp of brilliance and breaking through in ways we've never imagined, but we can't see ourselves crossing the finish line. We step to the front of the line, and our fears get the better of us. Our brain doesn't have a road map for where we're about to go, nor is it prepared to overcome the inevitable challenges that pop up along the way. Because of this, we end up sabotaging our success by focusing on tasks that are habitual, not helpful. When you can visualize reaching the goal in your mind first, it's easy to go there in real life. By initially focusing on your health and nutrition, we've fueled your brain for success, so it has the biochemical resources it requires for processing new information fast. Then, by short-circuiting fight/flight, we've put it into a state of neuroplasticity and optimal learning. According to the Oxford dictionary, "Neuroplasticity is the brain's ability to form and reorganize synaptic connections, especially in response to learning and experience."

Our brains are constantly evolving through experience; this is neuroplasticity in action. Changes in brain structure and organization occur as we learn, adapt, and evolve. With each repetition of thought, emotion, or action, we forge and reinforce new neural pathways. Neural connections are constantly becoming stronger or weaker depending on what we focus on, when we focus on it, and whether it's being used. Some of these pathways are being created daily, as we discovered in the previous chapter. For real change to occur, we need to visualize the new path in our minds, now that we have taken steps to calm the internal chaos. For this path to break old connections, we must get our brain into a state of neuroplasticity so change is easy and becomes permanent. If we want our brain to work better, we must progressively overload it so it adapts to change. And, just as we used various wearable devices to short-circuit and calm our fight/flight response, we can use the following strategies to prevent that response from occurring in the future.

Short-circuiting a fight/flight response is different from priming your brain for success. Priming allows us to mentally rehearse future events that require us to be at our absolute best. It prepares the brain for what is to come, to reduce any stress or anxiety related to the future event. Athletes prime their minds for success by mentally visualizing the competition they are about to enter. The more detailed this visualization is, the better and more consistently they perform. A study conducted by Guang Yue, an exercise physiologist at the Cleveland Clinic Foundation, had participants imagine flexing their biceps as hard as possible. The training lasted for 12 weeks (15 minutes per day, five days per week). After a few weeks, they showed a 13.5 percent increase in strength.[1] This demonstrates compelling evidence that the same neural pathways are activated while visualizing movements just as they are when the movement is being physically performed.

Mental rehearsal achieves five major outcomes:

1. It reduces mental noise that distracts us from what is important.
2. It tricks the brain into thinking you've already done the activity before; hence, there is nothing to fear and no reason to activate the fight/flight response.
3. You don't have to engage willpower to get work done; you enter a state of "flow" and become immersed in your task.
4. It alleviates fear, reduces stress, and helps you become more confident in yourself and the mission at hand.
5. You come into alignment and transform yourself into a Catalyst, an individual capable of getting what they want.

This method is by no means new. The problem many face is figuring out how to apply this strategy to everyday situations, particularly when it comes to reaching our goals. The visualization technique I will reveal to you in step two is powerful and effortlessly solves this problem. I have used it for the past ten years to prepare myself to speak in front of audiences of thousands, film videos without a teleprompter, deal with breakups, manage the death of my father, resolve internal conflicts, prepare myself for an intense workout, and write four books. In fact, I wrote 8,000 words in the past four days after priming my brain in the morning for no more than ten minutes per day before starting to write—a new personal best. There was a four-year hiatus between this and my last book because I had trouble writing; I couldn't even focus for longer than 30 minutes at a time.

During my 90-day mission, I decided to make it even more powerful by getting my brain into a state of neuroplasticity before I did my mental rehearsal for the day. This included enhancing my mental state with nicotine, alternating various nootropics (e.g., L-Theanine and L-Tyrosine), and wearing the TouchPoints to get myself primed to make strong neural connections. By no means are these steps essential to this mental rehearsal process; after all, I've successfully used it for years without the added help. However, they do amplify the method and make it even more powerful. I wanted to get myself into an optimal state of neuroplasticity by ensuring I was well-rested, which leads to our first step in priming your brain for success: sleep.

Step One: Sleep for Consolidation, Rest, and Rejuvenation

I was a walking zombie for four years despite getting the recommended eight hours of sleep each night. I would wake up feeling exhausted. Many factors contributed to this, including my digestive issues, nutritional deficiencies, and asthma medication. No matter what I did, I always woke up tired. Insufficient sleep is implicated in various mental health problems, including bipolar disorders, schizophrenia, and depression. Sleep is essential for memory consolidation, repair, and growth. I'm not alone, according to the Centers for Disease Control (CDC). The agency reports that between 50 and 70 million adults in the U.S. alone suffer from a chronic sleep disorder, with one in three adults logging under seven hours of sleep per night.[2] Connections between sleep deprivation, cancer, cardiovascular diseases, mental health, and obesity are being researched by the University of Oxford and the Royal Society for Public Health.[3]

What is profoundly interesting is that insufficient sleep affects the body the same way drinking alcohol does. One study at the University of New South Wales found that after 17 to 19 hours without sleep, a person's alertness is hindered to the same extent as someone with a blood alcohol concentration (BAC) of 0.05 percent.[4] This is considered legally "impaired" in the U.S. A person's impairment after a full 24 hours without sleep is equivalent to a BAC of 0.1 percent, significantly higher than the 0.08 percent required for being legally drunk. Lack of sleep causes a number of health issues that can compound over time, impact our mood, and send us straight into Guardian and Defender mode. The need for sleep will continue to increase until your brain forces you to take a nap. Too little sleep upsets our emotions and our ability to make rational decisions. Likewise, excess fatigue can cause stress and irritability and engage "decision fatigue" well before it would normally be triggered. Becoming a Catalyst requires strong emotional management, which is not possible when you are fatigued. It also requires being aware of what is pulling you out of your optimal state.

I wanted to get to the bottom of why I was so tired, so I purchased the Oura ring. This modern-looking finger ring worn day and night tracks body temperature, heart-rate variability, and sleep stages (timing, duration, and quality). It also tracks physical activity, respiration, and breathing variances, as well as inactivity, intensity, timing, and length of physical activity. The Oura ring is the first on the market to have been independently validated (conducted by SRI International).[5] The Oura ring takes wearable technology to another level. Instead of just inundating you with copious amounts of data, it provides daily suggestions to help you self-regulate. Every day, you receive a readiness score. This score is calculated by various factors, including how many hours you slept, resting heart rate, activity from the day before, and much more, and recommends whether you should have a highly active day or take it easy. It also adjusts how many steps you should do that day instead of the default target of 10,000. I noticed my readiness score jumped significantly if I got at least eight hours of sleep per night. And, because it was tracking my body temperature, I could also use it to indicate whether I was getting sick. The first week

I had it, my temperature one night went from 98.6°F (37°C) down to 97.7°F (36.5°C). I was sick. By keeping track of these statistics, you can take preventive steps before a cold or flu takes hold, like reducing the length or intensity of a workout, getting extra rest, or increasing various supplements. Female users can also detect menstrual cycle stages for better fertility management.

The Oura's most profound reading was my low levels of deep sleep, as shown in Figure 8.2. By early January, once my energy was returning and I was well into my recovery, my deep sleep jumped significantly, even while the duration of my sleep dropped. I was feeling much more mentally alert and my moods were improving. This coincided with a few interesting observations. My deep sleep increased as my nightly body temperature decreased and my respiration rate significantly improved (the number of breaths I take per night). When winter in Florida hit, I increased the temperature in my bedroom by one degree. Florida doesn't really have much of a winter at all. After observing that my deep sleep began to decline, I could link it to the temperature change and fix it. You'll learn more about this shortly. As you can see by comparing the diagrams, as my temperature dropped, my deep sleep increased. (See Figures 8.2 and 8.3.)

Remember that many factors play a role in feeling rested and rejuvenated. Over the years, too much emphasis has been placed on how much total sleep we need, when the quality of sleep, as well as understanding our natural circadian rhythm, plays an even more important role. We each have a unique circadian rhythm. It is an

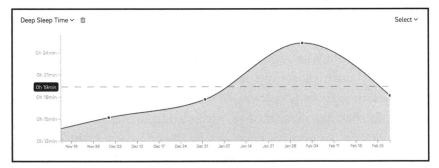

Figure 8.2 **My Oura Ring Correlation for Deep Sleep Pattern**

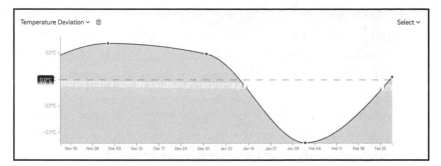

Figure 8.3 My Oura Ring Correlation for Body Temperature

approximately 24-hour rhythm that ticks away in the background of our daily life, setting the pace for our minds and bodies. This internal clock drives when we're active and when we need to rest, eat, and sleep. Any disruptions to our life, such as jet lag, can throw our circadian rhythm out of sync. By following our natural patterns as much as possible, we feel more rested and experience greater mental clarity. Not following our circadian rhythm can trigger various health issues. Unfortunately, this natural rhythm is being disrupted by our modern environment. Due to artificial light, we no longer follow the sunup and sundown cycle like our predecessors. This can affect the quality and stages of sleep. A normal sleep cycle includes the following stages:

1. *Light Sleep*: This is the phase in which your muscles loosen and relax, and your heart and breathing rates slow. This accounts for about 50 percent of total sleep time for most adults.

2. *Deep Sleep*: This is the most restorative stage and makes up between 0 to 35 percent of total sleep time.[6] It enables muscle growth and repair as human growth hormone is released, which is necessary for the stress triggered by exercise and weight training. Any interruption can suddenly stop its release.[7] Some research also indicates that deep sleep may be important in clearing the brain for new learning the next day. This is the most refreshing stage of sleep; if you are awoken from it, you may experience "sleep drunkenness," which is a particularly dangerous time to drive or perform other complex tasks.

3. *REM Sleep*: REM (rapid eye movement) is critical for reenergizing your mind and body. It is associated with dreaming, learning, creativity, and memory consolidation—all vital in preparing your brain to be mentally primed for the goals you would like to achieve.

4. *Awake Time*: This is the time spent lying awake after you have gone to bed. If you experience large amounts of awake time, it may indicate that you have trouble falling or staying asleep and you may feel sleepy during the day.

We all know how hard it is to focus during the day when our sleep is disturbed; hence, proper sleep habits are a crucial step in preparing for success. If disruptions to your sleep continue for too long, they may lead to exhaustion and eventual burnout, because your brain isn't consolidating the events of the day and your body isn't repairing your muscles. You're in a constant state of disrepair, putting stress on your body and brain. A 2016 meta-analysis of 11 scientific studies found evidence that sleep deprivation seems to cause a person to eat an average of 385 extra calories the next day.[8] Falling out of normal sleep range even a little bit can cause one's immune system to work against a healthy body.[9]

If you're considering the use of sleeping pills to manage your sleep, consider the following warning. A 2012 study showed that regularly taking prescription sleep aids increases mortality at a rate five times greater as non-users over a 2.5-year period.[10] Sleeping pills are not a long-term solution and come with potential side effects, including feeling groggy the next morning. A doctor should work with you to help you stop taking these medications.

So what are the alternatives to help improve the quality of your sleep and recharge your battery so that you're ready for the day ahead?

Top Seven Tips for Increasing Deep Sleep to Prime Your Brain for Success

The following list provides suggestions for getting a good night's sleep without the use of drugs:

1. *Block junk light.* Avoid using your electronic devices before bed, as they emit blue light that inhibits the production of the melatonin hormone, which regulates your sleep/wake cycle. This reduction makes it more difficult to fall asleep. Every time you look at the blue light from a screen, you're sending a signal to your brain that the sun is up. Most new phones now come with a built in "blue light filter." Have this set to automatically come on around the same time the sun sets. Second, be sure to get plenty of natural light during the day. Rodents exposed to sun produced far more melatonin at night than ones confined to an artificially lit environment.[11] Blue-blocker glasses with specially tinted lenses are also available to mitigate the effects of other light sources.

2. *Block social media.* You knew this one was coming! Social media's addictive nature can pull us into a news feed and not let us out for hours. What's more, many of us stare closely at that screen before we nod off. Have you ever dropped your phone on your face when looking at it in bed? Yeah, thought so! It's not just chipped teeth you should be worried about. Your social media use may also be causing you stress before bed. Allow at least one to two hours before sleep for your mind to wind down. Social media app blockers are available for both Android and iOS. I have mine set to block at certain times of the day. After a week, you'll realize how many times a day you check your phone, and how much better you feel once the pattern is interrupted. Social media can lead to decision fatigue as well. Reduce it and feel your mindset clear.

3. *Reduce stimulants.* Many people consume caffeinated drinks like coffee, sodas, or tea late in the day, leading to disrupted sleeping patterns. Caffeine has a long half-life, meaning your body will still be processing it hours later. Some of us metabolize caffeine slower, which could result in side effects much later in the day. If caffeine has left you jittery, dilute its effects with a dose of L-Theanine, as described in Chapter 6. L-Theanine partially counteracts caffeine-induced sleep disturbances. Also speak to

your doctor to see if any medications you are on could be disrupting your sleep or having a stimulant effect, such as asthma medication. This could be corrected by taking the medication in the morning instead of later in the day. A doctor will advise you as to your specific needs.

4. *Stick to a routine.* Prioritize your sleep. It is life giving and crucial to optimal cognitive functions that allow you to focus for lengthy periods of time. There isn't any specific time that you should go to bed; that is up to you and your unique circadian rhythm. If you've ever wondered why you get tired or hungry at the same time each day, that's your circadian rhythm at work. It's best that we follow these internal clocks and do what is right for us. Just because the habits of the ultra-successful include getting up at 5 A.M. doesn't mean you should, too. In fact, that could completely disrupt your natural rhythm and throw your life into disarray.

5. *Drop the temperature and increase your deep sleep.* According to Alex Fergus, research has found the "optimal room temperature for sleep is a cool 15.5°C to 20°C (60°F to 68°F)." My initial increase in deep sleep correlated with getting stranded at the peak of winter in Canada. It began to decrease again after I returned home to Florida, which doesn't experience much of a winter at all.

6. *Supplement with melatonin (sparingly).* Melatonin, an increasingly popular sleep-inducing supplement, comes with a warning. Taken by millions of Americans every year, it is only recommended for short-term use (a few months or less). Melatonin may also increase blood sugar, so anyone with diabetes or pre-diabetes should avoid its use. Too much can cause bad dreams and severe grogginess the next day. It should only be taken sparingly, as more research needs to be done.[12] I use it rarely, such as when I'm trying to recover from jet lag and resetting my circadian rhythm to a different time zone. For this reason, I would suggest not going with the cheapest brand.

7. *Address vitamin deficiencies.* As we've discovered, fixing nutritional deficiencies is the key to unlocking our mental capacity and

improving our sleep. Three key vitamins include vitamins A, B6, and D. Vitamin D3 deficiencies are also associated with sleep disorders. B6 deficiency has been linked to sleep disturbances, and Vitamin A is a vital contributor to setting and maintaining our circadian rhythm.[13]

Without quality sleep, remembering key facts, staying focused, and regulating your emotions becomes nearly impossible. Sleep plays a profound role in neuroplasticity and ensuring our brain can perform at its absolute best.

A study published in 2016 by the University of Freiburg found that the build-up of connectivity in our brains that occurs during the day is reset during sleep. They also discovered that missing one night of sleep is enough to stop this natural reset from happening, thereby hindering the brains ability to solidify memories from the day that was.[14] Quality sleep is vital for our brain's ability to remember and learn so we can adapt to the changing world around us.

While you may experience some benefits from doing mental rehearsal and meditation daily even when you are sleep deprived, you may find that you struggle to attain the level of focus required for long-term memory storage. This work requires nightly consolidation. You should take steps today to correct your lack of sleep and make use of wearable technology such as the Oura ring to track any changes so you can quickly correct problems when they arise. After all, sleep might be the most essential restorative bodily function required for neuroplasticity, and it prepares us for the next step in our journey, priming your brain for success and making new connections to an unstoppable you.

Step Two: Find Calm in Chaos

Neuro-linguistic programming (NLP) is the systematic study of human performance. It is grounded in the belief that an experience can be modified, improved upon, and even removed to help clear the mental blockages that hold us back. It provides a structural framework to help us manage our emotions as well as lay the foundation for future success. NLP originated in the 1970s in Santa Cruz, California, with Richard Bandler and John Grinder.

I was lucky enough to come across NLP in my early 20s and have used it for close to 15 years on an almost daily basis. NLP has been made massively popular over the years by Tony Robbins highlighting its benefits at countless events worldwide. Through years of self-experimentation, I have refined and combined specific NLP techniques that allow me to mentally rehearse future events and prime my brain for the task ahead in only 10 to 20 minutes per day.

If we are to take more purposeful steps forward in achieving our goals, our identity must come into alignment with who we need to become. Mental rehearsal is by far one of the most important steps you must take. If you can't see it in your mind, you won't see it in the world.

To achieve this, we need to take advantage of all the key aspects NLP provides to create real change. That includes becoming fully immersed in the daily mental rehearsals by making use of submodalities. Submodalities comprise our sensory representational systems; in other words, we see past and future events through these senses and the intensity associated with them. The way we use these submodalities dictates whether we see a situation as positive, neutral, or negative. They include all five senses:

1. *Visual submodalities* (what you see): Shape, color, focus, brightness/darkness, contrast, distance, speed, size, etc.
2. *Auditory submodalities* (what you hear): Volume, pitch, distance, movement, harmony, rhythm, tempo, phrasing, progression, etc.
3. *Kinesthetic submodalities* (what you feel): Temperature, weight, sharp/dull, wet/dry, pressure, texture, intensity, duration, etc.
4. *Olfactory submodalities* (what you smell): Sweet, fresh, perfumed, faint, mild/strong, putrid, etc.
5. *Gustatory submodalities* (what you taste): Savory, salty, sweet, bitter, hot, tart, etc.[14]

By manipulating a past or future event through adjusting its submodalities, we can lift the burden the event is causing for us and create new neural pathways and positive expectations for a happier outcome. This can lead to a positive behavior change while improving performance and reducing stress.

I asked Australian illusionist Sam Powers how he mentally prepares for the dangerous stunts he performs at 400 shows per year. He said, "When I am doing something new, I'll lock the dressing room door and in pure silence, I'll take about ten minutes to visualize specifically everything that is about to unfold right before I walk out onstage. That way when I do walk out, it's literally just happened minutes before, and all I am doing is repeating it in real life." He uses priming as a regular ritual to get himself in a proper state so he can give the audience everything he has, instead of worrying about what may or may not happen. Imagine how much easier your day will flow with this tool up your sleeve.

Exercise: Neutralize Negative Past Events

Let's examine how quickly you can change the way you feel about a past event or even a person. Think of a mildly upsetting event from the past. Rate it on a scale from 0 to 10 based on how much discomfort it causes you when you stop and think about it for a moment. Allow those feelings to expand. See it in front of you in your mind. What do you see, hear, feel, taste, and touch? How intense is it? Take a moment to experience it. Once it becomes uncomfortable, it's time to play a game with the submodalities to change the way you feel about it.

1. Change the picture to black and white and make it dull.
2. Shrink it down until it's the size of your thumb.
3. Hear your favorite song being played in the background.
4. Turn up the volume on this sound until you can feel the vibration from its bass (better yet, hit play on your favorite song while thinking about this event).
5. Make the image blurry while the song continues to play in the background.
6. Smell your favorite aftershave or perfume in the air.
7. Imagine sinking your teeth into your favorite food.
8. Replace this tiny, blurry, black-and-white image with a picture of an event that occurred later that had you bursting out in laughter.

9. What expression do you have on your face now? How do you feel when you think about this funny event? What can you hear? Immerse yourself in the experience.

When you think of that upsetting event now, on a scale of 0 to 10, how would you rate it for discomfort? Repeat this process multiple times.

What many people find after doing this exercise is they can barely remember the event or what they were upset about. If you still rate it as highly upsetting, try playing with even more types of submodalities to manipulate the image. I have always found that shrinking that image down to its tiniest size and replacing it with a happy image from after the event was over was by far the most effective way to relieve myself from all negative feelings associated with it. This simple yet powerful technique allows you to dissociate with all the factors that caused the event to be committed to long-term memory while associating it with more positive feelings. You thereby interrupt the pattern and how you respond to it—just like Trish did with her thalassophobia.

Step Three: Popping the Cork on Stress and Dropping into the Moment

Now that you understand how to neutralize an event by manipulating it, let's look at how we can relieve stress about future upcoming events and prime our brains to reach our goals. This time, we're not just taking in all the submodalities; we're also traveling through time. When we associate with our memories, they may be unpleasant or pleasant, which results in us responding to them as if the event just occurred. Our neurological responses to associated memories can be as strong as to the original events themselves. It is believed the brain can't distinguish between present, remembered, or imagined events. Because of this, mental rehearsal becomes a powerful tool for anyone who wants to become unstoppable.

By doing a mental dry run of an event in your mind multiple times before it occurs, we can alleviate any associated fear and prepare ourselves for what is to come. But one difficulty is that people often can't see life continuing on normally after the event in question has taken place.

Picture a couple who are about to get married. All their thoughts and energy are focused on that one date. They can't see past it. Pressure builds up between now and the wedding day to the point it becomes almost unbearable. It's almost as if life stops on this day, regardless of whether it's meant to be the best day of your life. The event has been "overamplified" and taken out of context with your life as a whole. This single-focused mindset allows no room for error. If something small goes wrong, people react as if it's a life-or-death situation.

But by simulating the event in your mind and going beyond it to see what you'll be doing in the days, weeks, months, or years that follow, you release the pressure. You've shown your brain that life goes on and gets better after the event has taken place. And, importantly, that it isn't a life-or-death situation. Better yet, you "drop into the moment" and become profoundly present, allowing you to enjoy yourself and the journey leading up to it.

I have had profound experiences using this technique. Many times I've spoken to an audience of thousands and walked off without any idea what just happened. I was so deeply in the moment that I just enjoyed myself. My thoughts flowed naturally, and I was free from being self-conscious, which was liberating. My brain had been there and done it before, which meant there was nothing for me to fear. It was all going to unfold perfectly because I had seen myself walking offstage after the event smiling to a round of applause. Think what could have happened if I had seen myself getting up onstage and fumbling to find my words. I would have negatively associated myself with an event that had never happened before, engaged my fight/flight response, and set myself up for potential failure and unnecessary stress.

Mental simulation can be used in the following scenarios:

▶ Priming your brain for the day ahead to help increase your productivity; this is part of your 90-day plan to an unstoppable you
▶ Progressively overloading your brain to adapt to future events that may stretch your comfort zone (e.g., taking a new job, ending a relationship, buying property, or starting your own business)

- ▶ Improving athletic performance, as I did in conjunction with Halo Sport to prepare myself for an intense workout
- ▶ Any other event you have coming up you want to be primed and ready for so you're on your best game

Let's walk you through the process now. But before I do, to ensure you have the best and most optimized experience, you may wish to do the following, although they are not essential:

- ▶ Have a green tea or coffee and some L-Theanine 30 to 60 minutes prior to help you get into the zone and increase the likelihood of unstoppable focus.
- ▶ If you have them, put on TouchPoints 30 minutes prior to get yourself into a state of neuroplasticity.
- ▶ Meditate for ten minutes to prepare your mind to focus on the task at hand, especially the first time you do this exercise.
- ▶ Read through the process multiple times before you try it. After time, it will be second nature and you can do it at a moment's notice when you need it.

If you would like a copy of the audio recording in which I take you through it step by step, visit www.areyouunstoppable.com to download a recorded version of this process you can add to your daily playlist. Check out the sidebar for a Quickfire Visualization technique you can start today.

Repeat this exercise daily after revising your goals for the day ahead. It is vital that you visualize yourself overcoming any challenges you may face along the way so your brain is prepared to deal with them calmly. You may find that your day flows more smoothly and you get more done in less time. Instead of spending all your time stressing over what might be, you instead focus on what can be. In this state, your mind is calm and rational, and you can handle problems easily. By snapping your fingers, or by making another gesture, you're anchoring that mental state with a physical gesture. This comes in handy when you're in the midst of doing the activity you've rehearsed. Simply snap your fingers, and you'll access those same emotions.

QUICKFIRE VISUALIZATION

(approximately five to ten minutes daily)

STEP 1: Get Quiet

Find a quiet place where you will not be disturbed for at least ten minutes, close your eyes, and take several deep and calming breaths.

STEP 2: Visualize the Upcoming Event

In your mind's eye, picture an upcoming event or goal on a TV in front of you that may be causing you stress or making you feel overwhelmed. Perhaps there's an event coming up where you need to perform at your best. It could be a major project or simply the activities you have scheduled for the day ahead that you want to complete on time.

STEP 3: What Do You See, Feel, Hear?

Think about it to the point that you start to feel some discomfort. What do you see, hear, feel, smell, and taste?

STEP 4: Manipulate the Image

Now, shrink that image down and place it on a screen, about the size of an iPhone, a few meters in front of you. Turn the image to black and white and take it out of focus.

STEP 5: Dissociate

Imagine floating out of your body and standing behind yourself. You're watching yourself watch yourself on the TV in the distance.

STEP 6: Rewind the Movie

Rewind the movie until just before this event, when you were laughing and having fun and everything was perfect. Really see it and feel it.

STEP 7: Fast-Forward the Movie

Then fast-forward through the event, seeing what you're seeing, hearing what you're hearing, and feeling what you're feeling. Picture yourself doing

QUICKFIRE VISUALIZATION, continued

what you need to do and everything going smoothly, not just around this event, but a day, week, month, and year into the future after the event is over.

Pause this image and turn it into color. Turn up the colors, sounds, and feelings of success to 10 out of 10. Take it from 2D to 3D. What do you see, hear, feel, taste, and touch? When you hit level 10, snap your fingers to anchor these feelings to a gesture.

STEP 8: Rewind the Movie

Now rapidly rewind this event, going as fast as you can, seeing what you're seeing, hearing what you're hearing, and feeling what you're feeling, until you're back at the start just before the event happened and you're laughing and happy again. Turn up the volume on these feelings and snap your fingers when you hit level 10 in intensity.

STEP 9: Step Into the TV

Step into the TV and actively visualize yourself doing what you want to do, everything unfolding exactly as you want it to. See yourself overcoming any challenges that may come your way with ease and grace until, once again, you're back at an image of success with a smile on your face. Amplify the volume on these feelings until you hit level 10, then snap your fingers.

STEP 10: Rewind/Fast-Forward

Rewind the event, fast-forward it, rewind it and fast-forward. Do it faster and faster each time. Repeat this at least 10 times and snap your fingers every time you reach either end of the timeline.

That's it! You're now ready to go about your day.

I have used this exercise for every book I have written. On the days I forget to do it, I write 50 percent less. My brain isn't prepared for the focus I need to get it done. This exercise will become your cornerstone for productivity and help you unlock your mental capacity in less than ten minutes per day.

Back to the Fire Walk ...

I made a fist to draw power into my body and mind. Then, with my head up, I began walking. Seconds in, I broke my state of concentration! Just as I was about to panic out of fear of getting burned, I snapped back into saying, "Cool moss, cool moss, cool moss," the auditory anchor Tony had successfully programmed into me. At the end of the fire walk, someone hosed my feet off with water to ensure I didn't have any hot coals stuck to them. One foot felt particularly hot, and I thought I had burned myself, but thankfully I hadn't. It took me a while to process what had just happened.

By using a powerful anchoring technique and mental rehearsal, we had put our minds into a state in which we could do something few of us thought possible. The fire walk demonstrated just how powerful simulating an event in our minds can be. By setting real intentions of making change and simulating that experience repeatedly in the safety of our minds, we can go beyond ourselves and close our identity gap between what we used to think was possible and what actually is possible.

What if you're not clear on your goals or you haven't been able to hear your soul's purpose yet? How would you use this exercise? It's simple: See yourself coming to the realization that you know what you're going to focus on. You don't actually have to know what that is just yet; you just have to see yourself realizing it's finally possible. As you're about to discover, many of us have buried our purpose out of fear and put our bodies into self-preservation mode. Well, it's time to turn off self-preservation mode, uncover your deeper purpose, and give yourself an even stronger reason to achieve your goals.

PART IV

YOUR PATH TO BECOMING
UNSTOPPABLE

CHAPTER 9

Uncovering Your Purpose
Upgrading Your Vision, Motivation, and Drive to Succeed

As I walked around the creek that wove its way through the family farm, I was hit with an epiphany. I knew I was destined for something meaningful—I just didn't know what. I was a spry ten-year-old farm boy at the time, and that was my earliest memory of longing for a life with meaning. Something to live for, stand by, and leave as a legacy. The shape it was going to take eluded me until my early 30s.

I had tried everything: metal sculpture, writing, music, fitness, life coaching, hosting monthly business-to-business events, consulting, and professional speaking. I went to the buffet of life and tasted everything to see what I loved and what I didn't care for. Each new challenge brought new excitement and experiences along with it, as well as a hit of dopamine each time. After a while, though, that excitement faded, and I was left with a lack of focus, drive, and motivation again. It took me many years to understand that purpose isn't fixed; it's fluid. Sometimes it flows freely, while other times it's a trickle.

Clinging to the idea that we are meant to do one thing for the rest of our lives is as absurd as walking around in the same pair of shoes until we die. The soles are going to wear thin until our feet are bare and bleeding, and we need to put on a new pair, get back up, and continue on our way.

We live in a society that expects each of us to name, claim, and die by one path alone. This can create great internal conflict and lead to frustration when we experience lulls where nothing excites us and happiness is elusive. At this point, we require a new way of thinking when it comes to finding purpose and meaning that evolves as we do and helps us achieve new levels of success. To do so, we must understand how identity, happiness, and purpose intersect and shape our daily experiences, driving us to achieve new goals.

To become a Catalyst, we know we must recharge our batteries with both biochemical and psychological/spiritual energy to light our vision. Purpose underpins psychological energy and helps reignite sparks that may have faded to an ember.

In March 2017, my spark was ready to go out. I didn't know what I wanted anymore, and I was ready to give up on everything. I kept asking myself the same question: "What's the point of all this?" It was going to take more than just a biochemical shift. I also needed to remind myself of my purpose, become aware of the identity I had taken on, and realize the identity I wanted to evolve into.

Our identity, the person we believe ourselves to be, dictates what we strive for and how we strive for it. Our purpose also dictates how our identity shifts. Even if you know what your purpose is, you must still shed old identities that no longer serve you. This is the never-ending cycle of life: a sudden shift of attitude and a longing for something more. Old goals and identities become no longer as relevant or meaningful to us as they once were.

This is the identity gap in action. When we finally evolve into the person we always hoped we would become, we may experience sadness because one journey has come to an end. It is the completion of a chapter in our lives. We may feel restless because we have nothing left to strive for. We experience our greatest happiness in this process of unfolding and becoming, in the beautiful gray area between who you are right now and who you are becoming. This is the area in which we must choose to consciously revel in and allow ourselves to be unapologetic creators of our own lives. When one journey ends, another must begin, otherwise we're struck with a lack of motivation, drive, and will to succeed.

Are You Standing Barefoot?

Finding your purpose is like slipping on a brand-new pair of shoes, lacing them up, and taking them out for a test drive. You may wear them for a while, but if it's not the right fit, you exchange them for a new pair. When it comes to your purpose, this process can take many years. But with each new pair you try on, you're adding to the cumulative experience that will lead you to your next adventure.

Every one of us comes to a crossroads multiple times in our lives when we will, once again, question whether our life has any meaning. The moment we feel stuck is the moment we end up standing at a crossroads. At this point, you will hold one of two identities that will influence how long you remain stuck there:

▸ Identity of a person *with a purpose*
▸ Identity of a person *without a purpose*

To completely transform into a Catalyst, we must clarify our current purpose and determine what meaning we ascribe to it. A Catalyst has a strong sense of purpose, as does a Synergist. That's not to say Defenders and Guardians don't have a purpose, but their biochemistry wants to turn left when their soul is desperately trying to turn right. This is the reason for the identity gap formula's existence. It recharges your battery when you're low on energy and lights up various goals (light bulbs) so you can narrow your focus toward them. It is the intangible momentum that pulls you forward, especially when your biochemistry is dragging you down into being a Defender or Guardian.

Without a purpose, you just plod along, like the countless millions living in limbo. People who hold the identity of an individual without a purpose have, consciously or unconsciously, chosen this identity. They've pushed their purpose so far down that all they can say to themselves is, "I don't know what I want to do." This gets stuck on repeat and becomes habitual. So despite opportunities landing in their lap that would be perfect for them, they repeat their preprogrammed response. This is the blind spot of their life. This response could have been triggered by any one of the following reasons:

1. The new goal requires significant change and energy, so it gets eliminated, especially when they are in Guardian or Defender mode and their brain is preserving any energy it has left over for vital bodily functions. This is why I didn't talk about purpose at the start of the book. Until we clear your path from any biochemical and cognitive challenges that may prevent your purpose from revealing itself, it can be incredibly hard for you to find it. Your brain hides your purpose out of fear that it will cost you your life, no matter how ridiculous that may seem to your logical/rational mind.

2. They are too scared to claim the goal. They can see or have seen what is possible, but because the goal sits so far outside their comfort zone, their fight/flight response is triggered, and they snap back into their current identity, in which they feel safe.

3. They are in a state of contraction, not expansion. When we're on a mission, every element of our being is geared toward expansion, or becoming more of who we are. At other times, we need to contract, cull whatever isn't important, and withdraw from life. This allows us to take stock of who we are, what we want, and where we're going next. Simply recognizing that you're in a state of contraction can give you the breathing space for your next project to reveal itself to you. The only time it doesn't is when you're too busy beating yourself up for not knowing what you want.

In the final stages of becoming unstoppable and closing the identity gap, we must first recognize we are constantly in a state of personal evolution. When we are born, we have twice as many synaptic connections in our brain as we have when we're grown. Our brain prunes our synaptic connections back to become more efficient (contraction). Children's brains are far more creative because they're experimenting with different configurations before settling on a specific structure. This reflects how we uncover our life purpose, through self-exploration and never-ending pruning, until we finally get to the essence of what we want to experience.

People with Purpose Are More Optimistic, Achieve Their Goals More Often, and Are Less Likely to Fail

Social studies have shown that people with a greater sense of purpose sleep better, have better sex, and live longer.

A year-long study showed that alcoholics were less likely to return to heavy drinking six months post-treatment if their sense of purpose increased during treatment. In addition, people experienced fewer sleep disturbances if they had a higher sense of purpose.[1, 2]

In a second survey of 999 entrepreneurs we conducted internationally, we found that people who had a strong sense of purpose achieved their goals 70 percent of the time as opposed to those who didn't have a sense of purpose, who said they only achieved their goals 6 percent of the time. I suspect this is because individuals with an overarching purpose were clearer on their overall direction each day and knew what they wanted to do. This increased the likelihood of success by narrowing their focus. Furthermore, we also uncovered the following intriguing findings (see Figure 9.1 on page 184).

People who had a strong sense of purpose vs. those who didn't:

- ▶ Were afraid of failing: 56 percent vs. 87 percent
- ▶ Doubted themselves: 52 percent vs. 87 percent
- ▶ Agreed to procrastinating: 72 percent vs. 95 percent
- ▶ Were optimistic about reaching their goals: 96 percent vs. 69 percent
- ▶ Had the mental stamina required to reach their goals: 93 percent vs. 59 percent

While this doesn't prove cause and effect, it does indicate a relationship between a strong sense of purpose and fear of failure,

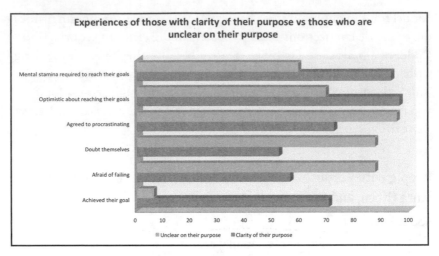

Figure 9.1 Clarity of Purpose vs. Lack of Clarity

doubt, procrastination, optimism, and mental stamina. I hypothesize that people without a clear purpose have no real beacon through which to channel their energy, making them more susceptible to doubting themselves, procrastinating, being less optimistic about reaching their goals, and lacking the required mental stamina to achieve them.

What Type of Well-Being Is Your Purpose Derived From? It Matters More Than You Think

It isn't just the psychological benefits we gain from having a strong sense of purpose that matter; it's the biological ones as well. In fact, a 2013 study by Steven Cole at the University of California, Los Angeles, delved into how having a purpose can affect our gene expression. To study this, Cole focused on two types of well-being:[3]

1. *Hedonic*: Derived from pleasure and rewards. This is based on how often an individual felt happy.
2. *Eudaemonic*: Derived from having a purpose beyond self-gratification; e.g., having a good sense of direction.

Cole measured this by having participants write down their well-being over the previous week, how often they felt happy (hedonic), or when their life had a sense of direction (eudaemonic). He found that even though individuals who scored highly on one area often scored highly on the other, both correlated to people having lower levels of depression.

But people with hedonic well-being had high expression of inflammatory genes and lower expression of genes for disease-fighting antibodies. This pattern is also seen in individuals who experience loneliness and stress. For individuals deriving eudaemonic well-being from an overall sense of direction in life, their biology looked completely different. Cole suspects eudaemonia, with its focus on purpose, decreases our nervous system's fight/flight response. This could be because when people are told to focus on something of value, the brain region called the ventral striatum is activated. This can help inhibit the amygdala, which promotes the fight/flight response. Research has also shown higher scores on a scale of purpose correlated with less amygdala activation.[4]

What does all this mean for you to ensure you reach your outcomes? There are greater health benefits from deriving purpose beyond self-gratification and having an overall sense of direction. In other words, reaching for something greater than yourself and having a clearer direction in life can decrease the fight/flight response and help us lead a life with less fear. As we've discovered, managing this aspect of the brain can help us experience greater mental clarity, become less emotional, and think strategically through situations and challenges, leading to better outcomes.

All the entrepreneurs and experts I interviewed on this journey had strong senses of purpose that drove them to pursue their goals. All of them, initially born out of an individual need to feel better (hedonic), evolved into a mission to help others succeed (eudaemonic). It is as if the only way we can find our sense of direction is first by focusing on ourselves. Once we're happy, we have enough energy to help others. Our sense of well-being flips into an identity that's biologically healthier for us. When we're not nourished, there's barely enough energy for us to function, let alone focus on assisting others for the greater good.

Is this evolution's way of driving us to help others by providing biological benefits to altruism? Who knows? What we do know is that you must pass through the first phase of helping yourself to get to the second phase of helping others. It's all part of learning who we are and what we stand for.

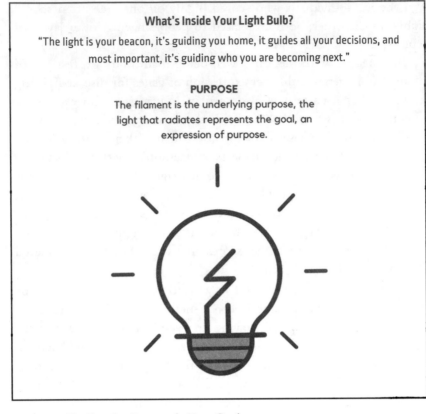

What's Inside Your Light Bulb?

"The light is your beacon, it's guiding you home, it guides all your decisions, and most important, it's guiding who you are becoming next."

PURPOSE
The filament is the underlying purpose, the light that radiates represents the goal, an expression of purpose.

Figure 9.2 **Finding the Purpose in Your Goals**

Some of us may already be clear on what our purpose is; others, not. Whichever camp you fit into, to achieve success and light a magnetic beacon that draws you in, you must have clarity on what that vision looks like and what underpins it. In the identity gap framework, the filament in the light bulb is the underlying purpose, the essence of how you want to feel. The goals (the light emitted) are an expression of your purpose. This light radiates in all directions, with different goals representing each beam. We have many beams of light shining from us because it is human nature to express the essence of who we are in many different ways. Goals will evolve over time, but as long as they are an expression of our purpose, we'll be on task and in powerful alignment. (See Figure 9.2.)

We often feel torn in two directions when the goal doesn't match the underlying purpose. Something feels off, but we can't always put our finger on what that is. To align these two elements, we use a combination of NLP techniques to tease it out and amplify it so we're strongly drawn to it. If you already know your purpose and your goals, I want you to pay even closer attention. We're going to turn up the volume on them so that you experience spontaneous behavior changes and overcome any challenges that may be holding you back from a psychological standpoint. If you're completely unsure of what your purpose is, by doing the following activities, you should gain a sense of relief and become clearer on what your purpose is and what you stand for. It is only through this experience that you switch from hedonic to eudaemonic well-being. When and how you do it is part of your personal journey. There are no set rules. You'll get there when you're good and ready.

The Tipping Point of Knowing

The "tipping point of knowing" is a mental state in which you may or may not have some idea about your purpose. It's bubbling just under the surface of the water. We need to free that bubble so it floats to the top and expresses itself.

Before we can uncover your purpose or find greater meaning in the sense of direction some of us already have, we need to get into a calm state so we can access our rational mind. We want to avoid engaging our fight/flight response, as that will affect the way you see your desires. If fight/flight is engaged, you may begin telling yourself, *it will never happen/It's too hard/I don't have the money/I haven't got the resources/I'm not smart enough*.

By proactively putting yourself into your logical/rational mind, you'll give your creative mind the space to explore so you can get to the essence of who you are and what you want. Your mind will be open and you'll access your intuition, free from fear and mistrust, where things will unfold exactly how they need to. Check out the sidebar on page 188 for another great exercise you can try, this time to uncover your purpose.

You could do a thousand different things, and as long as your goals are an expression of your purpose, you'll be on purpose, happy, and connected. The form and name your purpose takes in your life is unimportant. You can call it whatever you want, and you can allow it to take many different forms—in fact, I encourage

UNCOVERING YOUR PURPOSE AND LIGHTING YOUR BEACON

(Illuminate the Path Ahead of You)

STEP 1: Begin by doing the Quickfire Visualization you learned in Chapter 8. You want to reprogram your mind so it is open to the possibility of knowing your purpose, goals, and next project. This includes refining an existing goal to amplify it so it is intensely desirable and drives unconscious behavior change. You can do this by visualizing yourself coming to an awareness, acknowledging that you knew your purpose all along. You need to visualize that light bulb moment in which you have a blinding flash of the obvious.

When you do this visualization, see what you see, hear what you hear, and feel what you feel. Describe what this light bulb moment looks like. What are you wearing? Where are you when it hits you? What colors do you see? Who else is with you? What are you doing? What can you smell? How do you feel? Where do you feel it within your body? What facial expression do you have?

Be playful here. Allow your soul to take you wherever it wants to go in your mind's eye. Put your favorite music on in the background. Music can make us feel sexy, liberated, free, relaxed, or powerful. Pick something that perfectly suits how you want to feel when your purpose is revealed to you. Use this music to help you evolve into a person who knows what their purpose is; or, if you already know, allow it to give you an even stronger sense of power and meaning.

STEP 2: Once you've visualized yourself becoming aware of what your purpose/next project is, in a place free from distractions, ask yourself:

▶ How do you want to feel on a daily/weekly/monthly/yearly basis? Some examples for how you might want to feel include: empowered, adventurous, challenged, entrepreneurial, rebellious, connected, freed, unstoppable, unleashed, motivated, driven, abundant, rich, happy, connected, accomplished, generous, creative, calm, relaxed.

UNCOVERING, continued

▶ Revel in these feelings and turn up the volume on them until you hit 10 out of 10. What is it like to experience these feelings? Let them guide you to where you need to go. They are your road map to awareness.

▶ Now list the top four emotions you want to experience on a daily/weekly/monthly/yearly basis. This is your purpose. Write them down here:

1. _____

2. _____

3. _____

4. _____

STEP 3: While you're in a state of flow, answer the following questions. Don't think, just write as quickly as you can. This is how you express your purpose. Allow your higher self to take over.

▶ What motivates you?

▶ What are you drawn to?

▶ What makes you excited?

▶ What can't you stop thinking about?

▶ Where are your thoughts guiding you to?

▶ What can you see, hear, feel, taste, or touch?

▶ If you could do anything you wanted to do next, what would it be? What else? Just keep writing as long as you can.

▶ What skills do you have or would love to have that light a fire inside you?

▶ How are you expressing yourself through the skills you are applying?

▶ How does the application of these skills make you feel?

If you get stuck on any of these questions, ask yourself: If I did know, what would the answer be?

UNCOVERING, continued

STEP 4: Now we're going to combine the previous two steps.

▸ When you look at the top four emotions you would like to experience on a regular basis and the skills you would like to express through your work, do they align?

▸ Can you experience those feelings through those skills? If not, answer the questions again until the feelings you most want to embody at your core can be produced via your current skills, or the skills you plan to acquire.

▸ Finally, think of a time you felt really dissatisfied with your work: Were you experiencing those four emotions? No? Interesting.

it. To limit yourself is to deprive yourself of experiences that will lead you to a greater understanding of who you are becoming. I haven't named my purpose because my purpose is to experience my core emotions, including adventure, generosity, abundance, and challenges that allow me to grow. How I express those emotions can come through in a myriad of ways and take countless shapes throughout my lifetime. Becoming fixated on only one way of expressing yourself does a disservice to who you are as an individual. Ask yourself: Am I ready for my purpose to reveal itself? When you can answer with a resounding yes, it will hit you with a blinding flash of the obvious that you knew what it was all along.

When I realized this, I was finally free. Everything I had ever experienced culminated in the work I do today. The music I used to create on the computer gave me the skills I use to edit my cinematic videos. Developing online educational programs for entrepreneurs nurtured my creative side and allowed me to grow my brand and continually educate myself. Studying fitness at a young age has applied to this entire project, especially the four-week CrossFit challenge. Writing allows me to express myself in various ways that challenge me, give me a sense of abundance, and allow me to be generous by providing practical information that other people can use to make their lives better. This has expanded in recent years to helping others freely and without fee to reach their goals.

The medium in which I express my four core emotions will **continue** to evolve. Just because music was played on vinyl, then cassette, then CD, and now digital, doesn't mean it fundamentally changes what it is at its core. The essence of the expression of art through the artist remains the same. The medium through which it is expressed simply changes.

As long as my goals are an expression of my purpose, I will feel that I'm doing what I'm meant to do. I know that whenever I feel off-purpose, all I need to ask myself is: Am I expressing myself through my four core emotions? If I'm not, it's time for a reboot and a rethink. This might include a new project that will fulfill them, likely in an exciting new way that I have not tried before.

How to Use Progressive Overload to Become an Upgraded Version of Yourself

When people first realize that their emotions are at the core of their being and the guiding hand for their beacon, they can become overwhelmed. Suddenly a state of panic ensues. *What if I can't make this work? I don't have the money to get this business off the ground! I don't know if I've got what it takes to do what I have to do!* This is a normal part of growing as an individual. And, just like we discussed in Chapter 2 about preventing the snapback effect of getting thrown back into your old routine and your old identity, we need a new technique to stop it in its tracks. This is where progressive overload (PO) comes into play. PO is a technique used in strength training where you periodically increase the weight, intensity, or duration of an exercise to stimulate new muscle growth. You do it gradually over a period of time so the body has time to rest, recover, and grow. The body adapts to the change over time, so the increase doesn't cause a shock to the system or inflict real muscle damage. I have applied this same technique when I am in the process of evolving into a new identity. Here's how it works.

1. *Choose your next three major projects or goals.* I work in 13-week increments and focus on three major goals in that period. It's short enough to remain excited and not so long that momentum

is lost. Focusing on three goals during this process is manageable. I break them down into smaller goals on a weekly basis.

2. *Identify the "educational gaps" you need to fill to make this project possible.* For example, online marketing, public speaking, health, well-being, writing, product creation, starting a business, improving a relationship.

3. *Pick your educational resources.* Search for the top podcasts, YouTube videos, authors, educators, and experts within these educational gaps and then make a list you can reference. Listen to one podcast per day while showering, driving to work, or going for a walk. Sign up for online or in-person courses. Watch YouTube videos to fill a gap in knowledge and read or listen to books when you're working out. Keep a notebook close at hand so you can jot down ideas on the go or record them on a recording app on your cell phone. Do this weeks or even months before you start your project. This way, you will be progressively overloading your brain with new information that will force you to grow, and you will be primed to bring your project/goal to life. Once your educational gaps are filled, the fear of not knowing how to bring your goal to fruition suddenly disappears, excuses fade away, and you act without needing willpower to overcome fear. That doesn't mean you won't still occasionally be afraid, but now you'll have the techniques to deal with it.

4. *Decide who you need to become to reach these goals.* Do you need to be educated, empowered, fulfilled, confident, self-assured, motivated, driven?

5. *Do the Quickfire Visualization on a daily basis to prime your brain for the overall direction you are heading in.* Visualize the person you are becoming, the attainment of your goals, and the ease and joy you will experience along the way. Visualize as well any challenges you may encounter and effectively manage with style and grace. This allows you to grow into the person you're becoming and prime your mind for the changes you need to make, instead of throwing yourself out there, only to return right back to where you started like a boomerang. For my first book, I would stand

in front of the mirror nightly for months before I ever began writing and hold someone else's book in my hands with my eyes closed, visualizing it was my completed book. It mentally prepared me for the work ahead.

Enjoy this experience. This is the consolidation phase before the expansion phase, where everything you've learned will get put to practical use. At that point you cross the threshold from your old self to your new self, but thanks to progressive overload, the transition will feel natural and easy.

What Will Make Your Soul Happy Today?

I was staring at a dead body!

In February 2017, I visited New York for two months at the height of winter to get a feel for what it would be like to live in this incredible city. Having lived through Hurricane Sandy, I already knew it wasn't always going to be easy, but I was still excited about fulfilling a lifelong goal of relocating from Australia to the Big Apple. One day as I was walking through Bryant Park to grab lunch, I heard sirens from the emergency trucks screaming down the street on the other side of the park. On my way back to the co-working office, I came across the dead man. Five emergency personnel were standing a meter back from a middle-aged man face up on the freezing cold ground dusted with the previous day's snowfall. He was dressed in a gray suit, and his skin was blue; all color had drained from his face. It was clear they had given up trying to resuscitate him. It took me a while to shake this picture from my mind. It's not every day you see a dead body.

As we work toward our goals, there will be experiences that will catch us by surprise and possibly derail us from our journey. It is up to each of us to choose the right time to either pursue our goals or fall back and consolidate. Now isn't always the right time. When you are living in a state of constant fight/flight it becomes impossible to function normally, let alone access your intuition and trust that everything will work out perfectly. You will make decisions from fear, not logic. There will be times when you are faced with a challenge, and you have to ask yourself if it's worth it to keep going or if you should take a breather and reboot. The only person who has the answer to this question is you.

Remember, while fortune may favor the bold, it doesn't favor the dead. A purpose worth living for shouldn't put you in an early grave; it should nourish every part of your being. At times, it will challenge, test, and yes, even break you.

But there's only one question I want you to ask yourself: What will make your soul happy today? If the answer is rest, then rest. If it is to passionately pursue your goal, then pursue it. Just don't force yourself to do something when your gut is telling you now is not the right time, because there will be a right time. That time is when everything aligns and the need for willpower disappears. In our culture that applauds people working to the point of collapse, we need to follow our intuition and do what is right for us, not for others.

And, keeping that in mind, it's time to come up with your personalized 90-day plan to biohack your way to an unstoppable you, on your terms—no one else's.

CHAPTER 10

13 Weeks to Unstoppable
Your Personalized Plan

The New York skyline finally came into focus. After four years of working toward moving to Manhattan, I had signed a lease on an apartment. Writing the end of this book in one of my favorite buildings in the world, the New York Public Library at Bryant Park, a 15-minute walk from where I now live.

As I look up from my heavy wooden chair, I'm taken aback by the rich design and history of the building. The wood craftsmanship and the spectacularly arched windows that flood the room with light, even on a dark Manhattan day, inspire me to be better than myself. I still pinch myself when I realize I'd made it to New York City, especially considering I was on the verge of a mental breakdown less than 12 months ago and could barely string a coherent piece of writing together three months ago.

Moving to the Big Apple had been repeatedly delayed due to my health issues. These issues stunted my business growth, kept me from speaking onstage, and stopped me from consulting with clients one on one because I constantly felt exhausted and depressed. They prevented me from having any mental clarity, focus, and drive, leading to suicidal thoughts.

I was a Defender who desperately wanted to become a Catalyst. My identity gap was expansive, and it was going to take significant willpower to make the changes required to turn my mental and physical health around. At the start of this journey, I questioned my ability to get answers. My doctors could never pinpoint the underlying causes, offering only vague suggestions from a lack of evidence and limited openness to the latest research. Or, worse yet, no suggestions at all.

I began to question my own integrity. How could I solve this problem if the so-called experts can't? Who was I to write on a broad selection of health topics when my health was at its worst? I didn't have any credentials in any of these fields, aside from personal development. But ironically, that put me in the perfect position to delve into this arena.

Many who have been on this journey are so far detached from where they began, through doubt and lack of energy, they become overwhelmed on how to find answers. Their biochemistry must be pointed in the same direction as their underlying purpose so they are fully and completely living in alignment and living unleashed.

I had to try every possible option I could within a 13-week time frame in rapid succession, while still being able to pinpoint which attempted solution led to which result. While I don't claim my experience was a rigorous academic or scientific study, nor that everyone will get the same results, it was fascinating to see how at this fast pace, the answers came hard and fast. If I had spaced the tests and trials out over a lengthier period, the results would have come too slow to connect the dots between the actions I took and the outcome, or lack of outcome, that followed. I would have experienced progress in some areas but not others and lost momentum and hope. If certain areas weren't addressed in conjunction with others, they would drag any newfound results back down. I was tired of struggling to find the answers and break free from inadequate medical diagnoses. I had already spent more than 20 years on this problem to varying degrees, and I didn't fancy spending another 20 on it. I wanted more, but I knew I needed to do it in a way that was sustainable. And I know you want more too, right?

The Results of My 13-Week Mission to Become Unstoppable

The biggest changes from my 13-week mission to biohack my way to unstoppable were well beyond what I was expecting. As you can see in Figure 10.1, my body changed. In my first 30 days of the CrossFit

Figure 10.1 **The Physical Result**

challenge, I didn't just gain muscle, but cut my body fat from 16 percent to 13 percent, a number that had eluded me for years. I could also lift heavier and felt healthier for doing so. I experienced less muscle soreness when I pushed myself harder, and I could break through mental hurdles in the gym with greater ease.

I rid myself of the need to use my asthma medication by addressing candida, an inhaler that could have triggered the candida, a vitamin D deficiency, a gut imbalance, and more. This was an unexpected outcome that has truly changed my life. I no longer experience the anxiety I used to feel when I couldn't breathe properly.

My energy continues to improve to this day. Even if I am tired, I can still get work done without the need to exert willpower or beat myself up for not doing better. Writing this book in four months, especially with the countless studies I cited and interviews that had to be conducted, is testament to my newfound mental clarity and ability to focus. I can easily enter a state of mental flow I was never able to achieve previously, and work at a faster pace.

I feel more connected to who I am, and my relationships are deeper and more meaningful. I'm no longer as guarded, or experiencing worry or fear, or waking up in the middle of the night, unable to get back to sleep. My experiences of feeling overwhelmed have vanished. I love the challenge of a deadline again without feeling swamped by it. Many friends have told me how much wittier I am now. They see a spark in me that even I hadn't seen since my mid-twenties. I sometimes get emotional, realizing how much of my life has been wasted in a state of constant fatigue and bouts of depression. I will let go of this feeling in time.

This has been unlike any project I have ever encountered: gut-wrenching and personal beyond belief. I understand my body better and know that if I am feeling flat or tired, I can pinpoint it to a specific cause and correct course. I can record my weekly videos without a script and often get them in one take. I am excited for the first time in years to hit the speaking circuit again, knowing I will remember everything I need to say, and more. I feel liberated knowing that I can separate the cause from the effect, identify whether it is a biochemical or psychological challenge holding me back, and take action to rectify it without beating myself up. Most profound of all, I no longer feel depressed. My moods have evened out. If something catches me off guard, I am able to stop and think it through without turning on self-preservation mode. I still make use of the wearable technology I tried out when I was writing this book. It keeps me in check.

Could all this change? Absolutely! Life changes and evolves as I do, and as I am presented with new challenges. The difference is I have the tools to take in stride whatever comes my way. Now you do, too!

It's Not Just Me: More Successes

After my countless conversations with biohackers, neuroscientists, medical directors, doctors, and gut/brain health experts, I have devised a 13-week plan encompassing the best, most comprehensive way to biohack your way to unstoppable, a plan based on countless discussions, experiments, and consultations. This includes strategies from medical, self-help, nutritional, and therapeutic models to create a plan that covers all bases and leaves no stone unturned, no matter what your starting point. Most critically, this plan encourages an evidence-based approach to becoming unstoppable by seeking out a functional doctor where possible to help guide you on your journey. The collection of data is core to becoming unstoppable. Taking easy-to-do medical tests that can validate your experience is at the heart of uncovering anything holding you back from closing the gap between who you are and who you are becoming.

Living through this 13-week mission while actively having to solve lifelong problems allowed me to connect with others facing the same struggles in a deeply unique way. They watched with bated breath as I took various nootropics, interviewed experts, and wore the latest wearable technology in search of answers. And many became willing guinea pigs, who wanted to not only partake, but also share their experiences or their patients' successes. Some of their stories follow.

Stephanie

Stephanie, who you read about briefly in Chapter 5, was a Defender when I first met her. This changed rapidly after she added MCT oil, prebiotics, probiotics, and L-Tyrosine to her routine, along with cutting highly processed sugars and carbs from her diet to increase her energy. She obliterated her brain fog that clouded her judgment and overcame the debilitating depression that had been ruling her life for years. She underwent a candida diet protocol to reset her digestive system after discovering she exhibited every symptom of an intestinal fungal overgrowth, something she had never considered previously. (Note that a candida diet isn't right for everyone, which is why it's critical to personalize your plan.)

Stephanie shared, "After incorporating the candida diet into my life and adding some much-needed supplements, I felt a significant improvement! After the initial tiredness that comes from 'detoxing,' I felt much more calm and level-headed, more in control of my emotions, and less anxious. It was shocking to see what a significant impact food was having on my mental state. Physically, I felt *so* much better. Less bloated, the constant acid feeling in my stomach started to disappear, and I was sleeping better at night. Making such a huge change was *not* easy, I am not going to pretend it was. But for me, the benefits have completely outweighed the struggle!"

Adam

My lifelong best mate Adam, after being put on multiple hypertension medications, suddenly gained 30 pounds (13.6 kilograms) in less than three months. Adam had become a Defender, just like Stephanie, it just manifested in a different way. The medication caused him to become lethargic, emotional, and depressed; he was on the verge of taking antidepressants to address these side effects, a vicious circle many find themselves in. After seeking the advice of a functional doctor, he discovered other underlying causes that had been affecting his blood pressure and emotions. The doctor recommended an additional supplement regimen, and he began immediately. I noticed the difference in Adam within a week. He sounded alert and happy for the first time in months.

He said, "I certainly don't have anywhere near as much apathy as I did a few months ago. I'm now actively doing things like seeing a personal trainer at the gym for a session last week, cleaning out stuff around home properly, and doing things that I'd been putting off for far too long."

After taking a food sensitivity test, Adam also discovered that he was highly sensitive to eggs. Adam wasn't alone. A 1979 study of 15 hypertensive people who reacted to different combinations of foods like wheat, eggs, dairy, beef, oranges, corn, cane sugar, and yeast showed that their blood pressure regulated after removing those foods from their eating plans. The same study found that everyone with migraine headaches also saw those disappear after they stopped eating the reactive foods (migraines are commonly triggered by food allergies).[1] I asked Adam if he thought his egg consumption could be linked to the intense migraines he had experienced throughout his life. I have seen him throw up at their onset, call in sick, and stay in bed for days until they passed.

He responded, "Yes! I was eating anywhere from two to five eggs per day when I was doing CrossFit. I was having semi- or full-blown migraines every two to three months on average. Some had me out of action for a couple of days at a time. Since I fell out of that dietary routine and significantly cut down the consumption of eggs, I haven't had a migraine in about 12 months!" As I write this, Adam is still on hypertension medication, but it is not affecting him like it was before because he has addressed other nutritional deficiencies that were contributing to his fatigue and depression. Adam is now on track to reduce his hypertension medication as his blood pressure has begun to normalize in recent weeks.

Trisha

Trisha Hothorn, a licensed clinical social worker and a key advisor who always enthusiastically answered my questions as I went through this journey, shared a story of a patient of hers. M.I., a bright, well-educated,

50-year-old woman who worked as a CFO in several large corporations, was diagnosed by Trisha with anxiety and depression. M.I. chose not to add medication to her cognitive behavioral therapy, which focused on her daily difficulties in life.

Trisha shared that in therapy, although M.I. could develop insight about how her own behavior and expectations were connected to her "failures" (as she called them), she took that insight no further than to blame herself. She lacked motivation and energy to act on the changes that she cognitively understood would benefit her—and her pattern of "failed" life experiences continued to the point of suicide ideation last year.

Trisha said, "M.I. was followed by a family physician who noted no concerns over many years about her frequent illnesses and self-reported unhappiness and depression. M.I. sought out medical care at a 'doc in the box' clinic one weekend and was lucky enough to be treated by a wide-thinking physician's assistant, who, after taking a thorough history of her frequent illnesses—respiratory, GI—talked with her about the importance of vitamin D and suggested she seek testing and consider adding vitamin D to her daily routine. M.I. started vitamin D (1,000 IU) on her own and stated she felt different in a week! She reported more ability to concentrate and more emotional and physical energy in all areas of life. She did schedule an appointment with her own doctor, who agreed to test her D level, but suggested she stop taking it because it could cause liver damage. M.I. did not stop because she felt so much better. When the test came back, it showed M.I. had negligible traces of D in her system, even after weeks of taking 1,000 units. Her physician advised her to double her dosage!

In the weeks that followed, M.I. could do things she could only think about in the past ten years. She decided that she was unhappy in the financial corporate world. She gave notice of termination to her present employer and created her own LLC. She decided that she wanted to move closer to her family (with whom she had also broken emotional ties). She has reconnected with friends (after years of solitary life and seclusion) and is already much happier and more confident.

"I continue to provide supportive counseling for M.I., and it is truly overwhelming to see the changes that this patient has been able to make and the changes in her quality of life with one change—the addition of vitamin D to her daily routine. The energy that she now brings to her therapy sessions is truly extraordinary, and she can see life with much less self-reproach. Going forward, I have decided I will include vitamin D level assessment as a part of my baseline evaluations of my patients."

Derya

Always the picture of perfect health, Derya Gul, a friend from Melbourne, Australia, had never experienced any major health concerns until June 2017. She began slurring her words and experiencing hair loss, dry skin, premature aging, chronic fatigue, insomnia, low libido, unexplained bruising, intermittent hearing loss, brain fog, memory loss, muscle pain and weakness, swollen tongue, vertigo, sharp stabbing pains, depression, anxiety, and uncontrollable mood swings. Working as a flight cabin crew member, she attributed it to the fatigue of working long hours and went to her local general practitioner (GP).

She shared her experience on Facebook to serve as a warning to others:

> *Appointments with GPs got me absolutely nowhere. I had been exposed to first-round MRIs, endless amounts of blood testing, urine testing, endless amounts of physical neurological testing, all because I presented with symptoms of having MS (multiple sclerosis). My MRI results came back with slight white matter changes in my brain (lesions), however, not conclusive to MS. My symptoms were not only the same as MS, but vitamin D, B12 deficiency, and BII (Breast Implant Illness). I could not for the life of me explain myself to anyone, including family and partner, who all thought I was going insane. It would have been easier to say just hospitalize me in a psychiatric ward! [Since] it was not the suspected diagnosis (BII) [by the professionals, and] I'm not agreeing with what the professionals are saying! I'm listening to my body! That's insane, right? Your gut instinct vs. the professionals? How dare I question their diagnosis or authority? They have the years of education behind them, right? I was not going to rest! And thank God I didn't!*

Eighteen months prior, Derya had had breast implants done by a reputable, high-profile, and highly skilled plastic surgeon in Europe. Not for one moment did she think her implants would force her to present to the emergency department at the Royal Melbourne Hospital in January 2018. She was now displaying full symptoms of a brain tumor, stroke, and MS. CT scans confirmed that she didn't have a brain tumor; however, they still suspected she had experienced a mild stroke or had MS. Derya trusted her gut. She knew her breast implants were poisoning her. She insisted on a breast implant removal surgery, and in March 2018 they were removed.

She said, "They had degenerated so rapidly that they were both yellow in color, bleeding, and the outer shell was disintegrating—explains why I was feeling like death! Removing them was the best decision and investment I have made to gaining my health and life back!"

While at the time of writing, Derya was still on the road to recovery, she said, "I am optimistic and hopeful that with a complete diet and lifestyle change, my body will detox." She warned other women to be vigilant with their health and trust their instincts. Derya's drive to find an answer saved her life, and her willingness to share her story could help save others from an equally traumatic experience.

Your Plan Is as Unique as Your Fingerprint, So Personalize It

These stories underscore something of critical importance: Every person and every plan is truly unique. The keys that we each require to unlock our peak performing abilities are different. Sometimes we must fumble through many until we find the one that fits. That's why, in creating your plan, treat it as a framework. You need to allow for wiggle room so you can course correct based on your individual wants and needs. No plan is set in stone; it is a guide to get started and should evolve as you do. This is rarely considered in the many plans available in the marketplace that profess to help individuals become healthier, smarter, and more successful in just days. By creating a structure and suggesting steps, we can pinpoint challenges earlier and tackle them immediately, while addressing our biochemical and psychological/spiritual energetic needs. With this approach, we prevent the snapback effect, set us up for lasting change, and uncover the unknown factors holding us back. Who would have thought eggs were triggering Adam's migraines, food was impacting Stephanie's emotions, and a vitamin D deficiency was the root cause of M.I.'s suicidal thoughts? Or that coconut would send me into a funk for days, or a candida overgrowth was triggering extreme fatigue? None of these discoveries would have bubbled to the surface unless a framework existed to allow them to and the research or diagnosis existed to support them. We know this intellectually from all the studies that have been done, but we don't necessarily make the connection between the cause and our behavior. It's time to make that connection now and quantify it through data and research. It's the biohacker's way!

The signs are there; they're just not illuminated in bright lights, until we choose to take control of our thoughts and emotions and seek out the information we need. Everything is possible, even if others initially dismiss us or say "It's all in your head." Nothing is off the table when it comes to fixing your health and becoming an unstoppable Catalyst. Even doctors sometimes get it wrong.

The 13-Week Plan Isn't for the Fainthearted

If you are currently a Defender or Guardian, you have the farthest to travel, so you are going to find this framework the most difficult. However, like me, you also need it the most and have the most to gain from it. It's time to put an end to the fatigue that drains your spirit, emotions that rule your day, and insufficient focus that holds you back. Do not leave any stone unturned. You owe it to yourself.

I can't stress enough how important it is to seek the help of a functional or integrative medicine doctor who will help you feel better and uncover previously ignored causes. Use the Quickfire Visualization you learned in Chapter 8 to move past any doubt or fear holding you back. Prime your mind for the changes ahead. And remember to go easy on yourself. Separate yourself and your spirit from any biochemical imbalances, and allow yourself and your psychology to improve once these are in alignment.

We all have off days. If your soul is trying to turn right and your biochemistry still wants to turn left, acknowledge the misalignment and do what you need to do to recover. Ride the waves of discomfort until they die down. The second you stop resisting them, you free yourself from the stress of thinking the problem is all in your head. Use this 13-week framework as a complete reboot of your body, mind, and spirit.

Health is the core of your focus; your big goals can wait until you know the underlying causes of what ails you. Tread lightly with exercise. Exercise can cause inflammation, and if your body is unable to heal itself due to other issues, it may trigger new problems and exacerbate existing ones. Speak to your doctor about what is right for you.

If you are a Catalyst or Synergist, the focus of your plan should be fine-tuning everything from physical performance to gut health, focus, strategic thinking, energy, and problem solving. You are in the perfect position to try things you haven't done before. Your underlying biochemistry is up to speed or well on its way. Now it's time to dial in on your psychology and see what else you are capable of. Train your brain through meditation, interrupt negative thought patterns as you observe them, and ask more from yourself. There are always things you can tweak, like focus, concentration, and rejuvenation. Set yourself a new physical challenge along with the mental one, and drive a level of self-awareness that will propel you well into the future. Now is your time to become who you're next becoming and put your heart and soul into this transformation.

The Order, the Personalization

If I were to start this process all over again, I would have done some things differently, as you'll see in the plan outlined below. Specifically, I would have taken the lab tests, such as EverlyWell's food sensitivity test and Thryve's gut microbiome test, right off the bat. Why? Because if you suspect that food sensitivities, hormones, or nutritional deficiencies are impacting your psychology and biology, some of these tests can take a couple of weeks for results to come back, as they get approved by doctors and go through the labs. Thanks to companies such as

EverlyWell and Thryve, another option is to order these tests online and take them in the privacy of your home. Companies like EverlyWell are expanding the number of tests that they offer, putting us in charge of our own health and freeing us from judgment from many doctors. Find out the facts to avoid delaying your progress.

And take the tests before you start making changes. This is important because if the same issue occurs again, you'll know exactly how to correct course, instead of trying to figure out what is and isn't working. I delayed making other changes until I became fully aware of how food, my gut health, and my psychology were all interacting. This drove a level of awareness that has helped me get back on track whenever I felt like I was falling off. It is for this reason that nutritional changes are suggested only after you take all the tests and consult your doctor. Make this plan yours and revise it as needed. This is a suggested framework only, so you can change what you need to based on expert recommendations.

How to Use the Plan

This plan is unlike anything you have ever tried before. It's objective and offers a lifetime of benefits, not a five-minute quick fix. It is about educating yourself on what works best for you, not what the latest fad recommends. And, better yet, as research into our physical and mental health evolves, you'll be positioned to benefit from it with a firm understanding of what makes you tick. To make the most out of it, keep the following in mind:

▶ *Observe cause and effect.* What did you eat, take, or do that threw you off-kilter or optimized your performance? Record this in a journal that you can reference in the event of future setbacks. Collect as much data as you possibly can. Record your workouts: length, duration, and amount of weight lifted. Detail what made you feel better, more focused, and healthier. Incorporate any useful changes into your daily/weekly/monthly routine.

▶ *Find your baseline.* What is your starting point? How would you currently rate your energy, focus, drive, motivation, and well-being?

Record your baseline, so you can track your progress as you go. Recognize that you may not notice many of the health benefits until you run out of supplements or forget to do your daily mental rehearsal. Stephanie at one point came to me upset that she hadn't progressed, but when we took stock of where she started and how far she had come, her face lit with joy. We don't always see the difference because we're actively living the difference.

▶ *Don't do it all at once.* Isolate the experiments. Test each supplement or change individually, so you can pinpoint their effects. Yes, you may experience the placebo effect. However, as mentioned previously, you may also find you don't notice the benefits until you stop feeling your best.

▶ *Have a plan for setbacks.* I had many setbacks throughout these experiments, and I'll likely have more. Create a master list of steps you can take to feel better (e.g., visualization, meditation, improving sleep, supplements). List what works for you and stick it on your fridge so it stays in the front of your mind. Better yet, set weekly calendar reminders that ask you questions, such as "How are you feeling?" and "What steps can you take immediately to feel better?" This will be your prompt to bring yourself back into conscious creation. Be aware you may experience redirects. A redirect is a sudden realization based on test results that may cause concern and shape the weeks ahead. Take these in your stride, as they are built into the plan.

▶ *Plan when you are going to do the program.* Look over the steps and begin making a task list of what you need to arrange before you start to ensure everything flows smoothly (e.g., make doctors' appointments, order lab tests, buy supplements). I did this prior to my kickoff date, and instead of scrambling last minute, it was ready for me to experiment as I needed it.

Budget Requirements

Do you need to go out and purchase all the wearable devices and supplements I have talked about right away? The answer is no, because not all of them are going to be right for you. Second, as I mentioned, you don't want to try everything at once, so you can better isolate your results. Start with the basics: a checkup with a functional doctor and whichever supplements they recommend. Then build from there as you notice improvements.

Due to what was at stake for me, I was prepared to spend my last cent to feel better. My finances were at risk because I could no longer think clearly. I was ready to give up on a successful business that had taken me years of work and dedication to build. Saving it was worth any price I could pay on supplements that helped me feel unstoppable.

If your health is influencing your ability to think clearly and make intelligent decisions, it will negatively impact your income for years. This process is not just an investment in your physical health, it's an investment in your financial health and mental well-being.

Brief Plan Overview: Three Phases Over 13 Weeks

In Chapter 9, you identified your purpose, lit your beacon, and established goals that are a direct expression of your purpose. Now it's time to fuel yourself for success. That's why I've broken the plan into three distinct phases over 13 weeks. Some weeks are more intense than others, but all weeks build upon the ones that preceded them so you can better understand your brain and your body.

Weeks 1–4: The Accidental Biohacker (Biochemical Energy)

First you'll take the "identity gap" self-assessment quiz to gain insight on which identity you are currently operating in. Then you'll observe connections between your food, mood, and any medications you're taking to become an accidental biohacker, just like I did. Finally, you'll observe any physical ailments that may be hindering your performance on a physical or psychological level.

Weeks 5–8: Peak Performance Psychology (Psychological Energy)

In month two, you'll upgrade your psychological energy by optimizing your gut health, fueling your brain on healthy fats, ridding yourself of food cravings, visualizing who you are becoming, and experimenting with intermittent fasting. Intermittent fasting is by far one of the easiest eating protocols available; I'll show you how to do it. You'll also begin implementing recommendations based on any test results you have received from your doctor or other health-care provider, as well as gradually removing highly processed foods from your diet that affect your cognition and energy levels.

Weeks 9–13: Undeniably Unstoppable (Spiritual Energy)

And finally, in month three, you'll become unstoppable. You'll switch up your exercise routine and push yourself harder than usual because you'll be in a position to do so (unless your doctor advises otherwise). You'll adopt the "one cheat meal per week" protocol so you don't feel like you're restricting yourself, and you'll begin applying pattern interrupts to stop any self-sabotaging behaviors. In the final week, you'll self-reflect on your journey to date, observe your findings, and create a "master list" to add to your regular routine.

The 13-Week Plan to Biohack Your Way to an Unstoppable You

Let's dive into the breakdown of the program in more detail. Figure 10.2 on page 211 is a handy checklist/assessment to walk you through the process.

As you can see, this program is intensely comprehensive and focuses on *all* aspects that influence the way we feel, how we behave, and who we become. This is the complete picture, not just a piece of the puzzle, and it will fill in as you begin your journey to uncover the inner workings of your body and mind through neuroscience, biohacking, and psychology. To increase your chances of success, every Saturday and Sunday, in your journal, plan the week ahead and break down the week's tasks into easy-to-implement daily steps. To save time, order supplements and specific tests online that you don't need to consult a doctor for. At the end of each day, observe how you're feeling and note down what you ate and whether it nourished or depleted you. If you catch yourself in an angry outburst or engaging in self-sabotaging behavior, make note

Weeks 1–4
The Accidental Biohacker
(Biochemical Energy)

Week 1: Self-Assessment/Observation

❑ What will you do this week to work toward your three major goals as defined in Chapter 9?

❑ Visit www.areyouunstoppable.com to uncover your current identity.

❑ Observe your emotions on a daily basis on a scale from 0–10 for the following attributes: energy, mood, motivation, drive, and focus.

❑ Track the quality of your sleep on a scale from 0–10: 0 = not rested at all; 10 = well-rested and alert.

❑ Observe how much you need to use willpower to get through each day. Are you needing to persuade yourself to complete certain tasks? If so, why? Are you tired?

❑ If you suspect underlying biological causes are impacting your mood, visit a functional doctor for a full checkup.

❑ If you suspect food sensitivities, gut health, or hormones are influencing your energy levels and ability to focus, take the recommended tests. Visit www.areyouunstoppable.com. I suggest doing it in the first week, as some results may take a couple of weeks to get back to you. Budget for what you can and when you can. This is your plan; personalize it.

Week 2: Food, Mood, and Medication

❑ What will you do this week to work toward your three major goals as defined in Chapter 9?

❑ List all the medications you are taking and observe any mood or cognitive changes after taking each one. If you have been taking it for a long time, you may be unaware that it is influencing you. Speak to a functional doctor about the possible side effects and whether there are any options to go off the medication by identifying the underlying cause

Figure 10.2 Your Unstoppable Plan of Attack

of the original symptoms. Do not stop any medication without guidance from your doctor.

❑ Are there any medications that may cause side effects when combined?

❑ List all the supplements you are taking. Do they impact the effectiveness of any medications you require?

❑ Are you getting the most out of your supplements?

❑ Observe your mood after eating. Do you feel alert or fatigued? What did you eat? Was it high in sugar, refined carbs, or saturated fats?

❑ When does your energy peak during the day?

❑ When do you hit a wall? Does this coincide with the food you ate, or is it part of your natural circadian rhythm?

Week 3: Focus, Drive, and Motivation

❑ What will you do this week to work toward your three major goals as defined in Chapter 9?

❑ For the next seven days, you will rate your cognitive and emotional states on a scale from 0–10 to identify areas of improvement, including:

   ❑ Speed of thinking

   ❑ Decision-making abilities

   ❑ Memory

   ❑ Mental clarity

   ❑ Decision fatigue

   ❑ Mood

❑ Identify any connections between medication, food, sleep, and stress that are influencing your ability to perform and feel your best.

Week 4: Unlock the Keys to Your Kingdom

❑ What will you do this week to work toward your three major goals as defined in Chapter 9?

Figure 10.2 Your Unstoppable Plan of Attack, continued

❏ This week, you will observe how you feel within your body (e.g., are you bloated, cramping, suffering from diarrhea, experiencing muscle soreness or stiffness, having headaches, fatigue, insomnia, flushing, rashes, etc.)? Write down any observations you have at the end of each day, good or bad. This helps you become aware of any ailments that may have become the new normal.

❏ Note down any foods you suspect may be triggering any of these symptoms, e.g., artificial sweeteners, refined carbs, sugar, or artificial flavorings or colorings.

❏ Are you experiencing strong food cravings throughout the day?

❏ How are your energy level, focus, and mood? Rate them on a scale from 0–10.

❏ Track the quality of your sleep. If you can, purchase a high-quality wearable, like Oura, to collect data; otherwise, your sleep data will be inaccessible unless you perform a sleep study.

Weeks 5–8
Peak Performance Psychology
(Psychological Energy)

Week 5: Optimize Your Gut, Upgrade Your Mind

❏ What will you do this week to work toward your three major goals as defined in Chapter 9?

❏ What changes have you observed in yourself In the past week? How are your energy, focus, clarity, motivation, and drive? What can you improve upon?

❏ Take a doctor-formulated probiotic (e.g., the Garden of Life), or, if you have taken a gut health test with Thryve, begin taking your personalized probiotics on a daily basis. Probiotics need to be continued well after you finish your 13-week plan.

Figure 10.2 **Your Unstoppable Plan of Attack,** continued

❑ If you have seen a doctor, begin your daily supplementation routine based on their recommendations (e.g., magnesium, vitamin B12, vitamin D, etc.). Ask them if you need to supplement with these on a continual basis.

❑ Add more prebiotics into your daily routine to help with intestinal regularity. I use ones from Garden of Life.

❑ If your test results for food sensitivities are back, begin to remove problem foods from your diet. You may slowly reintroduce these foods at a later stage. Follow the recommendations on your test results or from your doctor. If you still react to it, like coconut for me, avoid it altogether.

Week 6: Fuel Your Brain on Healthy Fats and Rid Yourself of Food Cravings

❑ What will you do this week to work toward your three major goals as defined in Chapter 9?

❑ What changes have you observed in yourself in the past week? How are your energy, focus, clarity, motivation, and drive? What can you improve upon?

❑ Begin supplementing with MCT oils midafternoon and continue with prebiotics to prevent food cravings from occurring.

❑ Begin removing processed sugars and carbohydrates from your diet and replacing them with healthy fats and oils, i.e., olive oil, avocado, etc.

❑ Look at the labels on the food you eat. Note how much sugar is in the yogurt, bread, and other foods you consume daily. What is a healthier alternative?

❑ Revisit the list of nootropics in Chapter 6 and begin self-experimentation. Observe your response to them and remember to cycle them so your body doesn't get used to them and reduce the positive effects.

❑ Purchase organic produce where possible to reduce likelihood of consuming toxins present on food.

Figure 10.2 Your Unstoppable Plan of Attack, continued

Week 7: Visualize Who You Are Becoming

❑ What will you do this week to work toward your three major goals as defined in Chapter 9?

❑ What changes have you observed in yourself in the past week? How are your energy, focus, clarity, motivation, and drive? What can you improve upon?

❑ Begin your daily visualization practice. Start this step earlier if you are already in Catalyst, Synergist, or Guardian mode. In Defender mode, attempting to visualize may be difficult as your mental energy will be limited or fluctuate in extreme ups and downs. Do what you can. Do the Quickfire Visualization daily to set yourself up for the day ahead and see yourself constantly improving, laughing, and smiling. You can download this visualization at www.areyouunstoppable.com.

❑ Continue making changes based on any test results you may have done under your doctor's advisement.

Week 8: Boost Your Clarity With Intermittent Fasting

❑ What will you do this week to work toward your three major goals as defined in Chapter 9?

❑ What changes have you observed in yourself in the past week? How are your energy, focus, clarity, motivation, and drive? What can you improve upon?

❑ To increase your energy levels, heighten your focus, and improve your cognition, I suggest an 8/16-hour intermittent fasting protocol. It is easy for most people to do. You eat for 8 hours and then fast for 16. I begin eating at noon, and then stop at 8 p.m. I do allow for some flexibility. Your eating/fasting window can be altered to suit your individual routine. A great app for tracking IF, available for Android and iOS, is called BodyFast.

❑ Continue supplementing and removing any foods from your diet that deplete instead of nourishing you. Find substitutes (e.g., nuts and fruit instead of chips and a muffin for a midafternoon snack).

Figure 10.2 Your Unstoppable Plan of Attack, continued

Weeks 9–13
Undeniably Unstoppable
(Spiritual + Physical Energy)

Week 9: Upgrade Your Body

❑ What will you do this week to work toward your three major goals as defined in Chapter 9?

❑ What changes have you observed in yourself in the past week? How are your energy, focus, clarity, motivation, and drive? What can you improve upon?

❑ Decide on a brand-new workout program that suits you or revise your existing one if it has become stagnant over time. By this point, your energy should be increasing, your mental stamina improving, and your mood becoming consistent. Take advantage of this and use exercise to fuel your next stage of evolution.

❑ If you find it hard to maintain a workout routine, include exercise in your daily visualization so your mind is primed for it.

❑ Continue with recommended supplementation and clean eating.

❑ How do you feel about yourself and your goals?

Week 10: Switch to One Cheat Meal Per Week

❑ What will you do this week to work toward your three major goals as defined in Chapter 9?

❑ What changes have you observed in yourself in the past week? How are your energy, focus, clarity, motivation, and drive? What can you improve upon?

❑ Pick one meal per week to have as your cheat meal. Eat healthy 95 percent of the time, but allow for this flexibility in your plan so you do not feel restricted.

❑ Continue with recommended supplementation and clean eating until it becomes part of your life.

❑ Continue with daily visualizations to prime your mind for continued success.

Figure 10.2 Your Unstoppable Plan of Attack, continued

Week 11: Interrupt Negative Patterns and Break Free From Your Old Self

❑ Continue with your daily visualization practice as outlined on page 173. See who you are becoming and observe as many submodalities as you possibly can to amplify its impact and to lock in your desired behavioral changes.

❑ Continue your daily meditation practice for ten minutes at a time. Begin by focusing on your breathing and allowing your thoughts to flow free from attachment.

❑ Ask yourself, "Where does my soul want to take me today?" Listen to it and tune into its guidance.

❑ What will you do this week to work toward your three major goals as defined in Chapter 9?

❑ What changes have you observed in yourself in the past week? How are your energy, focus, clarity, motivation, and drive? What can you improve upon?

❑ Identify three self-sabotaging behaviors that you would like to obliterate this week. When you catch yourself doing one of these behaviors, change state, get up and move around, and put on an album that always made you feel confident or a silly song that breaks the pattern from continuing. If it is in your budget, use the TouchPoints before or while the behavior is taking place to reprogram your mind.

❑ Continue clean eating, supplementing with MCT oil and any other supplements your doctor has suggested.

Week 12: Find Your Flow and Increase Your Productivity

❑ What will you do this week to work toward your three major goals as defined in Chapter 9?

❑ What changes have you observed in yourself in the past week? How are your energy, focus, clarity, motivation, and drive? What can you improve upon?

❑ This week, observe which time of day you are most productive.

❑ On which days do you feel more rested? What time did you go to bed and wake up those days?

Figure 10.2 Your Unstoppable Plan of Attack, continued

❏ Which days of the week are you most productive? Schedule your most important projects on these days and make them your top priority.

❏ Observe your breathing. If your breathing is shallow and you can make yourself aware of it, pause and begin to breathe more deeply. If, like me, you need a pattern interrupt, I suggest getting the Spire trackable device, which will vibrate to make you aware of how your breathing is affecting your ability to focus.

Week 13: Master the Art of Becoming Unstoppable

❏ What will you do this week to work toward your three major goals as defined in Chapter 9?

❏ What changes have you observed in yourself in the past week? How are your energy, focus, clarity, motivation, and drive? What can you improve upon?

❏ Visit www.areyouunstoppable.com/week13quiz to uncover your current identity and check your progress.

❏ What did you discover about yourself during this journey?

❏ What tipped the scales for you and propelled you in a positive direction?

❏ What didn't work for you?

❏ What would you do differently?

❏ What will you adopt as part of your normal life?

❏ Which changes did you find hardest and why?

❏ What could you do to make these changes easier?

❏ Did you make use of supplements, visualization, and nootropics to make these changes easier?

Figure 10.2 **Your Unstoppable Plan of Attack,** continued

of it. Don't force yourself to change it yet. Observation is step one; step two is determining why that behavior occurred. Was it habitual, or was it sparked after you came crashing down after a sugar rush? Did you react to a food, even days later, that threw you off your game? These fine distinctions will enlighten you as to what works for you.

Will I continue to use this plan in the future? The answer is yes, and every time I will evolve it to the higher state I find myself in and progressively overload myself further to ignite new growth. It doesn't just allow for this—it demands it. Technology and science are evolving all the time; devices that help us become unstoppable will only get better. We're on the edge of a revolution in health. Individuals like Dave Asprey, Richard Lin, Daniel Schmachtenberger, Julia Cheek, Dr. Francis, Trisha Hothorn, and more are leading this charge by being the living embodiment of their work and sharing that work with millions of other people around the world. We will continue to understand the body and brain in profound new ways that we can use to better ourselves. And we will close each identity gap as it rises to the demands of our personal evolution.

Final Thoughts

My life has changed in ways I never imagined. Assumptions I had made about what I thought would give me the biggest breakthrough were disproved. Answers to lifelong questions were answered in ways I never thought possible, and I feel more settled and confident within myself and my body than I have in years. The biggest unexpected revelation has only just hit me as I write this. I realize that one year ago on that hot day in Australia when I was on the verge of my complete breakdown, it wasn't just in my head. I wasn't just depressed and exhausted. I was sick, and I needed help. I always thought I just needed to find the right person to fix me, make me get better, bring my drive back. I did, but it wasn't a doctor: It was me. I had put too much faith and trust in professionals and hadn't questioned their diagnoses. I had failed to stand up for myself. I recognize there was no way I could have when I was at my worst. I wasn't in the right cognitive state to do so. And neither are countless others. I got lucky in this journey, and I appreciate many others may not. Because of this, I have put in everything I could and more to come up with a comprehensive, well-researched solution, not just to becoming unstoppable, not just to closing the gap between who you are and who you are becoming, but to helping lift each other up when we've fallen down. It's time to cast judgment aside, quit accusing people of making excuses, and finally get to the bottom of what's holding us back from becoming the Catalyst we were always destined to become. Not just on an individual level, but on a global level as well.

So if you ever happen to find yourself stuck in a hurricane, stranded in Canada, at your breaking point, or ready to break through, I hope you revisit your identity gap, so you can rightfully not just reclaim yourself, but reclaim your life. You're capable of more than you know, and it's time you realized it.

—Ben Angel

The Accidental Biohacker

Endnotes

Chapter 1

1. Eva Ritvo, "Facebook and Your Brain: The Inside Dope on Facebook," *Psychology Today*, May 24, 2012, www.psychologytoday.com/us/blog/vitality/201205/facebook-and-your-brain.

2. Deane Alban, "Dopamine Deficiency, Depression and Mental Health," Be Brain Fit, https://bebrainfit.com/dopamine-deficiency/.

3. Deane Alban, "Serotonin Deficiency: Signs, Symptoms, Solutions," Be Brain Fit, https://bebrainfit.com/serotonin-deficiency/.

4. "Stress Effects on the Body," American Psychological Association, www.apa.org/helpcenter/stress-body.aspx.

5. "Stress Symptoms," WebMD, July 11, 2017, www.webmd.com/balance/stress-management/stress-symptoms-effects_of-stress-on-the-body#2.

6. R.J. Wurtman, "Brain serotonin, carbohydrate-craving, obesity and depression," November 3, 1995, www.ncbi.nlm.nih.gov/pubmed/8697046.

7. "Prefrontal Cortex," GoodTherapy.org, www.goodtherapy.org/blog/psychpedia/prefrontal-cortex.

8. Halo Neuroscience, "Department of Defense Selects Halo Sport to Train Special Ops Forces," August 4, 2016, https://blog.haloneuro.com/department-of-defense-selects-halo-sport-to-train-special-ops-forces-e0fd3b8d8c6a.

Chapter 2

1. Will Oremus, "What Controls Your Facebook Feed," January 3, 2016, www.slate.com/articles/technology/cover_story/2016/01/how_facebook_s_news_feed_algorithm_works.html.

2. Shai Danziger, Jonathan Levav, and Liora Avnaim-Pesso, "Extraneous Factors in Judicial Decisions," *PNAS*, April 26, 2011, www.pnas.org/content/108/17/6889.

Chapter 3

1. Farzin Irani et al., "Is Asthma Associated With Cognitive Impairments? A Meta-Analytic Review," PubMed.gov, December 2017, www.ncbi.nlm.nih.gov/pubmed/28325118.

2. "Reviews for Ventolin," Ask a Patient, accessed June 25, 2018, www.askapatient.com/viewrating.asp?drug=18473&name=VENTOLIN.

3. "Cancer Can Be Killed," https://cancercanbekilled.com/.

4. Andrew H. Miller et al., "Cytokine Targets in the Brain: Impact on Neurotransmitters and Neurocircuits," PubMed Central, March 6, 2013, www.ncbi.nlm.nih.gov/pmc/articles/PMC4141874/.

5. David Peterson, "Have You 'Weathered' a Cytokine Storm?" Wellness Alternatives, October 11, 2012, https://livingwellness-blog.wordpress.com/2012/10/11/have-you-weathered-a-cyto-kine-storm/.

6. David Scheiderer, "5 Reasons You Should Have Your Neurotransmitter Levels Measured," Integrative Psychiatry, March 8, 2017, www.integrativepsychiatry.net/blog/5-reasons-you-should-have-your-neurotransmitter-levels-measured/.

7. Andrew H. Miller et al., "Cytokine Targets in the Brain: Impact on Neurotransmitters and Neurocircuits," PubMed Central, March 6, 2013, www.ncbi.nlm.nih.gov/pmc/articles/PMC4141874/.

8. "Asthma Statistics," American Academy of Allergy, Asthma & Immunology, www.aaaai.org/about-aaaai/newsroom/asth-ma-statistics.

9. Chris Elkins, "Hooked on Pharmaceuticals: Prescription Drug Abuse in America," Drugwatch, April 18, 2018, www.drugwatch.com/news/2015/07/29/drug-abuse-in-america/#sources.

10. Gina M. Florio, "Signs Hormonal Birth Control Is Messing With Your Mental Health," *Bustle*, January 25, 2017, www.bus-tle.com/p/signs-hormonal-birth-control-is-messing-with-your-mental-health-32894.

11. Melinda Wenner, "Birth Control Pills Affect Women's Taste in Men," *Scientific American*, December 1, 2008, www.scien-tificamerican.com/article/birth-control-pills-affect-womens-taste/.

12. "Requip Highlights of Prescribing Information," GSK Source, February 2018, www.gsksource.com/pharma/content/dam/GlaxoSmithKline/US/en/Prescribing_Information/Requip/pdf/REQUIP-PI-PIL.PDF.

13. "Mental Illness or Caffeine Allergy?" Hippocrates Health Institute, September 10, 2012, https://hippocratesinst.org/mental-illness-or-caffeine-allergy.

14. Martin G. Bloom, "92% of U.S. Population Have Vitamin Deficiency. Are You One of Them?" The Biostation, February 3, 2014, https://thebiostation.com/bioblog/nutrient-iv-therapy/do-you-have-vitamin-deficiency/.

15. Bloom, Ibid.

16. Megan Ware, "What Are the Health Benefits of Vitamin D?" *Medical News Today,* November 13, 2017, www.medicalnewsto-day.com/articles/161618.php.

17. Kimberly Y.Z. Forrest and Wendy L. Stuhldreher, "Prevalence and Correlates of Vitamin D Deficiency in U.S. Adults," PubMed.gov, January 2011, www.ncbi.nlm.nih.gov/pubmed/21310306.

18. Rolf Jorde et al., "Effects of Vitamin D Supplementation on Symptoms of Depression in Overweight and Obese Subjects: Randomized Double Blind Trial," Wiley Online Library, November 11, 2008, http://onlinelibrary.wiley.com/doi/10.1111/j.1365-2796.2008.02008.x/abstract.

19. Maya Soni et al., "Vitamin D and Cognitive Function," PubMed.gov, April 2012, www.ncbi.nlm.nih.gov/pubmed/22536767.

20. E. Wehr et al., "Association of Vitamin D Status With Serum Androgen Levels in Men," PubMed.gov, August 2010, www.ncbi.nlm.nih.gov/pubmed/20050857.

21. Chuen-Ching Wang et al., "Testosterone Replacement Therapy Improves Mood in Hypogonadal Men—A Clinical Research Center Study," *The Journal of Clinical Endocrinology & Metabolism,* October 1, 1996, https://academic.oup.com/jcem/article/81/10/3578/2649928.

22. David Perlmutter, "The Vitamin That May Save Your Brain," DrPerlmutter.com, www.drperlmutter.com/vitamin-d-just-bones/.

23. "Sensitive Gut: Managing Common Gastrointestinal Disorders," Harvard Health, November 7, 2016, https://saludmovil.com/sensitive-gut-gastrointestinal-disorders/3/

24. "The Gut-Brain Connection," Harvard Health Publishing, www.health.harvard.edu/diseases-and-conditions/the-gut-brain-connection.

25. "Hormone-Replacement Therapy May Prevent Age-Related Declines in Cognitive Functioning," *Medical News Today*, December 3, 2013, www.medicalnewstoday.com/releases/269579.php.

26. Mary Elizabeth Dallas, "Testosterone May Protect Men From Allergic Asthma," MedicineNet.com, May 9, 2017, www.medicinenet.com/script/main/art.asp?articlekey=203446.

27. Joseph Mercola, "The Links Between Your Diet and Hormone Levels, and How Estrogen May Protect You Against Dementia," Mercola.com, February 23, 2014, https://articles.mercola.com/sites/articles/archive/2014/02/23/hormones.aspx.

28. Madeline Vann, "1 in 4 Men Over 30 Has Low Testosterone," ABC News, September 13, 2007, https://abcnews.go.com/Health/Healthday/story?id=4508669&page=1.

29. Randy A. Sansone and Lori A. Sansone, "Allergic Rhinitis: Relationships With Anxiety and Mood Syndromes," PubMed Central, July 2011, www.ncbi.nlm.nih.gov/pmc/articles/PMC3159540/.

30. Kayleigh Lewis, "Hayfever Drugs Could Reduce Brain Size and Increase Risk of Dementia and Alzheimer's, Study Says," *The Independent*, April 19, 2016, www.independent.co.uk/life-style/health-and-families/health-news/hayfever-drugs-reduce-brain-size-risk-dementia-alzheimer-s-a6991281.html.

31. Zen Vuong, "New Research: Increased Air Pollution Linked to Aggressive Behavior in Teens," USC Environmental Health Centers, December 13, 2017, http://envhealthcenters.usc.edu/2017/12/air-pollution-linked-to-bad-teenage-behavior.html.

32. Roger D. Masters, "Acetylcholines, Toxins and Human Behavior," *Journal of Clinical Toxicology*, May 25, 2012, www.omicsonline.org/acetylcholines-toxins-and-human-behavior-2161-0495.S6-004.php?aid=7795.

33. Glenda N. Lindseth et al., "Neurobehavioral Effects of Aspartame Consumption," PubMed Central, September 27, 2017, www.ncbi.nlm.nih.gov/pmc/articles/PMC5617129/.

34. Mohamed B. Abou-Donia et al., "Splenda Alters Gut Microflora and Increases Intestinal P-Glycoprotein and Cytochrome P-450 in Male Rats," PubMed.gov, September 18, 2008, www.ncbi.nlm.nih.gov/pubmed/18800291.

35. Amy Westervelt, "Phthalates Are Everywhere, and the Health Risks Are Worrying. How Bad Are They Really?" *The Guardian*, February 10, 2015, www.theguardian.com/lifeandstyle/2015/feb/10/phthalates-plastics-chemicals-research-analysis.

36. "The Science of Breathing," Spire, https://spire.io/pages/science.

Chapter 4

1. "HVMN Ketone," HVMN, https://hvmn.com/ketone.

2. Sue Hughes, "Boosting Brain Ketone Metabolism: A New Approach to Alzheimer's," Medscape, August 3, 2017, www.medscape.com/viewarticle/883743.

3. Louise Hendon, "What Are the Optimal Ketone Levels for a Ketogenic Diet?" The Keto Summit, https://ketosummit.com/optimal-ketone-levels-for-ketogenic-diet.

4. Joseph Mercola, "Magnesium—A Key Nutrient for Health and Disease Prevention," Mercola.com, December 28, 2015, https://articles.mercola.com/sites/articles/archive/2015/12/28/magnesium-atp.aspx.

5. Mark Sisson, "Managing Your Mitochondria," Mark's Daily Apple, October 20, 2011, www.marksdailyapple.com/managing-your-mitochondria/.

6. Sisson, Ibid.

7. Yann Saint-Georges-Chaumet, "Microbiota-Mitochondria Inter-Talk: Consequence for Microbiota-Host Interaction," PubMed. gov, February 2016, www.ncbi.nlm.nih.gov/pubmed/26500226.

8. Sandee LaMotte, "Woman Claims Her Body Brews Alcohol, Has DUI Charge Dismissed," CNN, January 1, 2016, www.cnn. com/2015/12/31/health/auto-brewery-syndrome-dui-womans-body-brews-own-alcohol/index.html.

9. "Candidiasis," Harvard Health Publishing, February 2013, www. health.harvard.edu/diseases-and-conditions/candidiasis.

10. "HIV-Related Candidiasis," AIDSinfo, April 1, 1995, https:// aidsinfo.nih.gov/news/174/hiv-related-candidiasis.

11. Qi Hui Sam, Matthew Wook Chang, and Louis Yi Ann Chai, "The Fungal Mycobiome and Its Interaction With Gut Bacteria in the Host," PubMed Central, February 2017, www.ncbi.nlm. nih.gov/pmc/articles/PMC5343866/.

12. "Gut Microbiota Info," Gut Microbiota for Health, www.gutmi-crobiotaforhealth.com/en/about-gut-microbiota-info/.

13. "Bigger Brains: Complex Brains for a Complex World," Smithsonian National Museum of Natural History, June 15, 2018, http://huma-norigins.si.edu/human-characteristics/brains.

14. Megan Clapp et al., "Gut Microbiota's Effect on Mental Health: The Gut-Brain Axis," PubMed Central, September 15, 2017, www.ncbi.nlm.nih.gov/pmc/articles/PMC5641835.

15. Carolyn Gregoire, "Probiotics May One Day Be Used to Treat Depression," *The Huffington Post*, April 17, 2015, www.huffington-post.com/2015/04/17/probiotics-depression_n_7064030.html.

16. Rasnik K. Singh et al., "Influence of Diet on the Gut Microbiome and Implications for Human Health," *Journal of Translational Medicine*, April 8, 2017, https://translational-medicine.biomed-central.com/articles/10.1186/s12967-017-1175-y.

17. Elizabeth Laseter, "Your Body Treats Fast Food Like a Bacterial Infection, According to Recent Study," *Cooking Light*, January 17, 2018, www.cookinglight.com/news/recent-study-shows-fast-food-may-damage-immune-system.

18. Emily Courtney, "Your Microbiome on Sugar," Hyperbiotics, www.hyperbiotics.com/blogs/recent-articles/your-microbiome-on-sugar.

19. Carol Potera, "Asthma: A Gut Reaction to Antibiotics," PubMed Central (June 2005), www.ncbi.nlm.nih.gov/pmc/articles/PMC1257633/.

20. P. Gumowski et al., "Chronic Asthma and Rhinitis Due to Candida Albicans, Epidermophyton, and Trichophyton," PubMed.gov, July 1987, www.ncbi.nlm.nih.gov/pubmed/3605797.

21. Abdulbari Bener et al., "The Impact of Vitamin D Deficiency on Asthma, Allergic Rhinitis, and Wheezing in Children: An Emerging Public Health Problem," PubMed Central, September–December 2014, www.ncbi.nlm.nih.gov/pmc/articles/PMC4214003/.

22. Joan Hui Juan Lim et al., "Bimodal Influence of Vitamin D in Host Response to Systemic Candida Infection-Vitamin D Dose Matters," PubMed.gov, August 15, 2015, www.ncbi.nlm.nih.gov/pubmed/25612733.

23. John H. White "Vitamin D Signaling, Infectious Diseases, and Regulation of Innate Immunity," September 2008, http://iai.asm.org/content/76/9/3837.full.

24. "Allergies and Asthma: They Often Occur Together," Mayo Clinic, February 13, 2016, www.mayoclinic.org/diseases-conditions/asthma/in-depth/allergies-and-asthma/art-20047458.

25. Claudia Wallis, "How Gut Bacteria Help Make Us Fat and Thin," *Scientific American*, June 1, 2014, www.scientificamerican.com/article/how-gut-bacteria-help-make-us-fat-and-thin.

26. Robert H. Lustig, "Sickeningly Sweet: Does Sugar Cause Type 2 Diabetes? Yes," *Canadian Journal of Diabetes*, August 2016, www.

canadianjournalofdiabetes.com/article/S1499-2671(15)30072-1/fulltext.

27. "Prebiotics Reduce Body Fat in Overweight Children," ScienceDaily, June 7, 2017, www.sciencedaily.com/releases/2017/06/170607123949.htm.

28. Joseph Mercola, "Neurologist Speaks Out About the Importance of Gut Health for Prevention and Treatment of 'Incurable' Neurological Disorders," Mercola.com, May 17, 2015, https://articles.mercola.com/sites/articles/archive/2015/05/17/gut-bacteria-brain-health.aspx.

29. Kathleen Doheny, "Eating Trans Fats Linked to Depression," WebMD, January 26, 2011, https://www.webmd.com/food-recipes/news/20110126/eating-trans-fats-linked-to-depression#1.

30. Food and Drug Administration, changes to the Nutrition Facts Label, www.fda.gov/Food/GuidanceRegulation/Guidance DocumentsRegulatoryInformation/LabelingNutrition/ ucm385663.htm.

31. John Casey, "The Truth About Fats," WebMD, February 3, 2003, www.webmd.com/women/features/benefits-of-essential-fats-and-oils#1.

32. Silvia Manzanero et al., "Intermittent Fasting Attenuates Increases in Neurogenesis After Ischemia and Reperfusion and Improves Recovery," PubMed Central, February 19, 2014, www.ncbi.nlm.nih.gov/pmc/articles/PMC4013772.

33 Mark P. Mattson, Intermittent Fasting and Caloric Restriction Ameliorate Age-Related Behavioral Deficits in the Triple-Transgenic Mouse Model of Alzheimer's Disease, April 2007, www.sciencedirect.com/science/article/pii/S0969996106003251.

Chapter 5

1. Dave Asprey, "Is Nicotine the Next Big Smart Drug?" Bulletproof Blog, December 1, 2015, https://blog.bulletproof.com/is-nicotine-the-next-big-smart-drug/.

2. Tabitha M. Powledge, "Nicotine as Therapy," PubMed Central, November 16, 2004, www.ncbi.nlm.nih.gov/pmc/articles/ PMC526783/.

3. John Heritage, "The Fate of Transgenes in the Human Gut," *Nature Biotechnology*, February 2004, www.biosafety-info.net/ file_dir/697848857c49a7da2.pdf.

4. Heritage, Ibid.

5. William J. Walsh, "Elevated Blood Copper/Zinc Ratios in Assaultive Young Males," 1996, www.ncbi.nlm.nih.gov/pubmed.

6. "Recommendation for Vitamin D Intake Was Miscalculated, Is Far Too Low, Experts Say," ScienceDaily, March 17, 2015, www. sciencedaily.com/releases/2015/03/150317122458.htm.

7. Atli Arnarson, "7 Signs and Symptoms of Magnesium Deficiency," Healthline, December 15, 2017, www.healthline. com/nutrition/magnesium-deficiency-symptoms.

8. Arnarson, Ibid.

9. Wisit Cheungpasitporn et al., "Hypomagnesaemia Linked to Depression: A Systematic Review and Meta-Analysis," PubMed. gov, April 2015, www.ncbi.nlm.nih.gov/pubmed/25827510.

10. S.W. Golf et al., "Plasma Aldosterone, Cortisol and Electrolyte Concentrations in Physical Exercise After Magnesium Supplementation," PubMed.gov, November 1984, www.ncbi. nlm.nih.gov/pubmed/6527092.

11. Nahla Hwalla et al., "The Prevalence of Micronutrient Deficiencies and Inadequacies in the Middle East and Approaches to Interventions," PubMed Central, March 2017, www.ncbi.nlm. nih.gov/pmc/articles/PMC5372892/.

12. I-Fang Mao, Mei-Lien Chen, and Yuan-Ching Ko, "Electrolyte Loss in Sweat and Iodine Deficiency in a Hot Environment," PubMed.gov, May–June 2001, www.ncbi.nlm.nih.gov/ pubmed/11480505.

13. Victoria Hendrick, Lori Altshuler, and Peter C. Whybrow, "Psychoneuroendocrinology of Mood Disorders—The

Hypothalamic-Pituitary-Thyroid Axis," PubMed.gov, June 1998, www.ncbi.nlm.nih.gov/pubmed/9670226/.

14. David Jockers, "Warning Signs of a B12 Deficiency," DrJockers. com, https://drjockers.com/warning-signs-b12-deficiency/.

15. Jockers, Ibid.

16. Willow Lawson, "Be Healthy With B12," *Psychology Today*, February 1, 2004, www.psychologytoday.com/articles/200402/ be-healthy-b12.

17. M.A. Reger, Effects of Beta-Hydroxybutyrate on Cognition in Memory-Impaired Adults, March 2004, www.ncbi.nlm.nih.gov/ pubmed/15123336#

18. Ward Dean, "Beneficial Effects on Energy, Atherosclerosis and Aging," April 2013, https://nutritionreview.org/2013/04/medium-chain-triglycerides-mcts/.

19. H. Takeuchi, "The Application of Medium-Chain Fatty Acids: Edible Oil with a Suppressing Effect on Body Fat Accumulation," 2008, www.ncbi.nlm.nih.gov/pubmed/18296368.

20. "10 Powerful Zinc Benefits, Including Fighting Cancer," Dr. Axe, https://draxe.com/zinc-benefits/.

21. Gabriel Nowak, Bernadeta Szewczyk, and Andrzej Pilc, "Zinc and Depression. An Update," *Pharmacological Reports* 57, 2005, www.if-pan.krakow.pl/pjp/pdf/2005/6_713.pdf.

22. Zinc & Aggression: www.organicconsumers.org/newsletter/ organic-bytes-55-food-and-consumer-news-tidbits-edge/junk-food-diets-promote-youth.

Chapter 6

1. Hannah Nichols, "What Does Caffeine Do to Your Body?" *Medical News Today*, October 16, 2017, www.medicalnewstoday. com/articles/285194.php.

2. "Caffeine," WebMD, www.webmd.com/vitamins-supplements/ ingredientmono-979-caffeine.aspx?activeingredientid=979.

3. "11 Science-Backed Health Benefits of Yerba Mate," Brain Wiz, https://brainwiz.org/brain-hacks/health-benefits-yerba-mate/.

4. Ibid.

5. Kenta Kimura et al., "L-Theanine Reduces Psychological and Physiological Stress Responses," PubMed.gov, January 2007, www.ncbi.nlm.nih.gov/pubmed/16930802.

6. "What Is It About Coffee?" Harvard Health Publishing , January 2012, www.health.harvard.edu/staying-healthy/what-is-it-about-coffee.

7. J.W. Bennett and M. Klich, "Mycotoxins," PubMed Central, July 2003, www.ncbi.nlm.nih.gov/pmc/articles/PMC164220.

8. Irène Studer-Rohr et al., "The Occurrence of Ochratoxin A in Coffee," ScienceDirect, May 1995, www.sciencedirect.com/science/article/pii/027869159400150M?via percent3Dihub.

9. Kieran Clarke, "Kinetics, Safety and Tolerability of (R)-3-hydroxybutyl (R)-3-hydroxybutyrate in Healthy Adult Subjects," October 2013, www.ncbi.nlm.nih.gov/pmc/articles/PMC3810007/.

10. David Shurtleff et al., "Tyrosine Reverses a Cold-Induced Working Memory Deficit in Humans," PubMed.gov, April 1994, www.ncbi.nlm.nih.gov/pubmed/8029265.

11. Marty Hinz et al., "Treatment of Attention Deficit Hyperactivity Disorder With Monoamine Amino Acid Precursors and Organic Cation Transporter Assay Interpretation," PubMed Central, January 26, 2011, www.ncbi.nlm.nih.gov/pmc/articles/PMC3035600/.

12. "L-Tyrosine," WebMD, www.webmd.com/vitamins/ai/ingredientmono-1037/tyrosine

13. Michael S. Ritsner et al., "L-Theanine Relieves Positive, Activation, and Anxiety Symptoms in Patients With Schizophrenia and Schizoaffective Disorder: An 8-Week, Randomized, Double-Blind, Placebo-Controlled, 2-Center Study," PubMed.gov, January 2011, www.ncbi.nlm.nih.gov/pubmed/21208586.

14. Chan Hee Song et al., "Effects of Theanine on the Release of Brain Alpha Wave in Adult Males," KoreaMed, November 2003, www.koreamed.org/SearchBasic.php?RID=0124K-JN/2003.36.9.918&DT=1).

15. Song et al., Ibid.

16. Gail Owen et al., "The Combined Effects of L-Theanine and Caffeine on Cognitive Performance and Mood," PubMed.gov, August 2008, www.ncbi.nlm.nih.gov/pubmed/18681988.

17. "L-Theanine," WebMD, www.webmd.com/vitamins/ai/ingredientmono-1053/theanine.

18. Ruud Vermeulen and Hans R. Scholte, "Exploratory Open Label, Randomized Study of Acetyl- and Propionylcarnitine in Chronic Fatigue Syndrome," PubMed.gov, March–April 2004, www.ncbi.nlm.nih.gov/pubmed/15039515.

19. Youn-Soo Cha et al., "Effects of Carnitine Coingested Caffeine on Carnitine Metabolism and Endurance Capacity in Athletes," PubMed.gov, December 2001, www.ncbi.nlm.nih.gov/pubmed/11922111.

20. "L-Carnetine," WebMD, www.webmd.com/vitamins/ai/ingredientmono-1026/l-carnitine.

21. Kate Kelland, "Is Nicotine All Bad?" *Scientific American*, www.scientificamerican.com/article/is-nicotine-all-bad/.

22. William K.K. Wu and Chi Hin Cho, "The Pharmacological Actions of Nicotine on the Gastrointestinal Tract," J-STAGE, January 9, 2004, www.jstage.jst.go.jp/article/jphs/94/4/94_4_348/_pdf.

23. "Ginkgo Biloba Benefits Energy, Mood & Memory," Dr. Axe, https://draxe.com/ginkgo-biloba-benefits/.

24. "7 Proven Benefits of Quercetin (#1 Is Incredible)," Dr. Axe, https://draxe.com/quercetin/.

25. "Citicoline," WebMD, www.webmd.com/vitamins-supplements/ingredientmono-1090-CITICOLINE.aspx.

26. Mendel Friedman, "Chemistry, Nutrition, and Health-Promoting Properties of Hericium Erinaceus (Lion's Mane)

Mushroom Fruiting Bodies and Mycelia and Their Bioactive Compounds," PubMed.gov, August 2015, www.ncbi.nlm.nih.gov/pubmed/26244378.

27. Matthew P. Pase et al., "The Cognitive-Enhancing Effects of Bacopa Monnieri: A Systematic Review of Randomized, Controlled Human Clinical Trials," PubMed.gov, July 2012, www.ncbi.nlm.nih.gov/pubmed/22747190.

28. Carlo Calabrese et al., "Effects of a Standardized Bacopa Monnieri Extract on Cognitive Performance, Anxiety, and Depression in the Elderly: A Randomized, Double-Blind, Placebo-Controlled Trial," PubMed Central, July 2008, www.ncbi.nlm.nih.gov/pmc/articles/PMC3153866/.

29. Lucilla Parnetti, Francesco Amenta, and Virgilio Gallai, "Choline Alphoscerate in Cognitive Decline and in Acute Cerebrovascular Disease: An Analysis of Published Clinical Data," PubMed.gov, November 2001, www.ncbi.nlm.nih.gov/pubmed/11589921.

30. Parnetti et al., Ibid.

31. Sana Ishaque et al., "Rhodiola Rosea for Physical and Mental Fatigue: A Systematic Review," PubMed.gov, May 29, 2012, www.ncbi.nlm.nih.gov/pubmed/22643043.

32. Bystritsky, A et al. A Pilot Study of Rhodiola rosea for Generalized Anxiety Disorder (GAD), 2008, www.ncbi.nlm.nih.gov/pubmed/18307390

33. Maciej Gasior, Michael A. Rogawski, and Adam L. Hartman, "Neuroprotective and Disease-Modifying Effects of the Ketogenic Diet," PubMed Central, May 5, 2008, www.ncbi.nlm.nih.gov/pmc/articles/PMC2367001.

34. "31 Surprising Health Benefits of Taurine—With Mechanisms and Side Effects," Selfhacked, www.selfhacked.com/blog/taurine-benefits/.

35. "KetoPrime," Bulletproof, www.bulletproof.com/ketoprime?utm_source=post&utm_campaign=13_nootropics&utm_medium=blog.

36. "Kado-3," HVMN, https://hvmn.com/kado-3.

Chapter 7

1. Kimberly Amadeo, "Hurricane Irma Facts, Damage, and Costs," The Balance, March 27, 2018, www.thebalance.com/hurricane-irma-facts-timeline-damage-costs-4150395.

2. Annual Stress Survey: American Psychological Association, 2017, www.apa.org/news/press/releases/stress/2017/state-nation.pdf.

3. Gloria Mark, Daniela Gudith, and Ulrich Klocke, "The Cost of Interrupted Work: More Speed and Stress," UCI Donald Bren School of Information & Computer Sciences, www.ics.uci.edu/~gmark/chi08-mark.pdf.

4. "Actual User Data Confirms That TouchPoints Reduce Stress By 74% in 30 Seconds," Shopify, January 25, 2017, https://cdn.shopify.com/s/files/1/1529/9657/files/TouchPoints_Data_Reducing_Stress_115f137b-10f9-466a-9a1b-2bc34aeb793e.pdf.

5. Richard J. Davidson et al., "Alterations in Brain and Immune Function Produced by Mindfulness Meditation," *Psychosomatic Medicine* 65, July 2003, https://journals.lww.com/psychosomaticmedicine/Abstract/2003/07000/Alterations_in_Brain_and_Immune_Function_Produced.14.aspx.

6. Melissa A. Rosenkranz et al., "A Comparison of Mindfulness-Based Stress Reduction and an Active Control in Modulation of Neurogenic Inflammation," ScienceDirect, January 2013, www.sciencedirect.com/science/article/pii/S0889159112004758.

7. Barbara L. Fredrickson et al., "Open Hearts Build Lives: Positive Emotions, Induced Through Loving-Kindness Meditation, Build Consequential Personal Resources," APA PsycNET (2008), http://psycnet.apa.org/record/2008-14857-004.

8. Wiveka Ramel et al., "The Effects of Mindfulness Meditation on Cognitive Processes and Affect in Patients With Past Depression," Springer Link (August 2004), https://link.springer.com/article/10.1023/B:COTR.0000045557.15923.96.

9. Albert J. Arias et al., "Systematic Review of the Efficacy of Meditation Techniques as Treatments for Medical Illness," Mary Ann Liebert, Inc. Publishers (October 11, 2006), www.liebertpub.com/doi/abs/10.1089/acm.2006.12.817.

10. Shauna L. Shapiro et al., "Mindfulness-Based Stress Reduction for Health-Care Professionals: Results From a Randomized Trial," APA PsycNET, 2005, http://psycnet.apa.org/record/2005-05099-004.

11. Hooria Jazaieri et al., "A Randomized Controlled Trial of Compassion Cultivation Training: Effects on Mindfulness, Affect, and Emotion Regulation," The Center for Compassion and Altruism Research and Education, June 13, 2013, http://ccare.stanford.edu/article/jazaieri-h-mcgonigal-k-jinpa-t-doty-j-r-gross-j-j-golden-p-r-2013-a-randomized-controlled-trial-of-compassion-cultivation-training-effects-on-mindfulness-affect-and-emotion/.

12. Traci Pedersen, "Meditation Produces Opposite Effect of 'Fight or Flight,'" PsychCentral, October 6, 2015, https://psychcentral.com/news/2013/05/04/meditation-produces-opposite-effect-of-fight-or-flight/54449.html.

Chapter 8

1. Vinoth K. Ranganathan et al., "From Mental Power to Muscle Power—Gaining Strength by Using the Mind," PubMed.gov (2004), www.ncbi.nlm.nih.gov/pubmed/14998709.

2. "Sleep Disorders," Health Resources & Services Administration (2011), https://mchb.hrsa.gov/whusa11/hstat/hshi/downloads/pdf/224sd.pdf.

3. Francesco P. Cappuccio, Michelle A. Miller, and Steven W. Lockley, "Sleep, Health, and Society: The Contribution of Epidemiology," Oxford Scholarship Online, January 2011, www.oxfordscholarship.com/view/10.1093/acprof:oso/9780199566594.001.0001/acprof-9780199566594-chapter-1.

4. A.M. Williamson and Anne-Marie Feyer, "Moderate Sleep Deprivation Produces Impairments in Cognitive and Motor Performance Equivalent to Legally Prescribed Levels of Alcohol Intoxication," National Center for Biotechnology Information, June 15, 2000, www.ncbi.nlm.nih.gov/pmc/articles/PMC1739867/pdf/v057p00649.pdf.

5. Massimiliano de Zambotti et al., "The Sleep of the Ring: Comparison of the OURA Sleep Tracker Against Polycomnography," PubMed.gov, March 2017, www.ncbi.nlm.nih.gov/pubmed/28323455.

6. Kaisa, "Understanding Sleep Quality," Oura, https://help.ouraring.com/sleep/understanding-sleep-quality.

7. John Cline, "The Mysterious Benefits of Deep Sleep," *Psychology Today*, October 11, 2010, www.psychologytoday.com/us/blog/sleepless-in-america/201010/the-mysterious-benefits-deep-sleep.

8. Haya Al Khatib et al., "The Effects of Partial Sleep Deprivation on Energy Balance: A Systematic Review and Meta-Analysis," Nature.com, November 2, 2016, www.nature.com/articles/ejcn2016201.

9. Elsevier, "Loss of Sleep, Even for a Single Night, Increases Inflammation in the Body," ScienceDaily, www.sciencedaily.com/releases/2008/09/080902075211.htm.

10. Daniel F. Kripke, Robert D. Langer, and Lawrence E. Kline, "Hypnotics' Association With Mortality or Cancer: A Matched Cohort Study," BMJ Open, 2012, http://bmjopen.bmj.com/content/2/1/e000850.

11. Maija-Liisa Laakso et al., "Twenty-Four-Hour Patterns of Pineal Melatonin and Pituitary and Plasma Prolactin in Male Rats Under 'Natural' and Artificial Lighting," PubMed.gov, September 1988, www.ncbi.nlm.nih.gov/pubmed/3185865.

12. Lisa Marshall, "Melatonin Benefits, Risks: What You Need to Know," WebMD, October 5, 2017, www.webmd.com/sleep-disorders/news/20171004/is-natural-sleep-aid-melatonin-safe.

13. Alex Fergus, "How to Increase Deep Sleep," AlexFergus.com, www.alexfergus.com/blog/how-to-increase-deep-sleep.

14. Ian Sample, "Sleep 'Resets' Brain Connections Crucial for Memory and Learning, Study Reveals," *The Guardian*, August 23, 2016, www.theguardian.com/science/2016/aug/23/sleep-resets-brain-connections-crucial-for-memory-and-learning-study-reveals.

15. "Submodalities," NLP World, www.nlpworld.co.uk/nlp-glossary/s/submodalities/.

Chapter 9

1. Elizabeth A.R. Robinson et al., "Six-Month Changes in Spirituality and Religiousness in Alcoholics Predict Drinking Outcomes at Nine Months," PubMed Central, July 2011, www.ncbi.nlm.nih.gov/pmc/articles/PMC3125889/.

2. Arlener D. Turner, Christine E. Smith, and Jason C. Ong, "Is Purpose in Life Associated With Less Sleep Disturbance in Older Adults?" *Sleep Science and Practice* 1, no. 14, 2017, https://sleep.biomedcentral.com/track/pdf/10.1186/s41606-017-0015-6.

3. Mark Wheeler, "Be Happy: Your Genes May Thank You for It," UCLA Newsroom, July 29, 2013, http://newsroom.ucla.edu/releases/don-t-worry-be-happy-247644.

4. Teal Burrell, "A Sense of Purpose Can Keep You Healthy," Support for People with Aspergillosis, January 31, 2017, www.nacpatients.org.uk/content/sense-purpose-can-keep-you-healthy.

Chapter 10

1. "High Blood Pressure and Food Allergies," IBS Treatment Center, https://ibstreatmentcenter.com/2012/05/high-blood-pressure-and-food-allergies-2.html.

Acknowledgments

This mammoth undertaking could not have been possible if it weren't for the endless encouragement, love, and support I received from countless individuals that spurred me on to make this the best book possible. I wrote this book to help others who have ever found themselves ignored by health professionals or felt less than because they didn't have the energy or support required to fulfill their soul's purpose. You drove me to ask more from myself and our medical community.

Thanks to my mum and dad for the endless encouragement and support you have both provided me throughout my lifetime. You will both forever be my heroes and my moral compass that guides everything I do. An enormous debt of gratitude goes to Jonathan, who has been by my side as we worked our way through what felt like endless health issues. Your love, support, and patience made this possible.

To all of the experts I interviewed for this book, I can't thank each and every one of you enough. You shaped *Unstoppable*, encouraged me, and challenged me to find the answers to my questions. Thank you for your time and commitment to getting to the essence of real health and sharing your own battle scars so that others can find inspiration in your stories. You each provided insights that will change countless lives and you are each pushing boundaries that few dare to.

To Dave Asprey, who inspired me to go on this journey. Your book, *Head Strong*, made me feel like I was no longer alone in this battle and ignited a fire within me to keep going when I was on the verge of giving up. The impact you are having on this world is nothing short of astounding. You are shaping lives in ways you may never be able to fully comprehend. Your legacy will pave the way for others to follow in your steps and for real lasting change to occur.

Special mention goes to Deborah Holmen, my next-door neighbor at the time, now lifelong friend who not only enthusiastically wanted to hear and participate in the biohacking experiments I undertook, but also assisted in editing and research for the book. Our countless conversations made it what it is.

To all of those incredibly special people I came across throughout my journey that provided wisdom, love and laughs, including; Trisha, Colt, Mary-Webb, Howard, Trish, Rick, Richard, Teresa, Steve, Jaya, Kristy, Stephanie, Scott, Rich, Melissa, Matt, Dean, Janeche, Sharon, Ashley, Michael and Derya. This couldn't have been possible without each of you. You have each impacted my life in ways you'll never know. Michael Smallbone, my agent, for throwing your full support behind me and getting me to the U.S. Thank you!

A huge thank you goes to the *Entrepreneur* teams that have shown unwavering support that made this entire project a reality. I can't thank you enough for putting your faith and trust in me to deliver something that was nothing short of a mammoth task in a short amount of time. You have welcomed me with open arms and have shown the utmost professionalism and commitment to making *Unstoppable* truly unique. You are changing lives! To the editors and fact checkers who worked tirelessly on this book to ensure it is accurate, thank you. I will forever be grateful to each of you. You are the unseen heroes that made this possible.

A big thank you goes to my best friend and Unstoppable team member, Adam Shepherd. Your tireless work behind the scenes allows me to do what I love and to help others while doing it. I have never come across a more loyal friend and dedicated team member. You inspire me each and every day.

And finally, to you, the reader. Thank you for picking this book up. It is my hope that this book shows you what is possible, no matter where your starting point. You drive me to do what I do.

About the Author

Ben Angel is a bestselling author of three game-changing business and personal development books, including, *CLICK: The New Science of Influence* and *Flee 9 to 5: Get 6-7 Figures and Do What You Love*. He's followed by over 250,000 internationally. His weekly inspirational videos have been viewed over 2.5 million times and have been featured by *Success* and *Entrepreneur Magazine*. Over 20,000 took one of his online courses In 2017. For the past 15 years he's helped entrepreneurs build strong and dynamic businesses and minds through a unique combination of advanced marketing strategies and peak performance practices. He's been featured across a diverse range of media, including; *The Huffington Post*, ABC, *Marie Claire*, *Vogue*, CLEO, and *GQ Men's* magazine, and is a weekly video network contributor for Entrepreneur Media.

Index

Are you

UNSTOPPABLE?

TAKE THE FREE ONLINE QUIZ AND FIND OUT!

I've got a few questions for you:

- Are you struggling to reach your goals?
- Do you feel like you're capable of more?
- Do you constantly feel tired or lethargic?
- Do you struggle to focus for long periods of time?
- Do you find yourself procrastinating or making excuses?

If so, visit www.areyouunstoppable.com and take your FREE 5-minute online quiz right now. By answering a series of simple questions, our software will analyze your results and provide you with a comprehensive report that will indicate your "identity" type, readiness to pursue your goals, susceptibility to stress/illness, your need to use willpower, current ability to assess consequences and focus, and whether you have both the psychological and biological resources you need to become UNSTOPPABLE.

What are you waiting for? Visit www.areyouunstoppable.com now.

How does it work?

STEP 1: ANSWER THE QUESTIONS

Answer a series of carefully selected questions designed to uncover hidden challenges in your life. The questions are based on your mindset, ability to adapt to changing environments, energy levels, memory, focus, diet, stress, sleep and more to determine key factors that may be influencing your mood and behavior and holding you back from feeling great and reaching your goals.

STEP 2: GET YOUR RESULTS AND TAKE ACTION

Download your free personalized report and start taking action immediately by teaming it with the 13-week plan in Chapter 10 of this book.